MONEY
AND
THE
MEANING
OF
LIFE

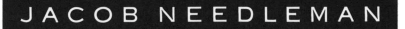

JACOB NEEDLEMAN

MONEY AND THE MEANING OF LIFE

DOUBLEDAY CURRENCY

NEW YORK LONDON TORONTO SYDNEY AUCKLAND

A CURRENCY BOOK

PUBLISHED BY DOUBLEDAY

A DIVISION OF BANTAM DOUBLEDAY DELL PUBLISHING GROUP, INC.

666 FIFTH AVENUE, NEW YORK, NEW YORK 10103

CURRENCY AND DOUBLEDAY

ARE TRADEMARKS OF DOUBLEDAY,

A DIVISION OF BANTAM DOUBLEDAY DELL PUBLISHING GROUP, INC.

BOOK DESIGN BY MARYSARAH QUINN

LIBRARY OF CONGRESS CATALOGING-IN-PUBLICATION DATA

NEEDLEMAN, JACOB.

MONEY AND THE MEANING OF LIFE / BY JACOB NEEDLEMAN.—IST ED.

P. CM.

"A CURRENCY BOOK."

1. WEALTH—RELIGIOUS ASPECTS. 2. SPIRITUAL LIFE. I. TITLE.

BL65.W42N44 1991

291.5'68—DC20   91-17775

CIP

ISBN 0-385-26241-8

FOR GAIL

ACKNOWLEDGMENTS

My first thanks are to Laurance S. Rockefeller for the extraordinary encouragement and generosity that enabled me to write this book, and to Sidney and Jean Lanier for the friendship that has made so much possible for my work.

Many people gave me the benefit of their own experience and thought about money. Among these, I wish especially to thank Rich Arnold, Russ Berrie, Joseph Ferrigno, John Levy, Danie Hulett, Michael Murphy, Joshua Mailman, Michael Gerber, Charles Schwab, and Marge Voyvodick.

I owe a special debt of gratitude to Rich Arnold, John Hunt, and William Torbert for reading the manuscript of this book and offering me much-valued comment and criticism.

I wish also to thank Cathy Grans, Jeffrey Kessler, Olga Madden, Carol Meehan, Gregory Porter, and Steve Zimmerman. And I wish to thank my students. Many of the events and characters portrayed in this book, especially the characters of Bill Cordell and Alyssa, are fictionalized distillations of numerous rich exchanges with students in my seminars and lectures.

The extent of the help given me by my wife and my gratitude to her are beyond acknowledgment.

CONTENTS

CONTENTS

MONEY
AND
THE
MEANING
OF
LIFE

INTRODUCTION:
THE FORCE OF MONEY

I once overheard the following advice: "If you want to take the true measure of someone, observe how he handles sex, time, and money." The target of this advice was a woman who had met an Oriental spiritual teacher and was ready to drop everything in order to follow him. As for the speaker, he was himself a teacher of considerable power, but a Westerner accustomed to moving in the rough-and-tumble world of business and government. Over the years that I had known this man, I had been deeply affected by his ability to guide others along the path of self-knowledge. But there was something essential about him that always eluded me, a capacity that set him apart from many other teachers and guides that I have met over the years. The moment he mentioned the word "money" in the context of spiritual growth, this feeling about him was again evoked in me. I began to grasp that part of his uniqueness was an ability to confront aspects of

1

human life that devour or confuse most people in search of the meaning of living.

Sex, time, and *money:* we know that the first of these is a force we all must struggle with, no matter who we are or what our aim in life may be. The teachings of every spiritual tradition and the writings of all serious thinkers offer insights of one sort or another about the question of sex. As for time, one may find at least theoretical treatments of this mystery in the scriptures, myths, and art of all ages, as well as in the writings of the philosophers. But one looks in vain for sustained guidance about money in the great teachings of the past or the books of the wise. It may even seem strange to mention it in the same breath with the other two issues. Yet the problem of money dogs our steps throughout the whole of our lives, exerting a pressure that, in its way, is as powerful and insistent as any other problem of human existence. And it haunts the spiritual search as well.

Usually, our concerns about money reduce themselves to getting or managing it, and there are countless books about that aspect of the money question. But it is almost impossible to find serious and useful thought about the relationship between the quest for *money* and the quest for *meaning.* What is the role of money in the search for consciousness, in the pursuit of that transformation of the self spoken of by the great teachers and philosophers of all epochs and cultures? The aim of this book is to open this question and to offer material for the task of answering it for oneself.

Why has this question never been squarely addressed before? Surely, it is because in no other culture or civilization that we know of has money been such a pervasive and decisive influence. In the world we now live in, money enters into everything human beings do, into every aspect and pocket of life. This is something new.

I do not mean to say that our culture is necessarily more

materialistic than those that have preceded it. I am saying only that money—that extraordinary device whose origins we shall soon discuss—now plays an unprecedentedly powerful role in our inner and outer lives, and that any serious search for self-knowledge and self-development requires that we study the meaning that money actually has for us.

It will not be an easy task to cut beneath the surface of this issue. The fact that money enters into everything means that we have to look at every aspect of our lives from the point of view of money and the force it conducts in the life of present-day civilization. Love and hatred, eating and sleeping, safety and danger, work and rest, marriage, children, fear, loneliness, friendship, knowledge and art, health, sickness and death: the money factor is a determining element in all of these—sometimes plainly visible, sometimes blended into the whole fabric like a weaver's dye. Think of our relationship to nature, to ideas, to pleasure; think of our sense of self-identity and self-respect; think of where we live and with what things we surround ourselves; think of all our impulses to help others or serve a larger cause; think of all our psychological and biological needs; think of where we go, how we travel, with whom we associate—or just think of what you were doing yesterday, or what you will be doing tomorrow, or in an hour. The money factor is there, wrapped around or lodged inside everything. Think of what you want or what you dream of, for now, or next year, or for the rest of your life. It will take money, a certain definite amount.

If we broaden our vision and consider the whole condition of the human family, we see the same penetration of the money factor into every facet of the crisis of the modern world: war, social injustice, the oppression of peoples and classes, crime in all its violent and nonviolent forms, our dying natural environment. We see money carrying and catalyzing the mammoth illusions of power, fame, and pleasure that move the masses of the world and to which our society devotes so much of its energy through the continually accelerating production of ever-new inventions and technologies.

We see to what a great extent the heroes we admire, if only for an hour, and the achievements and marks of "progress" of nations and cultures, are a reflection of financial forces, whose glory fades when these forces change, like eddies in a stream that have no reality apart from the currents of water that create them. We see how many of the dreams of empire, utopia, and religious salvation, as well as the paranoiac nightmares of mass resentment of new ideas or alien beliefs, are fueled and, to some extent, even created by money—directly or indirectly. To regard money in this perspective is to see who and what we are.

That is why now, in our time, the problem of money has to be faced as a problem of consciousness, as a problem of the being of man in the universal world. It is more than just a psychological or social problem which one strives to correct in advance of attending to questions of the spirit. It has become the key to understanding the great purpose of human life and what, precisely, prevents us from participating in that great purpose.

Because money is a problem that enters into the whole of human life, it cannot be dealt with in a piecemeal fashion on the level at which it presents itself—pragmatically, psychologically, or moralistically—any more than one can escape from prison by visiting the prison psychologist or social worker and improving conditions inside the prison walls.

The comparison of the life of mankind to existence in prison is rooted in a profound and very ancient vision of man's being and his possible inner development. In the following pages we shall see how this vision has been expressed in various images, many of which have lost their power for us and no longer support the search for liberation. But by relating these ancient teachings to the money question, we may begin to sound the depths of what has been called the *sleep* of mankind and discover what is required of us in order to awaken. Our relation to money can become a potent instrument in the search for self-knowledge.

We must understand this prison, this hell, this wheel of birth and death, if we wish to see clearly the immense greatness for which mankind was created. If we try to envision one without the other, it will lead us nowhere. It is necessary to grasp the true scale of man's place in the universe along with the extent to which he has missed the mark. To speak of man's intrinsic greatness without at the same time clearly picturing his actual degradation is to indulge in a daydream. Equally, to emphasize the illusions and corruption of man's existence without clearly envisioning his nearly godlike possibilities is to live in a nightmare.

A Freudian psychoanalyst once summed up to me his vision of the human condition by saying that man is not as bad as he thinks he is, nor can he become as good as he dreams of becoming. The assumption of this book is precisely the opposite of the psychoanalytic view: man is in a far worse condition than he believes, but he can become far greater than he imagines.

In this book, I shall try where possible to avoid using overly familiar religious language to speak about the human condition. But sometimes it will be unavoidable. For example, when describing man's ultimate possibilities, as they have been presented since the most ancient of times and by the wisest of teachers, it is impossible not to speak of man as serving a divine purpose on the earth and in the created universe. At the same time, it is necessary to break out of our conventional concepts of God as a merely external being. The point is that within *ourselves* there exists the possibility and even the necessity of experiencing and serving something unimaginably great and inconceivably real. The structure of human nature is without sense or meaning unless the idea of this inner possibility is understood.

Somewhere within every human being there exists an intimation of this possibility and often even a wordless, obscure longing for contact with this something. It is a longing, a wish, a call, that throws into question every other aim and purpose of our lives. We do not hear that call very often or very distinctly, but when we do hear it, we see that it comes from a part of ourselves that is disturbingly unrelated to the rest of us.

Paraphrasing the words of Goethe's *Faust,* "two selves dwell within our breast." One part of us is meant to live and function in the world we see around us—to eat, sleep, and produce our children, to answer the challenges of the natural and social world: in the words of Solomon in the Book of Ecclesiastes, to be born and die, to kill and to heal, to build and destroy, to weep and to laugh, get and lose, keep and cast away. This is human life "under the sun," the world that we see and know and call *real.* But God, that "something," is *above the sun,* above all that our eyes can see and our mind can name, and there is a higher part of ourselves that senses this and calls to us. We are two-natured beings. Such is the ancient teaching.

The legendary King Solomon, whom we shall have much occasion to call upon in this book, speaks of this life "under the sun" as a prison, a cage of vanities, a world of appearances and illusion. And the most terrifying thing about this prison is that we cannot see it for what it is.

Imagine, then, a prison where the prisoners do not know or remember the life of freedom outside the walls. All their efforts are spent trying only to better their conditions inside the prison. Those in crowded, dirty, or isolated cells envy other prisoners who have greater privileges. Some decorate the walls of their cells, paint pretty stripes on the bars, without suspecting what these bars are really for.

This is a very "enlightened" prison. There are recreation facilities, arts and crafts, there is a well-stocked library, though the prison authorities carefully exclude books with certain ideas about the world outside the prison. There are prison psychiatrists to help the prisoners adapt and adjust. There are prison priests to instill imaginary beliefs and form segregated little "monasteries." Over time, this prison has even evolved to allow political groups and meetings. Philosophers and critics arise among the prisoners to argue for more equality and liberty—*within the prison.* Honors are handed out, prizes are given, great names are enshrined in the rolls of prison-science, prison-art, prison-morality.

Occasionally, there appears a prisoner—sent from the outside—who speaks clearly and compellingly of a life outside the walls. What becomes of him or her? How is the messenger received? Sometimes he is met with mockery or hostility. Sometimes, the prisoners themselves kill him or dispatch him into isolation. Often his message, if it is particularly clear and persuasive, is taken up by the prison priests and psychologists, who adapt it to suit their purposes.

But sometimes this messenger from outside the walls convinces a few people that another world exists and shows them how to escape. These prisoners begin to understand that the only sensible aim they can have is to escape from prison and, if possible, to help others escape. A special, carefully guarded knowledge circulates among those who have "ears to hear."

A nightmarish fantasy or a fair representation of the life of mankind? And what are the bars and doors of our prison? What is its currency? Who are the jailers and administrators? For we must note that this metaphor, which accurately reflects teachings handed down over the millennia, is meant not only as a description of a materialistic society, but as a portrait of ourselves. The bars and chains are inside us, as are the "guards," the "priests," and the "psychologists." The spiritual paths or ways that have existed in all cultures and epochs of human history have sought to show us both the interior prison in which we live and the immensities of understanding and love that we are made for.

As for the "messenger," this also represents something both outside and within ourselves. The life of every man or woman contains glimpses of another quality of being, another state of consciousness; we need not rely entirely on metaphors and descriptions offered by others. But our culture does not help us appreciate these glimpses or understand them for what they tell us about our possible moral, mental, and emotional development. We are not helped to see these glimpses as "messengers" from another, higher part of ourselves which we need to study and cultivate.

We can begin to grasp what life could be like outside the walls of our prison by recalling what we are like during these rare moments. I am not necessarily speaking here of what are ordinarily considered "peak experiences" or emotional highs. Often, the glimpses I speak of are given to us in a moment of great sorrow or loss, or in times of extreme physical danger, of profound disappointment, when everything we have relied on is suddenly taken away or lost. Sometimes, they appear in moments of "super-happiness" when our ordinary perceptions simply cannot contain what is taking place.

In such moments, an individual *divides into two.* A second self appears and, most often, what it does is *watch.* Only that and nothing more. But it is a watching, a *seeing,* a presence, unlike anything else in our experience; it is an awakening to ourselves of utter lucidity and calm. It is a glimpse of inner freedom completely different from that to which we apply this label in the more familiar experiences of satisfying our desires or ridding ourselves of burdens. In this second self lies the seed of what in Christianity is called the new, arising from the old, Adam; in the Judaic tradition it is Jacob and Esau, the higher and the lower man within us; in Hinduism it is the imperishable atman existing within the mortal ego; in Buddhism it is the Buddha-nature waiting to flash like lightning within the darkness of the illusory sense of self.

What do we see when we awaken? Here there are many possibilities. In some cases, what is seen is a startlingly well-functioning ordinary self: this is often what happens in moments of physical danger when swift action, clear judgment, or unusual strength and fortitude are demanded.

But in other cases, what is seen is myself as I usually am, with all my weaknesses, deceptions, and failings, as sometimes happens when one sees oneself performing an action contrary to one's deepest moral values, or when one suddenly confronts oneself in the grip of some self-destructive habit. Such moments of seeing oneself can result in a complete change of one's life, freedom from an addiction, for example. Dramatic changes of this kind, however, tend to blur the most significant fact about these glimpses—namely, that they reveal the existence within ourselves of a second consciousness that is there all the time, but with which we are almost never in contact.

Experiences of this kind may occur spontaneously in the

midst of the most pedestrian circumstances of life, and they also appear with greater frequency when we are very young. But there is little to assist us in drawing the proper conclusions from them or in asking useful questions about them. Are they only the tip of a great mountain of possibilities lying dormant within us? What kind of people are we when these experiences are taking place within us? Do we not, if only for a fleeting moment, actually come closer to being the man or woman we wish to be—capable of impartial judgment, exquisitely precise action, deeply moral feeling? Are we limited to experiencing such states accidentally and sporadically, or is there a way of living that could bring us to a more frequent and more enduring relationship to these states? Who or what *is* this second consciousness that is sensed as more myself than my everyday sense of identity?

And what does it mean that this second self cares not at all for the things, such as money, that evoke so much desire and anxiety in one's usual state? What does it mean that there are two lives within us? Could they ever be brought into harmonious relationship? Could our ordinary functions of thought, feeling, and instinct ever become so attuned to this higher presence that they actually submit to it voluntarily and joyfully? And if this second self is indifferent to the aims of the ordinary ego, what then are *its* aims?—*its* values?—*its*—that is to say, *my*—real purpose in the universe?

In the light of such questions, one begins to sense that the perennial quest for the meaning of life must, without fail, take into account these extraordinary glimpses of our two natures. It may be that it is in these glimpses, and the deductions we can draw from them, that the whole question of the meaning of life lies. No wonder our attempts to answer this question without carefully considering these experiences almost always come to nothing. Is it any wonder that we have become a culture of cynics and dreamers?

There is more, much more, to be said about these moments and about the idea of man's two natures. We are not speaking here of what is ordinarily understood as "mysticism." This term has become useless, covering everything from the most exalted possible human contact with a higher reality to the most self-deceived, banal, or even psychotic experiences. But perhaps enough has been said for now to show why the great spiritual thinkers and teachers of the past, in every epoch and everywhere that man has lived, speak of man not only as the greedy, clumsy, cruel, and forgetful being he so often seems to be, but also as a being of colossal cosmic significance, a being meant to play a role of unique importance in the universal scheme. We need to listen more closely to what these teachers tell us about who we human beings really are.

But in order to be brought back to our present lives with all their actual difficulties, we must also ask another question of unsurpassed significance: what, in fact, keeps us from awareness of our true nature? What keeps us as though drugged, asleep to our possible inner life? Why aren't we terrified by our present condition? Why do we spend our precious psychic energy on craving better cells in our prison rather than seeking to escape? What is this *sleep of meaning?* Each day the jailers come to take one or another of us away. "It's the common lot," some of us say, with noble resignation. "It's the passage to immortality," say others of us, with the bright eyes of otherworldly passion. But there, in the corner of the common cage, quietly, unnoticed, two or three prisoners are whispering, examining a certain piece of paper on which is drawn a kind of diagram . . . or is it a map?

* * *

We are going to speak of money. What is its role in the search for meaning? Is our relationship to it one of the chief factors that keeps us in our prison, or could it also be a tool for breaking out, for awakening to a life filled with intensity of purpose?

I remember some conversations about money that also involved the businessman whose advice I quoted at the beginning of this introduction. The setting was a conference I had helped to organize in Madison, Wisconsin about fifteen years ago. He had eagerly accepted my invitation to join a panel of distinguished scholars, religious leaders, and local civic and government officials on the theme "Money, Power, and the Human Spirit."

In fact, he spoke very little during the three days, but when he did speak, there was such a remarkable evenness and authority in his words that invariably a special atmosphere of listening prevailed. Yet the things he said seemed more often than not slightly baffling to the panelists.

"I was thinking," he said at one point. "It's a real question for me. Is there a way of looking at money, of educating myself, and educating our children to look at money so that it is actually not dirty, so that it is a unifying factor in every scale, in every sense? Or is money only a problem? Money is dealt with by economics. That's treating money as a problem. But is there a way of reconciling ourselves to money, so that we actually discover an attitude, an idea with which one can approach money, educate people to approach money, in a way that gives it a place in the life around us as a unifying influence? That, to me, is *the* question."

At another point, several of the panelists had been excoriating the rich as greedy and selfish, and condemning the American economic system for making wage slaves out of everyone, including teachers of young people, forcing them to sell out their ideals.

Addressing the most vocal of these panelists, he broke in:

"Could I probe you about that—because I am very moved by your concern for the materially poor people. Is it impossible that you would be concerned for the spiritually poor people who have a lot of money? Because if you could get some of them on your side they might be able to help you accomplish what you have to do."

This was met with sarcasm: "Tactically, I wouldn't bother about them!"

With the slightest shade of impatience in his voice, he replied:

"I have been listening with good humor to the categorization of all rich people as being completely selfish and unintelligent. But, in fact, it takes a lot of character, a lot of imagination, a lot of determination to build a large fortune. It's not that easy. True, it is just money, but to work at it day after day in the changing, stormy, difficult economic climate we have—it's not that easy. You have got to allow that somebody who gets to the top of Continental Bank, or whatever, cannot be totally and hopelessly unintelligent.

"I think there are exceptions in all classes. There are morons among the poor and among the rich. Yet it seems that one needs to enlist the help of the privileged class in order to get anything done, even spiritually. It seems very odd, but even in the spiritual realm, money really does seem to help. I am being rather practical and this is the nub of my interest. It is very good to say that one should be poorer, but money seems to help."

Then, turning to the person who had accused teachers of being bought, he went on:

"Is it just the teachers who are bought? Or am I bought also? This is the heart of it. Are we speaking about a change, in the sense that some people are more vulnerable to the material power of money and *I'm not* like that and so I'm going to rescue civilization? Or, are we *all* being affected, and would the real change come when we're big enough to accept that the human psyche includes some tendencies toward the lower? We've got a very important question here, if it's change we're speaking about. Are we going to say, 'I know the answer' or are we going to say, 'We've got all these tendencies,' and in understanding them, in studying them, perhaps the change will take place by itself.

"We want to change because what we have is not working, even worldwide. But where does change begin? In the individual or in the social structure? It seems to me we are up against that question. Now, if change begins in the social structure, then, of course, I am with you. But if it begins in the individual, in myself, then it surely begins with myself becoming aware, for example, that I place too little value on things that cannot be quantified. If *I*"—he strongly emphasized this word—"become aware that I place too little value on these things, there's a redressing of the balance that takes place in myself, all by itself. If I really *see* that I'm going downhill, I start to go uphill."

Though he placed tremendous emphasis on this last sentence, no one around the table asked him to say more about what it really means to *see*. The discussion moved to other things, as it did almost every time he spoke.

Some years later, as a member of the editorial advisory board of the acclaimed *Macmillan Encyclopedia of Religion,* I asked this same businessman to contribute an article on "Money and

Religion." The essay he wrote was, in my view, full of extraordinary insight, but, lacking the requisite scholarly apparatus, it was rejected by the editors. Let me cite the last paragraphs of that unpublished article.

> In each normal child . . . there is a sense of adventure, a willingness to take risks to get what is wanted the most. In a world where money is part of everything, young people need much help in interiorizing this sense of risk in order to take hold of a truly [spiritual] understanding of what goes on within them and around them. Without this help, and without this inner understanding, passive obedience, out of fear, to the rules learned in Sunday school—not to steal, not to take what is not given—is unlikely to stand up to the stresses and emotional pressures of life, particularly in a big city. Sooner or later the rule will break down, unless that life, with its omnipresent money demands, is being lived in the light of a spiritual tradition. More and more, all over the world, responsible questions about money, such as how much does one actually need, how much is enough for a given purpose, are disappearing from view. The urge just to get more money is becoming a force, the action of which no one can easily deny, however ineffective he may be as a money-maker.

> A superficial understanding of the place of money in a spiritual life, and of its relation with religion through occasional and impersonal giving, is no longer much help. Without a long work on oneself, it is impossible in contemporary conditions to be generous and free in regard to the force of money. . . . To use the force of money intelligently is to become aware of its original function in uniting human beings in service to the highest; thus it may be

necessary nowadays for a seeking person to engage voluntarily in business for himself or herself for a certain period or to be faced with raising a large sum of money from nothing in a limited time for some inescapable reason. In other words, it may be necessary to have mastered the money game before one can see with certainty that the power of money over the human mind is limited and that there are things money cannot buy.

If the present book succeeds in opening the meaning of what is being spoken about here, then it will have accomplished its purpose. The aim is nothing more nor less than to sacralize the money question. This does not mean making money itself sacred. It means finding the precise place of money at the heart of the most important undertaking of our lives—the search to become what we are meant to be, in the service of that greatness that calls to every man or woman on this endangered earth.

PART I

THE AFFLUENT SOCIETY AND THE IMPOVERISHED SOUL

1.

"THE RICHEST AND MOST POWERFUL NATION ON EARTH"

What really makes our country so "wealthy"? I can remember the first time the question occurred to me. I was only twelve years old—long before I had even heard of the science of economics. It was just after World War II. In newspapers and magazines and in the schoolroom, I was constantly hearing the United States referred to as "the richest and most powerful nation on earth." Sometimes, the phrase was: "the richest and most powerful nation in history."

I could well understand that we were the most powerful— our military might, including the atomic bomb, was immense and invincible. But what did it mean that we were *rich?* How is a whole nation called *rich? I* was not rich; my family was not rich. Quite the contrary; we barely had enough money for the necessities of life. Nor were most of the people I knew rich, nor even "comfortable."

I knew that my schoolmate, Paul Meyer, who lived in a

big house at the corner of our block, was rich, the latest evidence being his new Schwinn bicycle. Whatever I wanted, Paul Meyer had. That's what being rich meant—you could get whatever you wanted. And that is what money always meant to me and to everyone else I knew.

But when I was quite a bit younger, eight years old, maybe, I visited Paul Meyer's house for the first time. We went down to his large playroom in the basement. My eyes nearly leaped out of my head when I saw what he had there. Every toy I had ever dreamed of having, and many I had never even heard of before, were neatly arrayed on wide shelves all around the room. Not one of them was broken, and that fact startled me as much as the sheer quantity and variety of toys. Every toy of mine sooner or later broke or wore out, if only because I had to extract all the joy and meaning I could from it before finding the energy to beg, really beg, my parents to buy me a new one. Subconsciously, I must have felt that Paul never really knew the intensity of that kind of desire.

When I saw his set of electric trains, I gasped and trembled. Half the floor was covered with gleaming silver tracks, crossing and looping beyond all comprehension, passing by exquisitely realistic switching and loading stations, bridges, and signal poles with tiny lights flashing, and through a long mountain tunnel that had an actual miniature village with little houses and streets nestled on the slope. As for the trains themselves, when I saw them I nearly exploded. They seemed a hundred times bigger than any toy trains I had ever seen. They were exact in every detail. I thought with shame of the miserable, tinny little set of trains that I owned; I had to squint to see them as real. But these trains of Paul Meyer's—and especially the heavy locomotive, with moving wheels and great rods and countless spinning, interlocking parts—were more real than reality itself.

Paul pressed the handle on the big switch box and the

trains—there were two of them—started moving. I was beside myself with excitement, but Paul—I could not understand his lassitude. He did not even watch them as they flew around the tracks, stopping and starting with magical synchronization. Instead of looking at them, he looked at me—with a weak, pathetic smile.

Here I was in wonderland and there before me was this weak, sad little prince. I could not digest the contradiction. When I returned home, I ran to get my own cheap trains and set the tinny locomotive on the small circle of tracks. Something had long ago broken in the rusting switch box, so I clumsily pushed the locomotive around the tracks. I remember experiencing two contradictory feelings: on the one hand, a devouring envy of Paul Meyer and, at the same moment, a sensation of emptiness that made my face feel exactly like the weak, sad face I had just seen when I was with him, and which gave me the first taste of what I much later recognized as the feeling of compassion. For that brief moment, I knew from inside what Paul Meyer felt about his trains and all his other toys.

I am not exaggerating when I say that this experience has stayed just below the surface of my consciousness during all the years that have followed, like a fragment of uranium irradiating my perceptions about money and wealth. In the household where I grew up, the most intense and violent emotions centered around money—the lack of it, the need for it, the desperate difficulty of having enough of it, and the fear of what would become of us without it. Money was power, reality, happiness. Money was a reality stronger than anything else, and the gods of money had no compassion; they were hard, unyielding, hostile. They broke my father's spirit again and again and, through his violent despair and anxiety, they continuously broke my own spirit. Yet, there was this Paul Meyer.

What Is An "Affluent Society"?

What I am trying to say is that we are all more alike than we may think. As a child, you may have had very different experiences with money, but we have all grown up in a "wealthy" country. And it was only much later in my life that I began to understand what this means. It means, at least in part, that *ours is a society that has given material wealth first priority in our common life.* As I studied the history of different cultures, I began to realize what was for me an astonishing fact: *not every civilization has wanted what ours has wanted!*

When I first glimpsed this fact about the history of human civilization, I was already far along in my career as a college professor; yet I experienced the same kind of shock that I experienced in Paul Meyer's playroom when I was eight years old. Here was a child who had everything I could have ever dreamt of having, but it was not what he wanted!

A New Definition of Affluence

Similarly, there had once existed civilizations, whole worlds, which had not wanted what we in our world have called "wealth"! But this must not be misunderstood or taken naively. Certainly, mankind has always needed and craved material things. And, certainly, human beings have always suffered from greed. But not every culture or civilization has measured itself principally by the standard of comfort and safety in the material world.

We live, then, in a "wealthy" country—what nowadays has been called an "affluent society." This means not only that we have much material wealth, but that *we want this wealth more than we want anything else.* This ordering of priorities has brought our civilization to the brink of ruin. We know we must find a way out, a way back to values and priorities that represent the real, whole nature of man. But all the ways that were once intended to help us find our authentic well-being and our authentic responsibility are themselves deeply stained by the money question. Religion, education, the pursuit of scientific knowledge, medicine, government, as well as most of our day-to-day relationships, have all been surrounded and captured by our compulsion for material wealth—and especially our fascination with the instrument we have invented in order to facilitate the acquisition and distribution of wealth, namely, money.

IN SEARCH OF A NEW ATTITUDE

What to do? How can we find a place to stand that is free from the influence of money so as to think impartially about it and then plot our course according to deeper values? We are like people adrift in a churning sea, desperately in need of finding even a tiny piece of stable, dry land upon which to take our bearings. Before we can solve the problem of our relationship to money, we must first understand it. And before we can understand it, we must study it. This requires that we adopt a certain attitude toward the whole range of our problems with money.

This new attitude is not easy to define or attain. We must not escape too far into abstractions, into philosophical outer space completely free from the pulls and bites of the money problem. Because it is precisely the seductions and anxieties of money that we need to have in view. On the other hand, if we stay too close to the problem, it will influence our perceptions in ways that will make impartiality impossible. We will start trying to *solve* the problem before we have really understood it and seen it as a whole. A great part of all mankind's suffering comes from this tendency in all of us.

We need to *orbit* the money problem, much as a spacecraft orbits the earth at a distance precisely between the gravitational pull of earth and the freedom of outer space. This freedom, as we now know, is actually the sum total of the influences of distant worlds, suns, stars, galaxies. We need to stay just within the gravitational pull of the money problem and, with a clearer view of the stars—the great metaphysical teachings of the ages— circle our ''earth'' with our eyes wide open and our observational instruments finely tuned.

2.

THE NEW
POVERTY

A number of years ago, I began to notice the same complaint coming from almost everyone I knew. People would say something like, "I'm going through a very bad time just now." Or they would say of someone else, "This is a rough period for her."

But I soon realized that these "rough periods" were occurring with greater frequency; they had become a permanent feature of people's lives. Yet my friends and acquaintances continued to speak as though they were only passing through something and would soon break into calmer waters. "We're coming on to the holidays," one would say, "it's a very bad time for people." Or, "You know how August is, everything goes to hell." Or, "Spring is always a tough time."

I began to be very interested in this phenomenon. These are all talented, mature people. Many are professionals—physicians, executives, editors, scientists, engineers, schoolteachers, artists.

Many live in beautiful homes and have fine cars or even boats. These are people who seem to "have it made."

Almost all these people admitted to being "better off" than they had ever been before—earning more money, living in better homes, having better cars, nicer clothes. Yet, almost without exception, they were all in a "difficult period."

It was only after a long time and a great many such observations that the question of the wealth of our society came together in my mind with the fact of the increasing unhappiness of its people. A huge contradiction loomed in front of me. It was obvious that in some deep, essential sense, we were not wealthy at all, but actually quite poor. We were all more or less like Paul Meyer.

What does it feel like to be poor? What is the psychological suffering usually associated with poverty? For myself, I have always pictured poverty as associated with fear and anxiety about the future, fear of abandonment, fear of physical danger, and fear of loneliness. I see the poor as trapped, tense, cunning, harsh. I see them bored, empty of hope, or consumed by absurd fantasies, or drugging themselves with some poison that destroys their bodies while offering only the relief of temporary oblivion. I see them living and dying like animals. Their lives are the very image of hell.

LIFE IN HELL

Now, call to mind the images of hell that have been offered through the ages by the great wisdom teachings of the world. Begin with the most obvious and common symbol, unquenchable fire. It is not hard to understand this to mean torture by one's own desires. A more modern word for this condition is neurosis—a condition in which one is trapped within an endlessly recurring pattern of emotional suffering, where obtaining the apparent object of one's desire serves only to intensify the desire itself. More recently, and more interestingly, the word *addiction* has been used to describe this pervasive psychological suffering. Exactly as one may become addicted to a narcotic like opium or heroin, so we each have our addictive cravings for sex, perhaps, or recognition, or food or clothes or victory or explanations, or any of the countless other things or experiences that form the object of what we call our *emotions.*

We need to understand that when the great thinkers of the past warn us about the evils of our desires, they are speaking of this. They are speaking of addiction. No great teacher, neither Christ nor Moses nor Socrates, ever condemned desire as such. No, what they have tried to show us is that we allow the desires to define our sense of identity. We fuel these desires with a certain precious psychic energy that is meant to serve a much higher function in our lives. Fueled by this higher psychic energy, desires become cravings, addictions; and there is no better representation of this state of affairs than the image of unquenchable fire.

In the first part of Dante's *Divine Comedy,* the author descends into Hell and begins by feeling pity for the men and women he sees there, writhing in filth and pain. But his guide, the great poet Virgil, admonishes him. Do not feel pity, Virgil tells him; they are getting exactly what they want. Hell is the state in which we are barred from receiving what we truly need because of the value we give to what we merely want. It is a condition of ultimate deprivation, that is, poverty.

In his vastly influential work, *The Affluent Society,* John Kenneth Galbraith characterizes the present economic structure of American society as based not only on the satisfaction of desire, but on the *creation* of desire. This aspect of our economic order is one of the chief factors that distinguishes it from the economies of almost all other cultures in history. In the following passage from *The Affluent Society,* Galbraith sums up his analysis of the dynamics of the production of consumer goods in our society. With very minor changes, it could pass for a traditional Buddhist description of hell:

> One cannot defend production as satisfying wants if that production creates the wants.
>
> Were it so that a man on arising each morning was assailed by demons which instilled in him a passion sometimes for silk shirts, sometimes for kitchenware, sometimes for chamber pots, and sometimes for orange squash, there would be every reason to applaud the effort to find the goods, however odd, that quenched this flame. But should it be that his passion was the result of his first having cultivated the demons, and should it also be that his effort to allay it stirred the demons to ever greater and greater effort, there would be question as to how rational was his solution. Unless restrained by conventional attitudes, he might wonder if the solution lay with more goods or fewer demons.
>
> So it is that if production creates the wants it seeks to satisfy, or if the wants emerge *pari passu* with the production, then the urgency of the wants can no longer be used to defend the urgency of the production.
>
> Production only fills a void that it has itself created.
>
> (JOHN KENNETH GALBRAITH, *The Affluent Society.* 4th ed. New York: New American Library, 1984, pp. 121–22)

THE DESTRUCTION OF TIME

The Buddhist symbolism of hell has much to teach us about our life in "the affluent society." In Buddhism, the world just beneath the human level is occupied by animals. In this symbolism, "animals" are understood as beings for whom the getting of food so completely dominates their daily lives that they have no "free time" to pursue any other aim. Moreover, the animal mind, with all its perception and feeling, is almost entirely in the service of this pursuit. The "animal" does not and cannot contemplate or ponder or even see anything that does not relate to its desire for food. In addition, the "animals" cannot live except by preying on each other.

Who can deny that, in this sense, we live like "animals"? Do we not everywhere hear the same cry: "I have no time!" "I'm so busy!" "I have too much to do!" Everywhere people are straining to "set aside" time for things that are felt to be humanly important—being with loved ones, enjoying nature, studying ideas, or engaging in some creative activity. And, more and more, it is becoming a losing battle.

Why has time disappeared in our culture? How is it that after decades of inventions and new technologies devoted to saving time and labor, the result is that there is no time left? We are a time-poor society; we are temporally impoverished. And there is no issue, no aspect of human life, that exceeds this in importance. The destruction of time is literally the destruction of life.

Leisure? Holidays? Retirement? Recreation? Anyone who has tried to turn to these activities in the hope of recovering his or her own human sense of time knows how disappointing they have become, how nearly impossible it now is to have real, full, and valid time. We rarely feel that our time is "our own." We rarely sense that we are consciously alive, now and here, free from compulsive worry about the past and the future, free fully to experience our lives. The coin of time has been degraded and cheapened to the point of vanishing.

In a very real sense, in a terrifyingly real sense, our lives have been growing shorter and shorter, even as medical science finds ever more ingenious ways of prolonging our biological or animal time. If we are going to find a new approach to the money question, it will have to enable us to bring time back into our lives.

As with time, so with space. Many are the images of hell that show it to be suffocatingly crowded. No freedom of movement is possible there. The denizens of hell cannot step away from the endlessly repetitive pursuit of what they crave. There is no perspective in hell, no distance from oneself. This absence of personal space is the visual symbol of what the wisdom teachings of all ages have referred to as the condition of self-identification with one's desires and fears. In the East this is called "attachment." In the West it has been called, simply, "capture." In all cultures, we find images of hell in which the devil or devils are pictured as eating human beings. Legends and fairy tales are full of stories in which monsters swallow and devour hapless men and women. This, too, is the condition known by the Fathers of the early Church as "capture."

A Day in the Life of Donald Trump

At this point, I cannot resist citing the portrait of his daily life offered by Donald Trump in his book, *The Art of the Deal*. It has been haunting me ever since I read it.

"I wake up most mornings very early," writes Mr. Trump,

and spend the first hour or so of each day reading the morning newspapers. I usually arrive at my office by nine, and I get on the phone. There's rarely a day with fewer than fifty calls, and often it runs to over a hundred. In between, I have at least a dozen meetings. The majority occur on the spur of the moment, and few of them last longer than fifteen minutes. I rarely stop for lunch. I leave my office by six-thirty, but I frequently make calls from home until midnight, and all weekend long.

(Donald J. Trump with Tony Schwartz, *The Art of the Deal.* New York: Random House, 1987, p. 3)

"It never stops," Mr. Trump continues, "and I wouldn't have it any other way." He then presents an hour-by-hour picture of his week, which consists entirely of meetings and telephone calls involving some of the most influential businessmen, the most famous or adored celebrities, the most highly placed government officials in America and Europe. It includes negotiations involving hundreds of millions of dollars, the buying and selling of giant companies and huge properties.

"I don't do it for the money," he writes. "I've got enough, much more than I'll ever need. I do it to do it. Deals are my art form. Other people paint beautifully on canvas or write wonderful poetry. I like making deals, preferably big deals. That's how I get my kicks." *(The Art of the Deal,* p. 3)

"My attention span is short," writes Trump in his most recent book:

Instead of being content when everything is going fine, I start getting impatient and irritable. So I look for more and more deals to do. On a day in which I've got several good ones in the works and the phone calls and faxes are going back and forth and the tension is palpable—well, at those times I feel the way other people do when they're on vacation.

(Donald J. Trump with Charles Leerhsen, *Trump: Surviving at the Top.* New York: Random House, 1990, pp. 5–6)

Why do I cite these passages? Why have they haunted me? Because there is a Donald Trump inside of me and probably inside of you, too. On my own small scale, I too *like* to be occupied with "important" people, "important" situations, "serious" problems. I, too, like challenges—of a certain kind, to be sure. There are other kinds of challenges which terrify me and, perhaps Donald Trump, too; we will speak later of the kind of challenges all of us run away from, and which are the most serious and necessary challenges for a human being to face.

But, for now, I am haunted by this image of the pleasure, the "joy" of being *busy,* of being busy with important things. I am haunted and disturbed by the part of myself that envies Donald Trump. How good it would be to live like that, dealing with big forces in the game of life, and *winning* most of the time, but in any case always being involved in something major, and being the central person, the one who makes the difference.

How did you get inside me, Trump? I don't remember letting you in. Do I really *like* having no time—or, to put it better—do I really prefer so many things, so much outer doing, to living consciously within myself in the present moment?

What I am asking is this: do I—do you—*need* to make that telephone call just now? Do I need to buy that car or suit or new VCR or that extraordinary carpet? Do you need to accept that invitation to dinner? Do I need to write that book, receive that honor? Take that trip? Do you need, now, to file those papers, dictate that report, do you need to be busy, that is, swallowed by your outer activity? What is it that makes all of us end each day with the sense that we have not lived our time, but have *been* lived, used by what we do?

Even those of us who are not so assailed by outer activities are part of the same tragedy. Even when we are not *busy,* we are often driven by envy of those who are busy. We continually look for ways to become busy—that is, to be devoured by some outer activity. We dread the prospect of not having enough to do. And as for the rest of us, who are neither immersed in outer activities nor yearning for them . . . our time is swallowed by dreams and fantasies or by the thousand little impulses, emotions, and thoughts that continually arise within us.

In sum, time disappears into outer action or inner impulses. Into doings, cravings, or dreamings. But human time is *conscious time*. And this has been lost, destroyed. In its place there is now animal time (doing, moving about, preying on others, eating, building, killing, etc.); plant time (dreaming, languishing, imagining); or "mineral"—that is, mechanical—time: the time of devices such as clocks and computers. What we call logical thinking is often just an internal version of these lifeless machines. Implicitly, we even take pride in the mechanicity of our thinking when, forgetting the metaphorical origin of the usage, we refer to a computer's "intelligence." This is mental time, "mineral" in its rigidity and sterility. We lay this logical cement over organic life out there and in ourselves. Carried to its extreme, this becomes the mindset that measures the whole of human life solely by the "bottom line."

THE REALM OF DIMINISHING BEING

These observations bring us to what is perhaps the most terrifying of all the images of hell to be found in the ancient teachings. In the Old Testament the lower world is called Sheol. Here there are no images of raging fire. No cacophonous sounds. No sulfurous fumes. Sheol is simply and solely the place of shadows, dark, weak existence, continually fading, ever-paler life. Sheol is the realm of *diminishing being*. This is what is meant by *darkness* when in Deuteronomy 33 God says to Man, "I have placed before thee life and death (darkness); therefore, choose life."

Sheol is the condition of human life proceeding with ever-diminishing human presence. It is the movement toward *absence,* the movement away from God—for let us carefully note that one of the central definitions of God that is given in the Old Testament is *conscious presence.* Moses asks God, "What shall I say to the people of Israel? Whom shall I say has sent me with these commandments?" The answer he receives, as mysterious today as it has ever been: "Say unto the children of Israel, I AM hath sent me unto you" (Exodus 3:14).

Sheol—the lower world or hell of the ancient Hebrews—is the condition of ever-increasing distance from *I am,* from one's own conscious presence in the midst of life. It is this state of the human psyche that is—for us—the most relevant definition of hell. Beyond all social criticism of our era and beyond all the progress and accomplishments we could name, the conditions of our culture more and more favor the diminishing of our being. Less and less is it necessary in this "affluent society" to be consciously present in order to accomplish the tasks that we are obliged to perform. The technologies, the inventions, the accomplishments we prize—all of them, almost without exception, are prized because they allow us to live and function more and more automatically, without conscious presence, without *I am.* I take the "happy life" of Donald Trump as a symbol of this state of affairs.

I should, of course, add that I have never met Mr. Trump personally. For all I know, he too wakes up in the middle of night asking himself what he is doing and why. Possibly he, like us, sometimes sees that he is not the hero of his life, that in fact he is being lived by his life rather than living it himself. Even though he writes as though he is consciously making great decisions and masterfully dealing with the vicissitudes of life, I do not for a moment take his books seriously in that respect, and perhaps he doesn't either. But as a symbol of one of the key aspects of our modern mythology, Mr. Trump serves very well.

The ancient Greeks had a view of hell similar to that of the Hebrews—the land of shadows ruled by the lord Hades. Homer tells us what the great and cunning explorer, risk-taker and trouble-seeker Odysseus learned when he was visited by the denizens of this realm, this underground world of the dead whose heads are filled with darkness as they wander forever among the silent fields of asphodels; who can never, the myth tells us, return to sweet daylight because they have drunk of the waters of the river Lethe, forgetfulness. They cannot remember the way they were brought to this dark realm, and therefore can never find their way back to the land of the living. Among those who appear to Odysseus is none other than the greatest of the Greeks, the king and warrior Achilles.

"Most fortunate man that ever was or will be," Odysseus greets him. And he continues:

> For in the days when you were on earth we Argives honored you as though you were a god; and now, down here, you are a mighty prince among the dead. For you, Achilles, Death has surely lost his sting.

"My lord Odysseus," replies Achilles,

> spare me your praise of death. Put me on earth again, and I would rather be a slave in the house of some poor and landless man, than king of all these dead men. . . .
>
> (Adapted from Rieu translation, Book VI)

When one begins to appreciate the significance of the fact that we are simply not consciously present in our lives, it becomes the central and most immediate question that we can have. The reason we are unable to find practical spiritual wisdom that can help us understand money is that we no longer can discern the teaching about *presence* in the doctrines and philosophies that have survived the passing of centuries. Once we reintroduce this notion into our understanding of life, there can appear a sort of aqueduct carrying good fresh water from the great minds of the past into the infernal wasteland of our contemporary existence.

We have all had intimations of the idea of hell as life lived without consciousness of self. I remember when I first heard about the Christian idea of hell—that popular version of the idea that takes it literally, horned devils and pitchforks—I felt strangely relieved when I started thinking about it. As a small child, my idea of death had come strictly from seeing animals killed, and from seeing my grandparents lying embalmed in their coffins. I thought of death as pure disappearance, vanishing. And when I tried to grasp the possibility of my own death, I became terrified beyond measure. I could not understand, I could not picture, I could not in any way accept that I, me, here, could ever *not* exist. And so, when as a child I heard about the souls of bad people spending eternity in a very hot place being jabbed by pitchforks, I said to myself something like: "That is not very pleasant to contemplate. I certainly do not want to be stuck and burned forever. But, however bad that might be, at least *I* would go on existing."

What a blessed thought! But in my guts I still feared that the other notion of what happens at death was the true one. And it continued to torment me. It was only long after I became an adult that something new entered into this fear. I began to have moments—in every other respect moments of balance and deep moral feeling—when I feared that I had *already* disappeared, vanished; moments when I understood what those earliest perceptions of death really were telling me. . . .

We will return to this subject, because in fact, this death and what it would mean to overcome it in our everyday lives are what this book is about.

3.

TAKING MONEY
SERIOUSLY

About twenty years ago, in a
Western called *Waterhole #3,* James Coburn played a high-
spirited cardsharp who snatches a chest of gold bullion away
from some bumbling thieves who themselves have just stolen
it from the U.S. Army. The film had the usual amount of
Hollywood guns and sex and perhaps a bit more than usual
good humor. It ran a few months and then faded into the
oblivion reserved for movies that will seldom be found even in
video shops.

But the last scene of the movie deserves to be remembered
and pondered. After a string of farcical amorous adventures and
gunfights, and after the gold has fallen into and out of many
grasping hands, James Coburn is about to ride across the Mexican border, his saddlebags filled with the precious metal. A
few hundred yards behind him rides everyone who is after the
gold—the sheriff, the sheriff's pretty daughter, plus the original

thieves, plus an Armenian shoemaker accompanied by a gun-toting madam, plus a trumpeting regiment of the U.S. Army. All their absurd gambits and conspiracies have failed and only James Coburn has come out ahead. They have all been greedy, but only Coburn never really forgets his aim of getting all the money for himself. All the others are at one point or another deflected from their greed by fears, emotions, fantasies, and wishful thinking. At the same time, Coburn is the only one who is able to separate himself enough from his desire for the money to allow himself some moments of tenderness for the girl and compassion for her comically beleaguered father.

As he is about to cross the border to safety, Coburn turns around in his saddle to face the viewer. "Maybe we take gold too seriously," he says to us with a smile. Then, amid the hoofbeats, shrieks, and gunshots coming from the horde of people chasing him, he calmly turns around again as the camera closes in on him. He is now quite serious, almost stern. His final words to us are: "We don't take gold seriously enough."

He rides off and the film ends.

We don't take gold seriously enough. *We don't take money seriously enough:* why do I cite these lines after just having claimed that our contemporary relationship to money has made our lives into an image of hell? It would seem that I should now be marshaling arguments to show how we must give priority to something other than money; that we should hearken to the admonitions of the great philosophers and spiritual leaders who have shown us over the ages how mankind gets swallowed by greed and avarice.

But something else is necessary before we can begin to understand what these men and women of vision are really telling us. The point I wish to make in this book is that money needs first to be *understood*—*before* we allow ourselves any moral stance at all. Surely a huge proportion of human unhappiness—

in all aspects of our lives—comes from trying to know what we ought to do before we see clearly the forces that are at play. Most so-called moral dilemmas simply dissolve when one gathers all the knowledge that is actually available. We waste an immense amount of our precious energy trying to make decisions before we really have to or are able to. Once we see something clearly, the question of morality more or less takes care of itself. *Authentic morality is the child of understanding.*

It may seem paradoxical, but what I am saying is that our lives have become a hell not because money is too important to us, but because, in a certain sense, it is not important enough.

MONEY AS ENERGY

One of the commonest views of money today is that it is a form of energy. Certainly, money is the main, moving force of human life at the present stage of civilization. Our relationships to nature, to health and illness, to education, to art, to social justice, are all increasingly permeated by the money factor.

It is not a question of regretting this fact; it is solely a question of understanding it. We live in the same world, metaphysically, cosmically speaking, as did Pythagoras, Gautama Buddha, St. Augustine, or Moses. The same forces are at play on this plane of being called earth, human life on earth. The Greeks gave the names of gods to these forces—Apollo, Aphrodite, Kronos. Today such forces are given names derived from modern psychology or science—for example, entropy, libido, homeostasis—which, however, convey only a pale reflection of their real power in human life and the cosmic scheme. And, in our time, the forces that define human life on earth manifest themselves through money.

In other times and in other cultures, money has not played

this role—but there has always been the same play of forces. What has changed is the medium through which these forces have flowed. In some cultures the "currency"—that is to say, the medium through which the main energies of human life has passed—has been land, or livestock, or human slaves, or a natural substance such as water or salt or iron, or weapons, or even ideas and symbolic forms, such as "beauty" or "honor." Walk into any museum, study any good book of history, look at any ancient document, and you will see that mankind has always put its main energy into one or another kind of thing, substance, or form.

We do not create the art of the Renaissance or medieval Europe; we do not worship the state as did ancient Rome; we do not build as did the Egyptians. But neither the Egyptians, nor the medieval Europeans, nor the peoples of the Renaissance—nor, for that matter, the cultures of ancient China, Greece, or Persia, nor the inhabitants of the North American continent before the white man—none of these created the immense global mechanism of finance whose penetration into every aspect of human life has been the chief feature of our contemporary culture. In other times and places, not everyone has wanted *money* above all else; people have desired salvation, beauty, power, strength, pleasure, propriety, explanations, food, adventure, conquest, comfort. But now and here, money—not necessarily even the things money can buy, but *money*—is what everyone wants. The outward expenditure of mankind's energy now takes place in and through money.*

---

* In his pioneering work, *The Philosophy of Money,* the sociologist Georg Simmel cited the unique interrelationship between modern technology and the invasion of money factors in every facet of modern life to a degree that sets our society apart from mercantile civilizations of the past. For Simmel, the importance given to the instrument of money epitomizes modern culture's enthrallment by means and instrumentalities. "The threads by which technology weaves the energies and materials of nature into our life are just as easily to be seen as fetters that tie

For anyone who seeks to understand the meaning of our human life on earth, for anyone who wishes to understand the meaning of his own individual life on earth, it is imperative that one understand this movement of energy. Therefore, if one wishes to understand life, one *must* understand money—in this present phase of history and civilization.

This outward movement of energy by itself has never been enough to bring ultimate meaning to human existence. Throughout all times and places, mankind has had to work to survive—to give out the energy necessary to fulfill the demands of biological and social existence on earth. But at the same time, he has been drawn to seek contact with something quite different. At all times, man has had to struggle not to be swallowed by the outer demands of life, not to disappear into these demands, needs, and desires which are a legitimate *part* of his nature, but only a part. All the great teachers of human history have brought ideas, methods, and symbols designed to help mankind in this struggle.

At the same time, the outward expenditure of energy constitutes an inescapable and essential aspect of our being. To turn away from that outward movement is to lose the authentic possibility of our life and essence as human beings. He who condemns this outward movement does not understand the human condition, the human structure, and the human possibility. And so the perennial question of humanity, the only question

---

us down and make many things indispensable which could and even ought to be dispensed with as far as the essence of life is concerned. . . . [What] nature offers us by means of technology is now a mastery over the self-reliance and the spiritual center of life through endless habits, endless distractions and endless superficial needs. . . . There has never been an age . . . [with] such an emphasis on the intermediate aspects of life. . . . Here, too, money shows itself to be not an isolated instance but rather the most perfect expression of tendencies that are also discernible in a series of lower phenomena. . . . Money . . . [is] the means of means . . . without which the specific techniques of our culture could not have developed.'' *(The Philosophy of Money.* London and New York: Routledge, 1990, pp. 483–85)

worth devoting one's life to, is: how are we, how am I, to live fully in the world of "birth and death," the world of organic life on earth, the world of society, responsibility, making and doing— while at the same time fulfilling the immensely higher and greater possibility that is offered to us as human beings?

The thesis of this book is that the chief representative of "life on earth," the world of birth and death, the world we are born to, but not necessarily destined to die in—that chief representation is now *money*. Our task, then, is to search for contact with something far greater than we can imagine, while participating rightly and truly in the forces of life on earth.

Two Worlds, Two Natures

The very essence of the idea of man that we find at the core of all the great teachings of all times and places is that we human beings are *two-natured*. I shall soon try to spell out more clearly some of the astonishing implications of this idea. For now, we may take from this idea the following direction: human life has meaning only insofar as we consciously and intentionally occupy two worlds at the same time. One force alone can never bring meaning into human life. *Meaning appears only in the place between the worlds,* in the relationship of two worlds, two levels, two fundamental qualities of power and energy.

Money is now, at this period of civilization, the chief representative of one of these fundamental worlds. That is its extraordinary, immense significance. We must understand it and respect it for that. This "lower" world of money is not evil. For us, as beings built to live consciously in two worlds, real evil consists solely of those factors in ourselves that prevent conscious awareness of both the inner and the outer world. It is not money itself which obstructs this awareness.

The challenge of our lives is to face the money question

without disappearing into it or running away from it. We must take money seriously. If we wish to live a human life, this can mean only that we participate humanly in all the forces of life—or, to put it another way, that we allow all the forces of life to participate in ourselves, to be embraced by our consciousness. We enter hell only when our consciousness is devoured, when we are absorbed by the outward-directed energy that constitutes only part of our true nature.

To be obsessed by money is certainly to be in hell. But there is another kind of hell, which we must also now acknowledge. We live in that hell when we refuse to participate in the realities of life, when dreams and fantasies, spiritual or otherwise, take the place of a real inner search. Let us now look at this other apartment in hell.

4.

IDEALISM AND
THE REALITY
OF MONEY

It is October 1967. I am walking in the Haight-Ashbury district of San Francisco. The Summer of Love has just made history, the Vietnam war is tearing out everyone's heart. Young people's minds are exploding and burning with drug-induced visions and paranoiac terrors. Incense fills the air. Beautiful young men and women drift through the streets dressed like houris, gypsies, Indians, sannyasins, prostitutes, derelicts, criminals, players in a drama of world revolution and mystical ecstasy. The tremor of sexual risk and erotic abandon is everywhere and in everything, secretly lending to all ideas and events a certain mixture of fury, courage and impending exhaustion. Strange handmade objects, as bold as they are ugly, are everywhere. Oriental images, lush, brilliant posters, crystals and excrement, and everywhere the aroma of marijuana; brilliant neurochemical eyes gaze at who knows what; gentle, paradisiacal smiles, soft glances, young bodieswithout spines, dogs without leashes crowd the sidewalk.

For some months now I have been researching and writing about the Eastern religions now attracting so many of these young people. Was there a real "spiritual revolution" taking place in America? Were these teachers, masters, and gurus from Asia really bringing something authentic to our culture? And were these young men and women really searching for higher values? Or was the whole "new religions" phenomenon only the high notes of a long, desperate scream? Were these followers of the new religions the antennae of an America seeking to regain its soul, or only the raw, oozing skin of an unhealed wound called Vietnam?

As a professor of philosophy and comparative religion, I had listened with great interest to people half my age speaking of spiritual experiences that I had only read about in the writings of the great saints and sages of India, Tibet, China, and Japan. My own personal acquaintance with the immense difficulties of the inner search made me very skeptical about the authenticity of the psychological descriptions I was hearing. Yet there was no doubting the sincerity of the need these young people felt for meaning and vision in their lives. There was no doubting that they had seen through the lies and hypocrisies of our society. They saw the materialism of America with the blazing clarity of fear, fear of dying in an ugly, selfish war against a tiny nation far, far away. Like an erupting volcano, their vision brought to America the light of a fire joined with a terrible heat and great dark clouds of vaporizing subterranean matter.

AN ENCOUNTER ON HAIGHT STREET

I enter one of the shops on Haight Street, breathing in the sickly sweet fumes of frangipani incense and marijuana. In the corner of the store, near the cash register, a pale beautiful girl is playing gentle chords on a small harp, her face rapt in happiness, her long blond hair flowing down to the floor. Behind the glass display counters is a profusion of Oriental jewelry, knickknacks, decorated boxes, scarves, copper urns, brass bowls, carved ivory and jade. The walls are covered with a wild mélange: photographs and portraits of spiritual teachers, paintings of religious symbols, silk scarves, statues, masks from Africa, Indonesia, and Nepal.

At first glance, it seems to me that the merchandise is in the display cases and the store owner's religious values are on the wall. Even so, I am startled to see these faces decorating the walls of a business. There is the nineteenth-century Hindu saint, Ramakrishna; next to him a photograph of the greatly revered twentieth-century master, Sri Ramana Maharshi; and there is a photo of another Indian teacher, Meher Baba; over there a famous portrait of the sixth-century Zen Master, Bodhidharma, together with a photo of the renowned scholar, D. T. Suzuki. There—farther along, several photographs of Sufi saints. And there is Krishnamurti. And a Russian icon of the face of Christ. There is Gurdjieff. And there are many others. There are great metal crucifixes, including a powerful Mexican carving of Christ wounded, bleeding, and dying. There are Jewish prayer shawls, Tibetan bells and *vajras* and countless other objects that I had never seen anywhere except in the solemn environment of churches or temples.

Suddenly I notice there is a price tag on the Russian icon; and then I am seeing the price tags on everything! Why had I not noticed them before? They are now all so obvious! I muscle through the crowd to get a better look and I am beginning to wonder why I am so shocked. The icon is going for $595.

The photo of Ramana Maharshi is $22.50. The Mexican cru-
cifix is $195 (a bargain?). Ramakrishna is selling for $14.95,
Krishnamurti $9.95. The prayer shawl is $35 and it is a
beauty—fine, delicately knotted fringes; rich deep pure white
silk. I want it. Badly.

The following little drama then unreels. Taking out my
checkbook, I ask the clerk—another pale girl smiling with
the same blurred ecstasy as the harpist—to let me see the
prayer shawl. "Oh," she says, in the gentlest, tiniest voice,
"we only take cash." For some reason, the word *cash*, coming from this flower child, hits me in the gut as though it
were an obscenity. I can feel my jaw thrusting forward and
I say, loudly and stupidly: "What do you mean, you don't
take checks!"

"It's the store policy," she says, a little frightened, but
not frightened enough for my liking. She puts the prayer shawl
down on the counter. I shove it aside without even looking at
it. And then I hear myself saying, in an even louder voice: "Do
you know who I am? I'm Jacob Needleman! I'm a professor
at San Francisco State University!"

As I am spitting out this absurdity, my eyes fall upon the
photograph that happens to be on the wall just behind her. Having
just heard my mouth expressing the most pompously egotistical
sounds I had ever consciously heard it utter, I now find myself
being observed by none other than Gautama Buddha himself,
whose teaching about the illusion of ego I had just that morning
so carefully explained to my students at the university.

The comedy continues. "Let me speak to the owner!" I
demand. The salesgirl disappears and returns accompanied by a
man in his late twenties with unkempt hair, soft, watery eyes,
a sickeningly loving smile, and a small photograph of a Hindu,
presumably his guru, hanging around his neck. I repeat my
demands, adding something to the effect—thank God, I don't

remember my exact words—that not only am I a professor, but a professor of philosophy and religion and give courses in the very people whose photographs are on the wall. As though that in itself entitled me to pay by check.

Suddenly, the man with the sickening smile develops eyes hard as steel and somehow, without his altering the smallest muscle in his lips, the "loving" smile is transformed into a sardonic grin. He picks up the prayer shawl—for a fleeting moment I actually imagine he is going to offer it to me as a gift—and while he is reverently folding it, he advises me to perform a sexual act upon myself.

Back in the street, a team of Hare Krishnas in full regalia and painted faces march by, chanting their Hindu mantra. I am trembling with anger—but at what or whom? And as one of the Hare Krishnas asks me to buy some incense or something, I suddenly burst into laughter. But, again, at what or at whom?

As I walk aimlessly around the Haight-Ashbury, my mind is a blooming jungle of thoughts about the confusion of money and religion—my own confusion and that of the flower children and hippies around me. The encounter at the shop allowed an impression to come into me concerning the hard reality of money, the kind of impression I used to have as a child when my own dreams and hopes were sometimes dashed by the realities of money or by the money fears of my father. As I walked in the streets now, I tried to understand what I had experienced in the shop—or at least to name it properly.

THE BARRIER BETWEEN THE WORLDS

In that shop I had seen the force of money in one of its most important manifestations. The shopkeeper had to be a businessman, he had to calculate rationally; he had to deal with the material facts of his business, the bounced checks he had no doubt had too much of. Yet he was also a "spiritual seeker." Maybe he was a disciple of some sincere Hindu teacher. Maybe he had in his heart dreams of freedom from the ego, God-realization. Or maybe he blasted his head with dope every day— who knew? But no matter how much "spiritual love" he sought or felt, he still had to deal with business facts.

This spiritual seeker was a lousy businessman—but he *was* a businessman. His money personality operated with no conscious relationship to his spiritual personality. His spiritual ideals prevented him from facing the needs of his business with anything like a human intelligence or care. These ideals had no room in them for the realities of everyday living that operate in the sphere of money. And so these spiritual ideals would probably forever remain *only* ideals, never entering into the details of his life. Lost in his extravagant religious ideals, he could not allow himself to face the kind of dealing with people that is necessary in order to be a good businessman. And therefore only the most primitive self-serving reactions could appear in him in a situation that demanded the ordinary control of these reactions that any sensible businessman can and must exercise.

He did not take money seriously enough. He did not give enough ordinary human attention to playing his role as a shopkeeper.

But what about me? Hard as it was to do, I had to accept that I was just as confused about money as the shopkeeper. Replaying the whole farce in my mind, I swung between tears and laughter as I remembered the antics of my preposterous ego in that situation. I saw that somewhere in my mind I too cherished the assumption that spiritual things should never be touched by money considerations. I too was afflicted with a hypocritical fantasy that dealings with God exempted one from dealing realistically with the world of money. I did not feel the *meaning* of money. Oh yes, I wanted money and craved money just as much as anyone else; and I feared money problems as much as anyone else. But I cannot say I *felt* the importance or significance of money in the conduct of life. So, while I could speak and write about spiritual, philosophical, and metaphysical ideas, not one ounce of my intelligence or sensitivity ever reached its way to perceiving and understanding money. I did not understand at that time that money was one of the chief ways in which man's life manifests itself in our world.

What a pathetic "purity" it is that prevents the better part of one's mind from attending to life with people and their needs, wants, and cares! What stood between these two parts of myself and screened one off from the other—so much so that in the face of the money problem—in this case a small purchase in a shop—only the lowliest manifestation of the ego/animal could show itself? I and that shopkeeper: were we not two ego/animals growling at each other? And these two ego/animals—didn't they each have great spiritual ideals in their minds somewhere, somewhere far off, screened, buffered from the parts of ourselves that dealt with our fellow man?

To take money seriously: this means to tear down that screen. This does not mean that one confuses spiritual strivings with material needs; on the contrary, it is necessary to see the real and true difference between these two human pursuits. But it does mean that one gives to one's material needs the energy and intelligence that is required for satisfying them, while allowing space in oneself for the appearance and action of the striving for transcendent meaning.

"Render unto Caesar that which is Caesar's, and unto God that which is God's." In my opinion, the entire problem of life in contemporary culture can be defined as the challenge to understand that saying of Jesus. It is not so simple; in fact, it is immensely difficult. It requires that we begin to understand what in ourselves belongs to the transcendent realm and what to the material realm. And then to give to each what is due to each—no more and no less. This is what it means to be human. Meaning can come from no other source than this.

The encounter between a philosopher and a "spiritual" shopkeeper, absurd and farcical as it is, illustrates many of the confusions that operate on very broad and significant levels in all our lives. In such personal and apparently trivial events, the likes of which are experienced daily by all of us, we may see what really lies behind our attitudes toward money, and in so doing we may hope to go beyond our usual reactions to what we call "greed," "heartlessness," "hypocrisy" and "immorality," both in everyday life and in business, religion, politics, education, medicine—in all aspects and institutions of our fragile civilization.

5.

GOD AND CAESAR

It may seem a long step from Donald Trump to an inept "spiritual" shopkeeper in the Haight-Ashbury, but they are not so far apart as it may appear. The first represents the attempt to find life's meaning in money; the other tries to make money out of the search for meaning. I know them both all too well—they live inside of me, and perhaps inside of most of us. They represent the confusion of two directions of life within us. This confusion prevents us from seeing the real difference between the search for God and the need to live normally in the material world.

The difficulty of accepting the idea that man is a two-natured being, and the challenge of living according to that idea, are not new. This has always been the challenge before mankind. It is possible to view the whole history of the human race as a drama in which this idea of the two natures is first given—by Jesus, Lao Tzu, Moses, and all the spiritual geniuses of the world—and then covered over or forgotten by whole peoples and cultures.

That man has both a spiritual and a material side, that he is both "good" and "evil," angel and devil, is, of course, the commonest of notions. But what, precisely, differentiates these two sides of human nature, and what attitude must we take toward them? And how can they be brought into relationship? *Ought* they even be brought into relationship? On these questions there is great confusion and discord throughout the history of civilization.

For centuries the institutionalized religions of the West communicated a strong condemnation—or at most a grudgingly limited toleration—of the "lower" part of human nature: the body, sexuality, and man's material desires. The attitude we label "puritanical" is part of that legacy, especially in the realm of sex.

In reaction, Freudian psychoanalysis spearheaded a movement that has taken many modern people in the opposite direction—even to the point of denying that man has a spiritual nature at all—and attempted to explain the "higher" aspects of man by reducing them to the twists and turns of animal instinct overlaid by inherently repressive human civilization. "Puritanism" condemns the animal; "modernism" denies the spirit. Both are equally pernicious if, as I am arguing, evil consists not in one side of man's nature, but in the failure to discriminate and respect both directions within ourselves.

THE SIN OF AVARICE

As with sex, so with money. The medieval Church tolerated the necessary exchange of money for goods, but considered business or trade, as such, to be morally dangerous. The task of the Church was to regulate the economic life of society so that the material needs of individuals did not become the cravings that pull one away from religious principles of behavior. For example, the laws against usury, or excessive interest on loans, were, at their root, meant to prevent exploitation of another's misfortune or need. In our capitalistic world, it is difficult for us to understand why religious traditions have always regarded the charging of interest with such strong disapproval. What we forget is that prior to our era, an individual usually asked for a loan of money only when driven to it by hardship. To charge interest on such a loan was to seek to profit from my neighbor's hardship—it was a form of *avarice.*

We must keep in mind how strongly the Christian Church considered man's economic activity in terms of the essential interdependence of human beings. Economic activity was understood in the context of individuals providing what was needed for each other in the material realm. In its most general and deepest sense, this interdependence is implicit in the commandment to love one's neighbor. Ideally, all activity in the material and social realm must provide what is needed or beneficial for others as well as for oneself. Thus, just as the pleasures of sex were justified only as an aspect of the duty of procreation, so material acquisition was justified only to the extent that it corresponded to the individual's authentic needs and those of the community.

THE UNFINISHED SELF

Man is a being endowed with spirit that flows within a mortal physical body. He lives in a physical world that is also suffused with spirit. This is his metaphysical destiny. His task is to live in direct relationship to both spirit and matter and, in so doing, forge within himself a new, godlike consciousness known as the *soul.* To this end, he must give both spirit and matter their proper due. Man, as Kierkegaard expressed it in the modern era, is meant to be a self (in medieval language, a soul), a synthesis of time and eternity, the finite and the infinite. It is his task, his destiny, but he is not yet this destiny; man is not yet a self.

How to direct man to the infinite in himself without neglecting the finite? How to render unto Caesar what is Caesar's and unto God what is God's? It took all the intensity and watchfulness of the greatest of spiritual masters to maintain this dynamic balance within the confines of the Christian monastery. Under a St. Benedict, for example, in the sixth century, the activity of the monk was carefully and creatively apportioned between meditative, mystical prayer and physical activity, communal association. This balance needed constantly to be reappraised and monitored by the leader of the monastery and by each monk within his own inner world. Temptation existed in both directions, and the writings of the Fathers of the early Church are witness to the great difficulty of this challenge, as well as the unfathomable rewards it brought.

If this quest was difficult within the dynamically controlled conditions of the monastery, it was all but impossible outside the monastery, in the vortex of everyday life. The ethics of the medieval Church, the laws by which it sought to regulate European society, could not effect what could be effected within the more controlled conditions of the monastery. But it could provide a religious framework which allowed men and women the possibility of searching for contact with something greater than the social ego. Much of what we now label as mere dogma—such as the doctrine that man was created in the image of God and fell into sin—in fact served to regulate both the outer and the inner life of men and women so that these two realities, these two aspects of human nature, did not depart irretrievably far from each other; so that the real difference between these two natures of man could, at least in theory, be appreciated.

The outer life of man, his lower nature, his "animal," his physical and social needs as a mortal being, were understood to be real, but secondary. The ethics of the Church aimed to prevent man from giving too much of himself to that outer nature; but it also aimed to respect it and satisfy its legitimate needs.

THE MOST DANGEROUS ILLUSION

Throughout human history, this teaching has proved so elusive that it has had to be continually rediscovered and re-created in the midst of the distortions that inevitably degrade it. One of these distortions has been the out-and-out condemnation of the lower nature of man—his physical and material needs and desires. Another distortion that often accompanied the first has been to overemphasize the "divinity" in man—to the point that the lower nature was neglected. In the first case, the result is what we term the "puritanical" attitude, with the hypocrisy and hidden psychological repression that comes in its train. The second results in the establishment of monastic conditions that are actually an escape from life, from the human condition. In this case, the monastery becomes only a shelter from the very truths about oneself that one needs to face. The great founders of the monastic system never organized monastic life in this way; on the contrary, the monastery was to be a place where the individual could experience a more intense encounter with the two natures, an encounter that could lead to the reception within oneself of the transcendentally reconciling force called the Holy Spirit, or grace—the gift of God.

In this context, the material and economic needs of man

were not considered evil; they were considered *secondary*. The tragic misunderstanding arises when that which is secondary gets taken as evil. It is a huge error. To give the lower nature its proper place in human life requires a fine and dynamic attention; to treat the lower nature as evil, on the contrary, invites a kind of violence toward an essential aspect of human nature. And this, in its turn, invites the reaction we have witnessed especially strongly in modern times, in which the unattended lower nature finally asserts itself like an unattended fire raging out of control.

The masters of the Christian teaching understood this dynamic as operating both within and outside of the individual human being. Both within the self and within the human community, the unattended legitimate needs and desires of the lower nature spread like wildfire—or like tares, to use the language of the Gospels. What were called the deadly sins were often to be understood in this way. Lust was what became of the normal sexual need when it lost its relation to the higher, spiritual nature of man. Avarice was what became of the normal material needs of man when they lost their relation to the spiritual nature of man.

And this, in fine, is why trade and commerce, and especially dealing in money, were so suspect. The economic life of man had to be conducted in such a way that the individual could see it as secondary to the aim of opening to the higher, to God. Secondary, not evil. An individual needed to live the life of the family and the body for his own well-being, while at the same time recognizing his dependence on the whole community and his obligation to serve the whole community—as a step toward brotherly love.

Under no circumstances was society to encourage man to feel self-sufficient, autonomous. This was the most dangerous of illusions, which would prevent his understanding his true nature as a divided, potentially exalted being whose true happiness depended on his receiving the spiritual force from above that could bind his two natures together and make of him a servant of God on this earth, in this creation. The amassing of material goods could not help but foster the illusion of self-sufficiency and, with it, the disease of self-blindness, the illusion of self-power, that hard, rigid hellish nightmare that the Fathers of the Christian tradition called *pride*. Pride is the self imagining it does not need to breathe the air of God. Pride is the illusion of false unity and power that prevents man from attaining authentic unity and power. The material world, like the lower nature, is not evil; but taken apart from its relation to the spiritual, it draws men away from their true possible glory and duty. Evil is the lack of relationship between higher and lower, between ontological, metaphysical levels in man and in society.

This is the real meaning of the sin of avarice, and indeed of all the deadly sins. All the sins are so many aspects of pride or egoism, understood as submersion in the illusion of self-power.

From Instrument to Idol

All the more was money itself a danger. As an instrument for broadening the passage of material help between human beings—and therefore the range of human love—it was an inspired invention. But as the modern world has discovered about all ingenious inventions, it was a sword with two edges. All by itself, as a *thing*, a *substance*, it was useless. It was meant only for helping people directly to live in the material world, while at the same time recognizing their dependence, first upon God and then upon each other. This is no doubt why, when coinage was first invented, it was administered by the priestly class; as this is no doubt why, in many cases, the earliest coins bore a religious symbol on one side and a secular symbol on other—God and Caesar. Coins, money as a thing, were intended as a tool, an instrument to facilitate necessary human interactions in the material world, while helping man to remember his dependence on God and God's moral laws. The ethical laws governing money exchange connected this activity vertically to the divine commandments; and the nature of money payment in itself was testimony to the horizontal, material dependence of human beings upon each other. The exchange of money could serve as a constant reminder of this mutual interdependence. In an economy based on need rather than desire, the "bottom line" is more than just an onerous limitation; it is an index for balancing one's own needs with those of others.

When the desire for "financial independence" grows excessive, it may breed illusions of self-sufficiency and thereby fuel the error of egoistic pride.* The spiritual meaning of independence was never intended to deny the individual's intrinsic obligation to the needs of his neighbor nor the fact of his dependence upon his neighbor's work. Spiritually, independence means complete dependence upon God's truthand energy acting from within the depths of one's own true self, and also freedom from slavery to humanly devised institutions and opinions—William Blake's "mind-forg'd manacles."

To deal in money in and of itself, with no immediate reference to goods and services, was to run a grave psychospiritual risk. Socially, such an activity cut the flow of human exchange

---

* It is worth noting, in addition, the Christian resistance, in medieval and early modern times, to the whole idea of *insurance* so prevalent in modern days, as an effort of human beings to blind themselves to the ultimacy of God's power. This view about insurance still prevails in certain Moslem countries and causes no little difficulty to Westerners doing business there.

by divorcing money transactions from the world of fundamental human needs; psychologically, it tended to foster the illusion that security exists in what can be devised by the mind alone: the illusion that the physical world and the mind that deals with the physical world are the most essential aspect of human nature. The Christian teaching, like that of all the great traditions, pointed man to a reality behind the world of sensory experience as regards both his view of himself and his view of the cosmos. To deal in money, money as a thing, a substance, was to run the risk of believing in the ultimacy of money's power, thereby losing sight of the idea of the higher reality in the universe and the need to cultivate an openness toward it in oneself. Money cannot do what the true causal reality of nature can do. The true causal reality—the more fundamental causes of what exists and happens in the world and in oneself—medieval man calls this God.

Do not take for God that which is not really God: this means, among many other ways of expressing it—not to look for power, safety, joy, service, love, or meaning from any other source than that which actually brings these about in the whole of reality. Do not take effects for causes. Do not take something that is an effect of the causal power for the causal power itself. This is the sin of idolatry.

Pausing now for a moment in the flow of our historical, philosophical discussion about the origin of money in our society, surely we are bound to ask—as the serious Christian must have asked in the Middle Ages:

What is God for me?

What takes the place of God for me?

What do I, what do we consider the cause of things that happen in and around us? And if our answer to this question is anything other than *money,* upon what is our answer based?

If our answer is anything other than: causes exist only in the material world outside myself, and inside myself causes only exist in my animal instincts and egoistic impulses—if that is not our answer, upon what is our conviction based? Have we really experienced metaphysical, invisible causes operating in the world—that is, have we really experienced God acting in the world? Have we really seen the great Mind and Purpose of nature? In oneself or in any human being or in any human event, have we really experienced causes, motivations, other than in the realm of the desire for sex, food, vanity, fear? That is, have we really seen the higher nature of man either in ourselves or in others?

At the heart of the great wisdom teachings of the world, including Christianity, is the view that really to experience the higher, divine nature of reality, in oneself and in the world, requires an intense and carefully guided way of life and practice. This higher reality, the real causal force in the world, God, exists and is a force of ultimate and unfathomable power. But we are blind to its reality, and to open our eyes to it requires a great work. Those who claim to know it and who believe in it are often only dreaming, or else are making far too much of a passing personal glimpse of something, in here or out there, of a different quality. Thus, each in its way, the great teachings have always warned us against false religions, shallow philosophies, and pseudospiritualities.

At the same time, human beings must be given indications of the higher reality—in the form of ideas, symbols, rituals, customs, images. There must be authentic religion, authentic ethics, authentic philosophy that can point man to the truth beyond what is experienced in one's ordinary state of consciousness. These indications are intended to evoke what, in the history of our civilization, has been given the name *faith*. Faith—authentic faith—is indispensable.

And the support for the arising and maintaining of faith must be very strong. Because the fact of the matter is that an honest man or woman, looking at his life and the life around him, is in his or her natural condition of mind bound to conclude that only material causes exist, that there is no higher reality. That is how the world and how the self appears to natural man living in the lower nature alone, the man of the senses.

This, in brief, is why there was such a thing as *dogma*—in the positive sense of the word: namely, a teaching, a worldview, a system of ethical rules and principles, customs, symbols, and images that could call men and women to that which they would never be able to experience in their everyday state of consciousness. It is a narrow prejudice of our own era that so many view *dogma* with complete disdain. At the heart of the Christian tradition, the teachers and priests were not all rigid, naive, power-hungry fools, as has sometimes been believed by modern people. At the same time, things did go wrong: something happened in the wide administration of the Church that turned the whole effort of transmitting higher values in the direction of failure and disaster—but we will come to that presently.

In the meantime, it is important to bear in mind this deep context in which the making of money, especially loaning at interest, was viewed with such distrust. The making of money, the accumulation of material goods, draws man to trust too much in the lower nature for his well-being. It draws us to give it first place. At the same time, *the lower nature has a place,* and a very strong place. The need for material well-being arises out of the transitory, but *real,* lower nature of man. And so the challenge of human life is that of rendering unto Caesar that which is Caesar's—*no more and no less*—and unto God that which is of God—no more and no less. The challenge is to live a two-natured life, according to the unique ontological struc- ture of the human creature.

THE FLIGHT FROM HUMAN NATURE

The monasteries decayed, the Christian life decayed—and human life in all societies decays—whenever these two aspects of our being drift too far apart. This drifting apart takes many forms, and in the history of Christianity it began on a world scale (it is always happening in the individual and always having to be struggled against) with the flight from the dec- adence of Roman society in the first centuries after Christ. In these first centuries many ardent individuals fled to the deserts of Egypt to escape from the horrors of Roman materialism and sensual excess. Many of these ardent early Christians sought to experience God under conditions of isolation not only from a decadent civilization, but from all other human beings. They tried to develop themselves in isolation, as her- mits. But the most intelligent and serious among them soon saw that it was impossible for men and women to perfect themselves in this way. The social aspect of the self was needed; isolated interiority could not develop normally with- out a relationship to the part of the self that is meant to exchange with other human beings. A sort of inner violence and spiritual egoism was developing as an overwhelming ob- stacle to true individual self-perfecting.

Spiritual communities were established—the beginning of what became the Christian monasteries. The wise leaders of these early monasteries, such as St. Benedict in the sixth century, established forms of organization which dynamically changed over the centuries, in which the necessary confrontation between the two natures of man could take place. Association with others was necessary; physical work was necessary—up to a point, and carefully monitored by the practical wisdom of the abbot or guide.

By the late Middle Ages, the drifting apart of the two aspects of human nature was again taking place on a very broad scale in the monasteries. Again, the monastery tended to become an escape from everyday life—that is, an escape from the lower human nature. Cut off from authentic awareness of the animal and social impulses in himself, the religious aspirant fears these aspects, fears the outer world. The lower nature itself begins to be regarded as evil. The body begins to be regarded as evil; normal human interaction begins to be regarded as evil. But these aspects do not die or recede. Their energy cannot be destroyed, but instead—without a presiding intelligence which they can voluntarily obey—their energy operates in disguise, and wildly.

While condemning lust, for example, an individual may simply lust after "God." Lust is one of the names for the process of being devoured by emotional or instinctual drives, and an individual can lose himself in "God" just as fully as he can lose himself in sex. Avarice is the process of being devoured by material needs and desires, and an individual can be just as avaricious about "salvation" as about wealth or money. To condemn either sex or money as such is only to deceive oneself. The real enemy is the tendency of the human psyche to be devoured—by whatever impulse. The all-consuming "flames of Hell" exist in our own nature.

The well-documented degeneration of the monasteries in the late Middle Ages, and the equally well-documented corruptions in the medieval Church, can be understood against this background of ideas about human nature. As the device called money took greater and greater place in the society of the Middle Ages, it became one of the chief objects of distrust, along with an often exaggerated condemnation of dealing in money and commerce. Mistakenly condemning the lower nature, religious practitioners were all the more subject to its force in their own lives.* This state of affairs is at the root of what we call *hypocrisy*.

THE END OF THE MEDIEVAL WORLD

The historically all-powerful reaction to this hypocrisy is known as *Protestantism*.** As we shall see later, Protestantism brought Western civilization an entirely new attitude toward living in the world, which led eventually to a new attitude toward the lower nature of man. Reacting to what it saw as the hypocrisy of the Church, Protestantism brought the idea that man could be free from obedience to the laws of any institution: that he could be guided solely by the light of his own reason. The whole arena of life was seen to be man's proper calling, and his role in the world could be as sacred as

---

* See, for example, R. H. Tawney, *Religion and the Rise of Capitalism.* New York: Harcourt, Brace and World, 1926, pp. 11–60.

** To prevent misunderstanding, it is necessary to emphasize here at the outset of this discussion that the term Protestantism is being used to designate only one element in the vast world of Western Christianity since the Reformation, namely the Protestantism that became a large-scale historical, social, and political movement, as distinguished from Catholicism considered in the same light. A deeper and more comprehensive view of Protestantism would embrace many of the greatest spiritual leaders and thinkers of our era and many noble communal experiments which have had lasting impact in countless ways. Also, as will be obvious, no attempt is being made to plumb the depths of Calvinist theology. It is also necessary to emphasize that the Brotherhood of the Common Life, which is singled out in the following pages, was itself but one of many movements throughout pre-Reformation Europe that sought to bring the Christian teaching into relation with the realities of the everyday life of men and women.

any priest's. Our modern economic system, as well as the ascendancy of science in our culture, springs in large measure from this view of the world; and our prevailing view of ourselves—including modern psychological categories and our exaltation of the intellectual function—springs largely from this view of the self. As we shall see, both on a broad social scale and on the scale of our individual inner world, the uniquely modern vision of the meaning of human life is reflected tellingly in the changes that have taken place since the Renaissance in the invented device we call money.

And so, when we take out our wallets or our checkbooks or our credit cards, we are handling part of a huge instrument of social technology in which almost all the forces of human life on earth come together in a way that uniquely defines the modern era. When we are buying or selling or worrying about paying our doctors or our lawyers, or sending our children through college, or signing a lease, or putting together a down payment on a house, or shopping for a car, clothes, or a vacation, or looking for a better job, or looking for a loan, applying for a grant or whatever it may be that we are going to give most of our energy to today, we are reaping the legacy of a long historical encounter between specific spiritual teachings and the necessities of material life—or, more exactly, the encounter between the striving of man to make contact with God and the needs of man to survive in the world of nature and society.

The Middle Ages ended. What we call the Renaissance and the rise of humanism began. The forms, symbols, and expressions of the Catholic Church were shaken by changing events on a world scale. The monasteries lost the vigor of their original vision. Villages became towns, towns became cities. The New World was discovered and great quantities of gold and silver were brought into Europe. What we know as Protestantism, starting with the dramatic confrontation between the

Church and Martin Luther, stepped onto the stage of world history and soon the names of all the world forces underwenta change. The forces remained the same, as they always will. But the garb of the players changed, new subplots and subtexts were introduced.

We cannot say whether by the end of the Middle Ages the monasteries had become more corrupted or whether they had lost the ability to see and accept the place of man's lower nature. In the end, it comes to the same thing. The lower nature becomes a force for degeneration only when it is not seen with the strong embrace of an accepting consciousness, only when the lower nature becomes cut off from the spiritual aspiration and therefore manifests in destructive ways.

Nor can we say that regarding the lower nature (the body and its material needs) as evil, rather than as secondary, was the cause or the result of misunderstandings and carelessness among certain leaders of the Church. It is no doubt a reciprocally acting phenomenon: to turn our attention away from the lower nature is to invite its blind action in our lives. And since we do not see and accept this action for what it is, since we no longer see the secondary nature, we become what the world calls "hypocrites." But it is not the fault of our human nature, it is the fault of our awareness. The struggle against being dominated by the secondary nature ought to be the struggle to see it. But it became the struggle to kill it. It cannot be killed, for, if it is killed, man ceases to be man either metaphysically or physically. Such was the core teaching of the Christian religion, as it is the core teaching of all the great spiritual traditions.

The secondary nature resists the spiritual aspiration, but at a certain point this resistance does not hinder inner development. On the contrary, at a certain point, when the awareness is strong enough, the secondary nature serves the spiritual aspiration. This is one aspect of the mystery of the cross, that is, the intersection of two opposing directions. At that intersection there is great struggle, great suffering of a unique kind, but also great joy and the possibility of a new birth. This is also part of the mystery of the two natures of Christ, a doctrine which itself was the subject of much controversy in the history of the Christian tradition.

The challenge of economic life, the challenge of living in a way that is adequate to our material needs, is to make that life serve the spiritual aspiration. The understanding of that challenge is what formed the monasteries in the first place; the loss of that understanding led to their degeneration. And the attempt by some Christian leaders, such as Pope Gregory VII, to apply monastic standards to the arena of everyday outer life led to further hypocrisies and ultimately to what we now call neurosis. This is fairly clear in the area of sex, where the rule of celibacy, which was no longer viable even within the monasteries, was transferred to priests working and living in the uncontrolled conditions of everyday outer life. But it also happened with a vengeance in the economic sphere as well.

In sum, the Christian Church presented a picture of hypocrisy and corruption. Condemning the sexual nature of man, the leaders of the Church indulged their sexual needs. Warning against greed and avarice, the Church and monasteries amassed wealth and political power which they were unable to deal with in ethically balanced ways. Much later in history—in the early part of the twentieth century—the question of sex became largely excluded from the rule of religious influence. That is what the Freudian revolution effected. But as for the material desires of man, these became separated off from the influence of the Christian teaching much earlier, under the banner of Protestantism. The earliest name for this state of affairs in which the conduct of economic life became cut off from the influence of spiritual ideals was and now still is: *Capitalism.*

MONEY AND THE SEARCH FOR SELF-KNOWLEDGE

Our coins, so to speak, no longer have two sides—a sacred symbol on one side and a secular symbol on the other. Money in the modern era is a purely secular force, reflecting the lower nature of man. Cut off from any relation to spiritual aspiration, it has become the most obvious example of a fire raging out of control. Our challenge is to bring money back to the place where it belongs in human life. It is not a question of getting more money, although for you or me that may be necessary. It is not a question of giving up money, although, again, for you or me that may be necessary up to a point. It is not even a question of ordering one's life—tidying up one's affairs, necessary though that may be for you or me sometimes. It is solely a question of restoring money to its proper place in human life. And that place is *secondary.* Our aim is to understand what it means to make money secondary in our lives. As a principal representative of the lower nature, the outward, physical body of man, money must become secondary, as the body must become secondary.

Secondary to what? Not to what we call ethics. For, to be honest, what is ethics in our world and lives? Look about you; look squarely at yourself. Very little if anything is left of the absolute demand from Above that is the essence of authentic ethics. What we call ethics is mixed inseparably with hidden pragmatic aims of strictly "local" character—health, satisfaction; family, tribal, or other advantages involving nation, ethnic group, or any other of the countless associations that modern and especially American life has produced. What are called ethical rules of behavior thus often serve only the transitory nature of man, though dressed in names and forms echoing ideas and teachings that refer to the Higher—God, for example. We cannot get to ethics until we can separate the higher from the lower in ourselves. Therefore, ethics for us—in our present condition of confusion about these levels—can only be that which enables and leads us toward this separation, which in turn can make possible the real relation of the levels. Therefore, money cannot serve what the world now calls ethics.

Secondary, then to what? Not to love—who now can separate a love that is pure from a love that is of the ego/animal?

No, name any human value you wish—service, charity, peace, health—and you will find that in order to pursue these values past a certain point we have to be free from the tyranny of the unmastered lower nature. The pursuit of such values presupposes a level of inner freedom that we do not as yet have, an inner freedom that allows us to see the real difference between the two natures within us. To love as we would wish to love, we have to discriminate between selfless action and disguised egoism. To serve the planet as we would wish to serve it, we have to discriminate between an understanding of the earth in the cosmic universe, and our perceptions of the impact of the environment on our merely physical and social needs. To pursue health as we would wish to, we have to know our whole human nature, not only the body with its mind and personal emotions.

All the values we recognize, whether religious or humanistic in nature, presuppose our ability to discriminate the two natures within us in such a way that, under the force of our awareness, these two opposed natures, these radically different levels of life, actually move into relationship with each other.

Therefore, our only realistic aim can be the attainment of this power of discrimination, this unique quality of self-knowledge and inner freedom. And if money is to be secondary in our lives, *it can only mean that money serve the aim of self-knowledge.*

Here, at last, we have found our question. Here we find the key to the place that money can—and must—occupy in our lives. Money must become an instrument of the search for self-knowledge. Money must become a tool in the only enterprise worth undertaking for any modern man or woman seriously wishing to find the meaning of their lives: we must use money in order to study ourselves as we are and as we can become.

PART II

THE

COIN

OF

GREATEST

VALUE

6.

"MONEY AND THE MEANING OF LIFE"

Those are not the eyes of a certified public accountant. That soft, forgiving blue was meant to reflect the summer sky or a clear mountain pool, not endless columns of numbers on tax forms. How and why did this gentle woman sitting in the front row ever become a CPA?

The class is called "Money and the Meaning of Life"—a one-day workshop that I am offering through the University of California extension program. About eighty people have come, and from a surprising spectrum of backgrounds—lawyers, financial planners, owners of small businesses, as well as a number of students of philosophy and religion. But none draws my attention more than this blue-eyed woman with the face of a poet. From the moment she identified herself as an accountant, I found myself addressing most of my remarks to her. How old is she? Thirty-five? Fifty? Impossible to say. Crow's-feet surround her eyes and mouth; her dress is neat, simple, and youthful; she moves like a young girl, but her hands are rough and wrinkled. When she smiles she is like a child. Instinctively, I feel she holds some kind of key to the question I need to explore in this workshop.

I began by surveying the historical background of the money problem in modern times. After sketching the medieval background, I outlined the brilliant theory of the early twentieth-century sociologist Max Weber about the origins of capitalism. Although Weber's theories had formed an essential part of my education when I was in college, and were still an important part of the contemporary academic milieu, I suspected that these people had no knowledge of Weber, apart from a few of his phrases like "Protestant work ethic" and "charisma" that have become household words. They were probably unaware that Weber, in his field, and in his influence on modern thought, was more or less on a par with Freud and Einstein.

CAPITALISM AND RELIGION

It was Protestantism, said Weber, that was the chief cause of capitalism. Astonishing! Freud shocked the world by arguing that a thwarted sexual drive was at the root of culture. Einstein shocked the world by showing that there were no absolute physical realities in the universe. But no less startling and no less revolutionary was Weber's thesis that it was a form of Christianity itself that had bred the worldly materialism of the modern era!*

---

* Weber took pains to forestall exaggerated interpretations of his thesis. He writes, "But it is, of course, not my aim to substitute for a one-sided materialistic an equally one-sided spiritualistic interpretation of culture and of history" (The Protestant Ethic and the Spirit of Capitalism. New York: Charles Scribner's Sons, 1958, p. 183). Nevertheless, while Weber made room for the interdependence of religious teachings and social and economic conditions, his persuasive argument that Protestantism was at least a principal causal force in the creation of the spirit of

According to Weber, the corruption of monasticism and other corresponding developments within the Catholic Church broke down the otherworldly ideals of the Church in the minds of many serious thinkers. The way was open to seek salvation in the very midst of worldly life. Through the teachings of John Calvin (1509–1564), and in the whole vast context of the Protestant Reformation that was moving through Europe, the goal of salvation was now intimately related to action in the world, not in a monastery. And now the "world" was the *city*—in the beginning of its modern form. The *city* in which now all the gold and silver of the New World, all the forces of the scientific-industrial revolution—material wealth, goods, inventions—were gathering.

It was in the cities—Amsterdam, London, Venice—that processes of material exchange began developing to accommodate the new wealth, the new powers of technology—that is to say, the new instruments of dealing with the outer world of nature and society. Within this crucible of forces, there emerged many innovations in the sphere of financial exchange— innovations which we now recognize as the origins of modern banking, including the widespread use of paper money and promissory notes representing money. The whole meaning and function of *credit* was undergoing transformation: a loan was made not merely to answer *need* in times of hardship, but to satisfy *desires;* it was an instrument to help in the functioning of business in general. And money was no longer a *thing*, valuable in itself—or at least substantially physical. Money was a promise, a representation—almost a *thought*. Money itself be-

---

capitalism has had nearly the same cultural shock effect as if he had argued for its being the main or only cause. In general, when great innovative theories begin to have broad cultural influence, they rarely carry with them the important nuances and qualifications that their founders attached to them.

came a loan, a promissory note, while the thing it represented was elsewhere. Money became one step more removed from reality—whatever reality was. And what reality *was* became ever more a question.

Because money became a representation of a representation—this is the meaning of credit in our world—it was able to move more freely. More freely because more on the surface of life. From being a great ship following the ocean currents, money became a light vessel responsive to the swifter-moving flows closer to the surface. Material life skimmed more quickly and more "efficiently." Money and wealth became more and more something in movement. Ah, but what kind of movement? We shall always have to ask this kind of question, as we consider the inventions of modernity. For example, the printed word, the telephone, the computer. There is more communication by far now in the world among peoples, more quickly, over greater distances—but what kind of communication, at what level of life?

Protestantism, in its Calvinistic mode, sanctified life in the world of the city, the world of business. The term used by Max Weber was *worldly asceticism.* The very qualities of self-discipline and self-denial that once characterized the monk seeking salvation under the special conditions of the monastery were now to be pursued outside the monastery in the conditions of worldly life. The circumstances in which one found oneself were to be regarded as one's *calling,* the station in one's life in which one could and must serve God. It was neither necessary nor efficacious to seek specially protected or favored conditions in which to work for God. All human life, all of civilization, all the world, was the creation of the all-powerful God and therefore, strictly speaking, the world was man's "monastery."

THE WAY IN LIFE

At this point in my presentation, I noticed a certain agitation in the woman sitting in the front row—her name, as I learned, was Alyssa.

"Is there something you want to ask?" I said to her.

"Well, yes," she said, setting her pen down on her notebook. "What you're describing—isn't this the whole idea of a way in life?"

I was taken aback to hear this phrase coming at me from my audience. This was precisely the idea, and in the very words, that I was planning slowly and indirectly to open up during the course of the day. One of the main ideas of the twentieth-century spiritual teacher G. I. Gurdjieff was that the search for self-knowledge and inner development can take place—and for most modern people must take place—in the midst of ordinary life. Like all of Gurdjieff's teachings, this was an idea of extraordinary subtlety, however simple and clear it might appear on the surface. It shook me a bit to hear it mentioned flat out like this and reminded me that the ideas of this powerful teacher had—at least here in California—entered into the everyday language of contemporary culture. At least, the verbal formulations had so entered—terms like "state of consciousness," "self-observation," "essence and personality," and many others.

Alyssa was waiting for my response, her eyes boring into me like lasers—ah, yes, *that* look could certainly see through a financial report or a business plan.

"Yes and no," I answered her, "and it's interesting that you bring this up. It's an aspect of the history of Christianity that Max Weber was not aware of. And because he wasn't aware of it, there's a tremendous gap in his theory that no one seems to have seen."

A MISSING LINK

I decided then and there to change the plan of my presentation to the group. The cat was out of the bag—that is, the idea that dealing with money could be approached as an instrument for seeing ourselves, thereby awakening and supporting the wish for inner freedom toward life. I had planned to allow that idea just to emerge by itself and gradually to bring out the vision of man's cosmic destiny that gave the idea its real depth and subtlety. But now I would have to speak about it first and be much more explicit about the power the idea of a way in life has exerted over the centuries, a power that, in my opinion, neither Weber nor any other recognized thinker—psychologist, historian, or sociologist—has seen.

Max Weber had stunned the modern world by claiming that Protestant Christianity decisively furthered the development of modern capitalism and the uniquely modern forms of greed, obsession with money, and materialism that we generally associate with our present economic system. Weber's theories easily lead to the notion that our modern obsession with money is, in large measure, a *misplaced religious quest.* We turn to money as though it were God, or close to God!

But what Weber had neither seen nor appreciated was that the turning toward the world that we identify with the known forms of Protestantism was only a partial expression of an idea and a direction that had long existed within Western Christendom, and in a much more complete and psychologically effective form. If what we know as Protestantism—which at root was and continues to be religiously motivated—had somehow and unwittingly spawned our modern obsession with money and wealth, it may have been because it was offering only part of the great idea of a way in life. History is full of such things: ideas which are an awakening force in their complete form and in the proper context, becoming a soporific or even a destructive influence when only a piece of them is used or understood. The noblest and most powerful ideas can make the strongest poison for the mind and soul.

Before explaining how Weber had stunningly captured the essence of the American love affair with money, and before I could open the question of how that love affair had become for us a form of psychospiritual prostitution—and certainly before we could discuss how the money question could serve the regeneration of our inner lives—there was no choice but to outline the whole idea of the way in life. And that would take us not only into the hidden history of Christianity and Judaism, but into Islamic mysticism, into the Oriental ideals of the "householder" and the "warrior," and perhaps even into the ancient symbol of the "great magician" as it still speaks in the legends and fairy tales that we heard as children. I saw that the financial planners, lawyers, and businessmen in the audience were going to get something other than they might have expected, and I was already wondering if there would be time to find our way back to our bank accounts, credit cards, salaries, and the buying and selling that makes up so much of our daily lives. I needed coffee.

7.

IS THERE A WAY
IN LIFE?

I began the second part of the morning by remarking to the class about the historical *hiddenness* of the way in life. Fortunately, I had brought along my usual load of books and could hunt out references to illustrate my points.

"Throughout history," I began, "the idea of the way in life has been spoken of as the 'path of the warrior' or as the 'teaching for kings.' Both the warrior and the king represented, in literal fact and symbolically, the individual engaged in all the forces of life, as opposed to the priestly class or the ascetic removed or protected from many of the influences that permeate the greater world. Often, this idea of the way in life was transmitted as the 'way of the magician,' that is, in the language of sorcery. Again, it is a matter of the individual who confronts and masters all the forces, high and low, that constitute reality.

"These symbolic languages—represented by the images of the warrior, the king, the magician—have become distorted, and the form this distortion has taken is a fascination with 'powers' and pleasures of an egoistic kind. And so the religion of the larger culture acts to turn the masses of people away from these symbols—with good reason. The broader religion, that which shapes the mores and ethics of a whole culture, insists on turning people's minds solely toward God and away from the ego. The first necessity always and everywhere in man's search for a rightly oriented life is to recognize the existence of a greatness—whether it is a being—God; a force—the Absolute; or a truth—the Buddhist doctrine of non-ego. Until this turning is reached, until this attitude gels within man's psyche, the way of the warrior, the king, or the sorcerer is fraught with peril. But for those who have assimilated this attitude, or who are gifted with an intense hunger for the transcendent, the way in life becomes an especially effective and intense path toward regeneration and inner development. Thus no one can be a warrior unless he is first *obedient:* obedient to the Higher—Plato's warrior caste, the medieval Templars, etc.; no one can rule as 'king' unless he is under the rule of God—the divine King, under the tutelage of the great priests, as in ancient Egypt, for example; no one can become a magician unless called to it by God—as was Moses and, we shall soon see, Solomon."

I paused in my lecturing. Some illustrations were in order.

ARJUNA THE WARRIOR

"The Bhagavad Gita, for example, is the most widely revered single text in India. The whole vast ocean of Hinduism is summarized and epitomized in this dialogue between God and man, written some twenty-five hundred years ago and inserted in the middle of the great Indian epic, the *Mahabharata*. What is this epic? It is nothing less than a mythic representation of the war between the two cosmic forces as they confront each other in man, symbolized by two great families of royal intermixed blood—king against king, brother against brother, army against army, a war of long duration, filled with flowing blood, tears, deception, naiveté, courage, foolishness, sacrifice and sorrow—on an immense canvas. And where does the dialogue between man and God—Krishna—take place? On the field of battle itself, as the armies mass for combat on either side. Who is man in this dialogue? He is Arjuna, the noblest warrior of all, the most feared, and strongest—*but Arjuna does not want to fight!* 'I owe veneration to my teachers,' he tells Krishna, 'and to my uncle and king.' The enemy king is blind Dhritarashtra, symbolic of that inner false 'king,' the ego. 'How,' Arjuna asks, 'can I take bow against these fathers and sons, wives, brothers, teachers, and other kinsmen marshaled against us? I do not want such a war, nor such a victory.'

"When Arjuna the great warrior has thus unburdened his heart, he says simply: 'I will not fight.' And then falls silent. Krishna smiles and speaks to Arjuna.

"There, between the two armies, between the two cosmic forces, Arjuna is given the teaching of the way in life. 'Take up thy bow and fight!' says Krishna. 'Prepare for war with peace in thy soul.' Plunge into the battlefield of life, and make your inner world the true battlefield. Act, live, as you are ordained to live, amid all the forces that every man and woman must face. Set your heart on inner freedom, on opening to the Absolute, and fight! Act, move, lead—but search always for inner freedom from the very impulses and forces that cause you to act. Separate the inner awareness from the everyday self, discriminate the eternal from the transitory in yourself. First separate, and then embrace these two great levels. Be a warrior!

"Says Krishna: one man in a million is called to this path; and of those who are called to it, one man in a million follows it to the end. That is to say: to the very end of this path, the way remains always and everywhere hidden, difficult and infinitely subtle. Yet it is the greatest and highest path a human being can take.''

I took a breath and reached for another book.

THE ZEN MASTER HAKUIN

"In eighteenth-century Japan, the most revered Zen master of his time, and one of the most influential of all Zen Buddhist teachers, was the artist and calligrapher Hakuin. Here he writes of the way in life to his illustrious pupil, Nabechima Naotsune, governor of Settsu province. This pupil, deeply enmeshed in political, economic, and military affairs, is given the following counsel regarding his search in the midst of human activity. Hakuin begins by assuring him that those who practice under the protected conditions of monasticism are in no way advantaged in the inner search. On the contrary:

Frequently you may feel you are getting nowhere with practice in the midst of activity. . . . Yet rest assured that those who use the quietistic approach can never hope to enter into meditation in the midst of activity. Should by chance a person who uses this approach enter into the dusts and confusion of the world of activity, even the power of ordinary understanding which he had seemingly attained will be entirely lost. . . . The most trivial matters will upset him, an inordinate cowardice will afflict his mind, and he will frequently behave in a mean and base manner. What can you call accomplished about a man like this? (p. 33)

Hakuin goes on:

How does one obtain true enlightenment? In the busy round of mundane affairs, in the confusion of worldly problems, amidst the seven upside-downs and the eight upsets, behave as a valiant man would when surrounded by a host of enemies. . . . (p. 65)

And finally:

In my later years I have come to the conclusion that the advantage in accomplishing true meditation lies distinctly in the favor of the warrior class. A warrior must from the beginning be physically strong. In his attendance on his duties and in his relationships with others, the most rigid punctiliousness and propriety are required. His hair must be properly dressed, his garments in the strictest of order, and his swords must be fastened at his side. . . . Mounted on a sturdy horse, the warrior can ride forth to face an uncountable horde of enemies as though he were riding into a place empty of people. . . . Meditating in this way, the warrior can accomplish in one month what it takes the monk a year to do; in three days he can open up for himself benefits that would take the monk a hundred days."

> (*The Zen Master Hakuin,* trans. Philip B. Yampolsky. New York: Columbia University Press, 1971, p. 69)

THE BATTLEFIELD OF MONEY

Having heard these and other citations from the Oriental teachings, the class was ready to hear the idea of the way in life presented in the language of our own Western teachings, a language that has unfortunately been covered over with naive literalism or sanctimonious religiosity. Before taking that step, however, I needed to make sure they kept in mind where the discussion was leading. In our time and culture, the battlefield of life is money. Instead of horses and chariots, guns and fortresses, there are banks, checkbooks, credit cards, mortgages, salaries, the IRS. But the inner enemies remain the same now as they were in ancient India or feudal Japan: fear, self-deception, vanity, egoism, wishful thinking, tension, and violence.

In the language of the warrior, these are enemies of inner development, enemies which one cannot hide from in overly protective monasteries. At the same time, one cannot defeat them without extraordinary help and knowledge of a kind that was perhaps not accessible within the broad cultural movement known as Protestantism.

What Max Weber did not see was that as a social movement, Protestantism turned religious man toward the forces of life without providing adequate "weapons" or precise knowledge of how to fight on that clamorous battlefield. And Weber did not know that, behind the scenes, there was another kind of "protestantism"—hidden from view—that opened man to the way in life armed with a specific inner discipline of self-inquiry, a discipline or art of living which has to be rediscovered now and here in our time.

Historically, these inner enemies also had another name. In the language of magic and sorcery, they were called *demons*. It was time for the class to examine our own Western expressions of the way in life. It was time to meet the figure of King Solomon.

8.

SOLOMON THE
WISE

I began as follows:

"Unique among all the legendary figures of our culture, Solomon represents the blending in one individual of godliness and worldliness. Here, a great double symbol rises before us: the *king* and the *magician*. Now, almost every ancient spiritual teaching in history speaks to us of the *divine king*. It is a universal symbol of the challenge before every man or woman to live simultaneously in the two worlds—the inner world of the spirit and the outer world of matter. Even Plato, whom many regard as the father of scientific rationalism, made this symbol central to his teachings in the image of the philosopher king.

"Ah, but King Solomon! He was also a magician. *He* understood about demons. Many a saintly man has been portrayed to us as a destroyer of demons—and that is certainly a high attainment. But the figure of Solomon offers us an even greater possibility. Through the power of his magic ring, Solomon does not kill the demons, but makes them into his servants. As one legend has it, Solomon outwitted the demons even after his death, which occurred, according to this legend, while he was leaning on his staff supervising the labors of the demons on some sacred edifice. In that posture, so the story goes, his body remained a full year after his death, and only when a worm gnawed away the end of his staff, causing his body to fall, did the demons discover he was no longer there.

"The figure of Solomon in lore and legend, as well as much of what is attributed to Solomon in the Bible, comprise one of those traces strewn throughout the history of civilizations that indicate an art and even a science of living, one that shows us how to open fully to the forces of outer life while at the same time experiencing within ourselves the all-penetrating energy that sustains the universe. Over the centuries, these indications are covered over like signposts in a windy desert. Again and again they have to be unearthed. You may read the Bible a hundred times without noticing these signposts. You can read about Solomon, for example, and not see that he is waiting there to counsel you in the very midst of your present life with all its contradictions, anxieties, and tensions.

"The Old Testament, like many ancient documents, can therefore be viewed as a scarred battlefield where life-giving new ideas once fought with old, entrenched attitudes about the conduct of human life. Always and everywhere the old fights against the new, striving to dampen the real meaning of the human adventure. Safety wars against risk; piety wars against the inner search; moralism wars against conscience; traditionalism wars against spiritual existentialism.

THE DREAM OF HAPPINESS

"Look, for example, at what the legendary figure of King Solomon is trying to tell us about the dream of happiness. In fact, these are passages that are well known to many of us. But what do they really mean?

> What profit hath man of all his labor wherein he laboreth under the sun?
>
> I have seen all the works that are done under the sun; and behold, all is vanity [in vain] and a striving after wind.
>
> I said in my heart, Come now, I will try thee with mirth, and enjoy pleasure; and behold, this also was vanity.
>
> I searched in my heart how to pamper my flesh with wine, and, *my heart conducting itself with wisdom,* how yet to lay hold on folly till I might see which it was best for the sons of man that they should do under the heaven the few days of their life.
>
> (Ecclesiastes 1:3, 14; 2:1, 3)

"King Solomon tries everything, experiences everything; but, be it noted, without allowing himself inwardly to be swallowed by what he does, his heart—that is, his inner self—"conducting itself with wisdom." He tastes the whole range of human experience in order to understand the real sense and aim of his life:

> I made me great works; I builded me houses; I planted me vineyards; I made me gardens and parks. . . .

I acquired men-servants and maid-servants, and I had servants born in my house . . .

I gathered me also silver and gold, and the peculiar treasure of kings. . . .

And whatsoever mine eyes desired I kept not from them. I withheld not my heart from any joy. . . .

Then I looked on all the works that my hands had wrought, and on the labor that I had labored to do; and, behold, all was vanity and vexation of spirit, and there was no profit under the sun.

(Ecclesiastes 2:4–5, 7–8, 10–11)

"What lesson is being offered here? Is it only a sanctimonious injunction against the striving after material goods? That is how it is often taken, and even those who compiled the Bible seem sometimes to have changed or added words in order to deliver that point of view. But if we tear away that veil, we see rather clearly the image of a man engaging in the fullness of life—studying, questioning, observing. For King Solomon, human life with all its desires, dreams, and fears becomes an arena in which we can experience the play of universal forces in ourselves. And it is this engagement, this study, which can bring what we seek. The things that we desire—material objects, physical and psychological pleasures—do not bring happiness. Solomon exposes that illusion to us. It is a striving after wind. But the study of life frees us from the dream. Freedom is the study of slavery. Happiness is the study of sorrow and false pleasure. This is a revolutionary attitude toward life. Everything else 'under the sun' is vanity."

SOLOMON'S WISH

In speaking about Solomon and the way in life, I felt it necessary to start from the story of his deeply inner wish for that which transcends all worldly aims. For me, Solomon represents a man in whom there exists a balanced relationship between metaphysical vision and worldly realism, at home in two utterly different realms.

I continued:

"The Old Testament tells us that after the crown of Israel had passed to Solomon, God appeared to him and offered to give him whatever he wished. We are told that Solomon asked for only one thing: *an understanding heart*. And God said to Solomon:

> Because thou hast asked this thing, and hast not asked for thyself long life; neither hast asked riches for thyself, nor hast asked the life of thine enemies, but hast asked for thyself understanding to discern judgment.
> Behold, I have done according to thy words; lo, I have given thee a wise and understanding heart. . . .
> And I have also given thee that which thou hast not asked, both riches and honor . . . all thy days.
> And if thou wilt walk in My ways, to keep My statutes and My commandments, as thy father David did walk, then I will lengthen thy days.
>
> (I Kings 3:11–14)

"How are we to take this? Does it mean that the material and psychological things we all desire and need cannot be our first priority in life? And that they will come to us only as a result of our inner wish for something of another level in our lives—namely, an 'understanding heart'? How many fairy tales

92

have told us the same thing! If inwardly I seek the good, then outwardly I will be given great rewards. Is this really something more than a childish fantasy? Or does it have a meaning that a grown-up man or woman, experienced in the ways of the world, can respect?''

Suddenly I remembered who these people in my classroom were. They didn't need to be persuaded that there was a higher dimension of life. These men and women already yearned for something, dreamed of something higher and greater than their lives in the world of money and the bottom line. But time and time again I had seen that people who begin to hunger in this way simply cannot keep their eyes on both the metaphysical and the worldly at the same time. And who could blame them? Who *can* reach for what transcends earth while still remaining *on* the earth? Who can find his way into the exalted human center between heaven and earth, a center that not even the angels occupy, a center that is the sole destiny of the being called Man? Not I, not anyone perhaps that we know. In speaking of the goal of the way in life, we are speaking of a reality of an entirely different level, moving in an entirely different direction, serving an entirely different aim, than our calculating, dream-ridden, egoistic lives, our sense-based lives, our little earth of the animal/ego. And we are supposed to live in these two worlds? Impossible, yet necessary. Impossible, yet the only life that gives our lives human meaning.

I was determined not to make this other level of being seem all sweetness and light, not to make it all sound like a New Age fairy tale or its sentimental religious equivalent in Christian or other language. Didn't I spy some of the students carrying recent books with titles like *How to Achieve Enlightenment and Become Filthy Rich* or *Praying for Profit* or

Do Whatever Gives You Immediate Pleasure; Wealth and Substantial Real Estate Holdings Will Follow, or something of the kind.

But, joking aside, it was imperative that I communicate to the class the scale of this higher level of life and the difficulty of the struggle between man's two natures. Only then could a new attitude toward money be spoken about. To do this, however, I had also to remind *myself* of the immensity of the struggle to be open to both worlds within myself. And so I began to relate the legend of Solomon's throne: it is through myth and legend that the vast scale of spiritual ideas was communicated in ancient times.

THE LEGEND OF THE THRONE

And so, I began again:

"The legend of Solomon's throne is not dwelt upon in our Bible. The Old Testament speaks of the magnificence of Solomon's temple, yet the legends speak also of the throne—the strange, hidden legends, whispered somewhere, held closely somewhere. A throne, after all, is even more at the center than the temple. The throne is the center of the center. The hidden of the hidden, the heart of the heart. To speak of the throne is to speak of the precise point from which all creative power emanates.

"We are told that the splendor of Solomon's throne was such that all the kings of the land—all other aspects of oneself that exercise sovereignty within their limited realm—prostrated themselves in awe before its glory. It was an immense construction, this throne, completely covered with gold and precious stones. Six great steps led up to the seat and on each step were two golden lions and two golden eagles. But, in addition, at either side, two other creatures were placed, each pair symbolizing in its own way the spiritual and material forces that man must harmonize within himself.

"To climb to the seat of the throne, Solomon had first to pass between the lion and the ox, ancient representations of the sun and moon—that is to say, the active and the passive forces in the cosmos. On the second step he passed between the lamb and the wolf, symbols of the pure heart and the devouring passions; then the goat and the leopard, symbols of self-sacrifice and aggression; then the eagle and the peacock, representing the striving toward transcendence and the earthbound vanity of the ego; then the falcon and the cock, representing obedience to the higher and the satisfaction of lust; then the hawk and the sparrow, representing courage and timidity. At the very top of the throne, also fashioned in pure gold, there rested a dove surmounting a hawk, the dove being the great symbol of the force that reconciles the primal opposing energies within the being and life of man.

"But there is more in the legend, much more. Solomon's throne was not only an awesome but immobile structure; numerous extraordinary mechanisms were automatically set in motion the moment Solomon set foot upon the first step. The golden creatures on each step guided him to those on the next step, all this 'machinery' indicating that infallibly acting laws were at work.

"But in addition to these ingenious machines, there stood upon each step a herald whose task was to remind Solomon of the law for kings. The first of these heralds approached him when he set foot on the first step of the throne and spoke to him thus: 'The king shall not multiply wives to himself.' At the second step the second herald spoke: 'He shall not multiply horses to himself.' At the third step: 'Neither shall he greatly multiply to himself silver and gold.' And so on, up to the seventh step. There, having passed between all the symbols of man's two natures, and under the sign of the dove—symbol of the reconciliation of opposites—the seventh herald cried out to Solomon as he prepared to assume his place: *'Know before Whom thou standest!'*

"At that moment Solomon takes his seat upon the throne and the royal crown is set upon his head. A huge snake rolls against the machinery, forcing the golden eagles and lions upward until they encircle the head of the king. The golden dove descends, removes the scroll of the Torah from a casket, and gives it to the king. Now, only now, is the great Solomon ready to carry out his duty as king and judge of Israel!''

SOLOMON'S FALL

My recounting of this legend accomplished what I wished. Everyone in the classroom sat rapt in wonder and puzzlement. They might have easily accepted that the story of Solomon contained hidden meanings, hidden ideas. But this particular idea was not the sort they would have expected—namely, that the spiritual and the material impulses in man were so deeply opposed to each other and yet had to exist together in harmony. They could have accepted either one or the other—either that the two natures were opposed and the lower nature must be destroyed, *or* that they could never be reconciled in this earthly life and that inner peace could be found only in some other world or in some imagined life after death. But they could not take in the notion that these two aspects of human nature were diametrically opposed to each other and yet had to live in relationship.

This is nothing less than the paradox of human life that has silenced all great minds throughout history. Out of this paradox comes the eternal and ever-new question: what must we do, what can we do to allow this reconciliation to take place? From where will the force come that brings together the "lion" and the "ox," the "lamb" and the "wolf," "God" and "mammon"?

The question had to be answered in some way. But I no longer felt the vitality of the "answer" that was in my mind. This answer lay in the idea of a way in life, but at that moment the whole idea of a way in life seemed like only words to me, an empty symbol. I did not want to give this class empty words. They had come for the purpose of understanding something about a very real, living problem of their own lives.

Together, the class and I were squarely in front of a question that was as urgent as it was—at the moment—unanswerable. In fact, it is exactly this situation that I now wait for and look for in speaking with people about the great questions of life. This is the creative moment.

Yes, this moment between people who are brought up short and stopped in front of the questions of contemporary life, these questions that our society and our era—perhaps only our era—has delivered to us because of our utter loss of spiritual tradition and trust in ancient principles of ethics and laws of conscience—these questions of a society lost in materialism and technological change in which the lower nature has been sated again and again, a society in which the ancient traces of higher feelings are vanishing like so many fragile life species: this is the moment, the situation, I believe, that we need to cultivate together.

No one person can answer the questions of meaning in this world today. And, as has always been the case, no one person who has an answer (and there are such people) can simply give it to another ready-made. No, it is in thinking together, under strong conditions of serious search, that a new understanding can be approached. Group communication, group pondering, is the real art form of our time.

In that situation in front of the class, I knew I had to resist the temptation to latch on to the answers my professorial mind was offering to me. It is always very difficult. I had to stay with my students in the state of unknowing and, with them, wish—only wish—for a grain of real understanding. Under these conditions a certain quality of silence sometimes appears. Staying in that silence even for a few seconds is like breathing fire. The ego wants only to talk, to "keep things going." But understanding always has to be paid for, earned, by staying in front of two opposing impulses—in this case, the impulse to talk like a professor and the other impulse drawing me toward the taste of new understanding.

In that purgatorial silence a new voice must always appear—sooner or later. But one can never know in advance from where it will come or who will speak. In this case, it was external; it was Alyssa, my gentle poet and certified public accountant:

"Dr. Needleman," she said, "there is something about Solomon I've always wanted to know ever since I was a child. If God gave Solomon an understanding heart, if He gave him such great wisdom, why does the story tell us that Solomon sinned and was punished?"

Some of the class looked puzzled. Not everyone knew the Bible as well as Alyssa apparently did. I quickly summarized the Old Testament story for the others, how Solomon "did evil in the sight of the Lord" by taking wives from other nations who "turned away his heart after other gods," and how the Lord was angry with Solomon and "commanded him concerning this thing, that he should not go after other gods." And we are told: "Solomon kept not that which the Lord commanded." As a result, disunity and division returned to the land of Israel.

And, in fact, this aspect of the biblical story of Solomon is one of the most puzzling in the whole of the Old Testament. It is true that the Bible continually tells us of divinely favored men and women who disobeyed God's decrees and, after paying the price for their disobedience, emerged even greater than before. It is a paradox that confronts every student of the ancient wisdom—not only in the Old Testament, but in most of the spiritual teachings of the world. Man, it seems, is tempted— perhaps we should say "invited"—to fall; invited, it seems, by God Himself. Through this fall a certain definite struggle is offered to man. If he refuses this struggle, he dies. If he accepts this struggle, he is brought to a destiny so exalted that—as it is sometimes said—even the angels in heaven bow down before him.

But, even knowing this pattern in the sacred writings, the story of Solomon presents an almost intolerable paradox, because before his fall he already had the qualities that come to other heroes *after* they fall away and return. Almost from the very beginning,

> . . . God gave Solomon wisdom and understanding exceeding much, and largeness of heart, even as the sand that is on the sea-shore. And Solomon's wisdom excelled the wisdom of all the children of the east and all the wisdom of Egypt. For he was wiser than all men. . . .
>
> (I Kings 4: 29–31)

How could such a man crave things of the world? How could he "multiply wives unto himself," wives and concubines numbering a "thousand"—to the point that God sends down punishment that utterly breaks the power of Solomon and the integrity of the land of Israel? What is Solomon's story telling us about the meaning of the way in life, the specific struggle that is demanded of us if we are to ascend, step by step, to the throne foreordained for us—step by step, between the lion and the ox, the lamb and the wolf, the eagle and the peacock?

Thank you, Alyssa, for your question. And now, from where will come the response?

9.

WHAT MONEY CAN AND CANNOT BUY

From the legends. The response will come from the legends. It is there that the grace notes of the biblical tales are often found—those all-important grace notes that can evoke in modern people the feeling so needed to help us hear the hidden teachings of our Western scriptures. It is in the legends of Solomon that we may see how Solomon struggled between the darkness and the light. The Bible seems to tell only what God gave him and what God took away. It does not dwell on how Solomon *earned* his understanding. For the understanding that man is made for can never just be given. Or, rather, it can be given only to the individual who is able to receive it. The legends of Solomon tell us of the struggle needed if we are to be able to receive the gift that is offered to us as human beings.

And with whom or with what did Solomon struggle? None

other than the king of the demons himself—the redoubtable ruler of this lower world, *Asmodeus.*

THE BUILDING OF THE TEMPLE

The tale begins with Solomon building the great temple that God had ordained him to build. But he cannot break the stones, for he is forbidden by Mosaic law to use metal to cut the stones of the temple. To build this great structure, he cannot use what comes from "lower down" in the scheme of things—iron. He gathers together his elders to receive their counsel and they tell him that there is somewhere in this world a wondrous creature named the *shamir,* a creature whom God created at twilight on the eve of the first Sabbath, among the very last of His wonders. Smaller than a grain of barley, the *shamir* has such power that with the merest touch it can cleave rocks and cut through the hardest of stones. "Command that the *shamir* be brought," the elders say.

"Where can he be found?"

"We do not know," answered the elders. "Summon the demons and inquire of them."

The king brought all his demons before him.

"Where is the *shamir?*" he asked them. These were the demons who served Solomon, whom Solomon had mastered, the dark forces in man that the great king had seen and overcome.

"We too do not know where the *shamir* is to be found," the demons answer, "but perhaps Asmodeus our king will know."

Asmodeus, the king of the demons! The one demon that Solomon had not yet conquered. Powerful as he was, Solomon had not mastered nor even seen the chief demon within, the source of all the dark forces within oneself. Until a man has struggled with this demon he cannot take the place prepared for him from above.

"But where is Asmodeus to be found?" asks Solomon. Where can I find the central demon of my life, the dark source of all that takes man—myself—away from consciousness?

To this question, the demons reply:

"Asmodeus dwells upon one of the great mountains in the land of darkness. . . ."

MONEY AND THE EMOTIONS

As I was telling this story, I was struck by the way the class was changing. Some were utterly rapt with the tale, but most were getting restless and looking uncomfortable. I hadn't really gotten to the main ideas of the story, the truths about ourselves which indeed can make any of us feel uncomfortable. Were some of the students already sensing the subtle ideas behind this legend? Or, was it only that I had gone past the time for the lunch break? I laughed to myself, announced the break, and went toward Alyssa—who was coming toward me.

"I only wish some of my clients were here at this workshop," she said. She explained that when she had some years before decided to become a CPA, she had assumed it would only be a matter of arithmetic, mathematics, rules and regulations. She had coldly and calmly chosen that because, after years of fighting a losing battle as an artist, she had no choice but to make herself "marketable." She had assumed her work would be more or less mechanical from that point on, and she would do it until she had saved enough money to go off somewhere and return to her art. "But I had no idea of the people element in this profession. I'm not dealing with forms and figures. I'm dealing with people. I'm dealing with lives. I'm dealing with hearts. Maybe even with souls?"

I knew exactly what she meant. Time was, in our society, when it was the clergyman, the physician, or the psychiatrist who was most privy to people's secret lives, their fears, desires, anxieties, their shame and misdeeds, their private sorrows, all their psychic "beauties." But now this role was occupied more and more by the accountant and tax preparer. In many cases, it is the accountant or tax preparer or estate planner before whose eyes and ears an individual spills the details of his life— wittingly or unwittingly.

"But," I said, "that is exactly what people need now. Maybe it's even a whole new profession or role in our society: the priest-accountant, the therapist-accountant."

We both smiled and we were both serious.

"That's exactly what I've been pushed into," she said. "And I don't know how to deal with it. When I see someone's financial records—or lack of them—I'm seeing more about them than I want to see. I'm seeing their lies, their contradictions, their hypocrisies, their sexual hangups, their hatreds and petti- ness, their phenomenal cruelties and their incredible wishful thinking. Their selfishness, their . . ."

As we were leaving together by the faculty exit, I heard my name called. I turned around. One of the students was hurrying toward me.

"May I have a word with you?"

I stopped in the doorway.

"Is it possible to get my money back?" he asked in a voice crackling with tension. He was a tall, youngish-looking man, not more than thirty, with short, dark hair and a neatly trimmed full mustache. He was wearing a maroon school tie and a tweed sport coat.

"This is not the course that was advertised in the catalog." Straining at the edges of courtesy, he reached into his folder and brought out the Extension catalog. "This man is a law-yer," I thought to myself. He began reading:

" 'Topics to be treated will include:

> *How Much Money Is Enough?*
> *Money and Sex*
> *How Can You Tell if You're Selling Out?*
> *What Money Can and Cannot Buy*
> *The Meaning of Luck'—*"

I stopped him. He had a point. I offered to buy him lunch. His eyes lit up and all anger passed away from his face.

I had wanted to use the lunch to talk more with Alyssa, to understand something about her relationship to money. Why not use this young man to help me?

As we crossed the street to the restaurant, I couldn't help noticing how affable this young man had now become. The demand to have his money refunded had been mainly an ex-pression of an emotion, and my asking him to lunch had com-pletely changed his emotional state. How far, I wondered, has money become an instrument of emotional expression in our lonely society—a language of the emotions, the only such lan-guage left for many of us?

What a strange and strangely unexpected thing! Without anyone noticing it or naming it properly, this ingenious instru-ment of material exchange, money, has turned into the only means or the principal means of human communication in a society that has lost the meaning of so many of its laws and customs of mutual relationship. I filed that thought away for future consideration.

We entered the restaurant, a marginally upscale sushi bar crowded with the students from my class. As we waited to be seated, I took stock of how things stood with the course. As often happens to me, I had opened up more lines of thought than I could possibly pursue in the time remaining that afternoon. First of all, there was the whole Max Weber issue—extremely important. I had promised the class I would indicate what this great sociologist had left out in his epoch-making analysis of the relationship between Protestantism and capitalism—and how this missing element could point the way to the possibility of the inner search right in the heart of the world of money—the world of today and tomorrow. I was referring to the historical emergence, starting in the fourteenth century, of a group of men and women who were practicing the way in life right within the bosom of Christianity. What we know as Protestantism was a reflection of this way in life, but a reflection that left out a most essential aspect of it.

I'd had no choice then but to bring forward the whole idea of the way in life, an idea that goes back to the deep source of all wisdom teachings in the history of mankind. So, I was obliged to speak to the class explicitly of this immense idea. And to communicate something of its true immensity, to prevent its being taken as a merely interesting psychological theory or, even worse, as some new piece of overcooked meat in the New Age stew, I'd had to draw on mythic language that could be felt, but not easily intellectualized. And so, I went to the legends of King Solomon, where the idea of man's two natures, so central to the teaching of the way in life, is communicated with equal measures of dramatic power and symbolic subtlety. And that in turn meant explaining the real meaning of the devil, the chief of demons, Asmodeus himself, in Solomon's—and man's—struggle for an enduring contact with the God within oneself.

And now, on top of all this, a student—this now amiable young lawyer—insists that I actually speak about the topics mentioned in the catalog description of the course. And he is perfectly justified.

His name was William Cordell III, a name perfumed with money and destiny. But he was not at home inside his name or his body. Or his probable destiny.

"Please call me Bill," he insisted, nervously smiling and fidgeting. Why didn't he just introduce himself as Bill?

Even before the menus were brought, he was at me. At the same time, I was fascinated by him. I had never before seen a man whose life and character were so easily visible in his face, his posture, his name: this was a man who had too much money.

And that was exactly his question. As Alyssa and I exchanged glances, he launched into the following:

"Please forgive my rudeness a moment ago," he began, "but when I saw the description of your workshop it really raised my hopes. Especially the question of what money can and cannot buy.

"Only five years ago," he continued, "it seemed to me I understood something about that question. I was in my second year at law school, looking forward to a happy future. I had good friends, I was interested in helping people in the field of civil rights law. My parents were very wealthy, but never overindulged me. They provided for me very well, but I always understood that I had to earn my way in life. I knew I would take a position in my father's big law firm sooner or later, but I felt free to follow my own star.

"Almost overnight, all that changed. My mother and father died in an automobile accident and, as I was their only child, the entire family fortune fell into my hands. For a long time, I was numb with grief, but eventually I was able to take an interest in my situation. When I registered how much money

I had inherited, the shock was nearly as great as when I heard about my parents' accident.''

"How much was it?'' That was Alyssa.

"Sixty-five million dollars,'' said Bill in a strangely flat voice. I gasped, but I did not take my eyes off Alyssa. Her eyes merely narrowed in an expression of intense interest, like a scientist coming upon an unusual phenomenon of nature. Bill continued:

"I had already taken a leave of absence from law school, and when I applied for an extension of the leave, the chancellor of the school himself came to see me to offer me whatever help I needed. What kindness, I thought, that such an important person would be so solicitous to an obscure student like me. But soon I began to realize how nice everyone had been to me. People I had not seen for years or did not even know particularly well came calling, or wrote to me. I'm not stupid. I saw what was happening. Yet I couldn't help myself from believing they were all sincere. It was pure self-deception. But I couldn't help myself.

"But the most difficult thing was the way my closest friends started to behave. Every single one of them came to me for money—and always as though they were doing me some kind of favor, or as though I was morally obliged to share my wealth with them. I would have been glad to give them money, but they didn't allow me the chance. They didn't let me give out of my own heart. . . .''

As Bill was speaking, I noticed that the students at the nearby tables had grown silent, their ears cocked to hear our conversation. The waitress took our order.

Bill went on:

"I became more and more lonely. I gave them money and then long periods would pass when I wouldn't give anyone anything. I had financial managers, but I began to distrust them also. I bought everything I had ever dreamt of and when that paled I bought things I didn't even want. I bought a horse ranch, I bought a big boat. I gave money to causes and charities. I bought a small publishing business. I bought a mansion."

"You were trying to throw your money away?" asked Alyssa.

"No," said Bill, after a long pause. "No, I don't think so. In any case, that's not what happened. The more I spent, the more kept coming back. At the end of a year, I had more than I started with. It's not so easy to piss away sixty-five million dollars. Short of just burning it."

"How much are you worth now?" asked Alyssa.

While the waitress placed the delicate food on our table, Bill stared at Alyssa with slitted eyes.

"Why do you want to know? Why are you so interested in the exact amount of money I have?"

Oh! Here was the other Bill—or should I say William Cordell III. This was getting interesting.

Alyssa was unfazed. Her blue eyes sparkled, her lips curved in a smile. "Because," she said, "when it comes to money, precision is essential. If you don't know exactly how much money you have, you will never be in charge of your life, or that part of your life where money is necessary."

Bill turned his face away from her in disgust. He looked at me and sadly shook his head, as if what Alyssa had said was just another sign that the world was against him. Where had I seen that kind of look, that particular brand of self-pity, before? That particular mixture of weakness of will and a sort of attractive innocence? A sort of beauty, almost, but a rotting beauty. . . .

My God! It was the face of Paul Meyer, my childhood friend sitting sadly with his wondrous roomful of electric trains!

Fascinating, but there was more than that going on. I had

seen that face in other people as well, people who were not rich at all. It was coming to me slowly: it was the face of a man compelled to hide from his own inner contradictions, who had found the means to escape from every prompting of conscience except for one piercing, agonizing cry from somewhere far back in his mind. A man who had to prove the world was against him, even to the point of killing himself, if necessary. It was the face of a man who could not see even for a moment his own contradictions, who needed pity in order to prove—to prove what? A man who heard the call of conscience for a terrifying split second and who had at all costs to close it down. But wait! Isn't this the meaning of all our sorrow in this life? That one thing in each of us that blocks us utterly from seeing the main and central contradiction of our selves? Isn't this, after all, the meaning of our impoverished soul? Isn't this the *chief of the demons?*

It was now quite clear to me what Bill looked like. There are certain alcoholics—we have all known them, we have most of us suffered from them and loved them, many of us *are* them— who have a certain compelling beauty, charm, creativity that compels us to love them or care for them, but who at the same time are deeply and irrevocably frightened, weak, childishly incapable of seeing or listening either to another or to themselves in the midst of the difficulties and responsibilities that life brings to all of us. That, after all, is the spiritual definition of neurosis—the constitutional inability to see oneself. Spiritually posited, neurosis has nothing to do with how one behaves or suffers; it has nothing to do with the fact that the psyche is infused with contradictions; it is primarily the failure of the capacity to attend to the truth about oneself, whatever it may be, with an awareness free of emotionalism—a capacity, by the way, which the great spiritual masters of early Christianity and Sufism called *sobriety.*

Thus a man, at one level, can seem to the world to be an alcoholic by the amount he drinks and the way he behaves, but spiritually speaking, within the most authentic realms of his psyche, he can be utterly sober and responsible to the power of self-attention within him; while another man may drink very little or not drink at all, and may seem reasonable and responsible, yet within himself he may be a roaring alcoholic, only not necessarily with the chemical substance alcohol as his drug.

Bill's drug was money. He was like a man who had been given whiskey or cocaine without being prepared for its effects on him, or like a man whose body was genetically vulnerable to a certain substance, or like the young people of the sixties, many of whom were raised with a conventionally moral but rigid upbringing and threw it all off under the power of drugs, half-truths, and an unusually hypocritical, stupid, and brutal war. Like marijuana in the unprepared person, like alcohol, sudden wealth had blunted and even reversed the development of will in the psyche of William Cordell III. He turned to his wealth to escape the inner contradictions that all human life is heir to, while at the same time his money allowed impulses to flourish and be implemented that would otherwise never have come to the surface. It was all in his face.

For Bill, money was an instrument of the emotions, those emotions that obstruct our vision of the real world. But for Alyssa, as I now began to grasp, money meant something entirely different. For her, money was an instrument of the mind!

What Money Can Buy

All this became clear to me as the discussion continued. Bill picked up on something I had said in passing during the morning lecture. I had challenged the class by claiming that there were very few, surprisingly or even shockingly few, problems of life that could not be solved with a finite amount of money, a distinct, specific dollar amount. Almost all the difficulties that we think of as ethical problems, problems of sensitivity, human relations, problems involving love, honor, duty, could be resolved with a definite dollar figure. I had asked the class to think of the problem in their own lives that was particularly troubling them at the moment, and then sincerely to ask themselves exactly, *precisely*, how much money it would require to deal with the problem.

Many of the students were disturbed by what they took to be my cynicism. But I did not mean it cynically at all. It was only my way of showing the actual power of money in our lives and then showing the weakness, or limitations, of that power. A few of the students had honestly tried this little exercise, with results that were eye-opening for them. One spoke of a specific and prolonged medical treatment that would, he felt, definitely solve a problem he had up until now thought of only as a moral dilemma involving his relationship to his aging parents. Another mentioned the same sort of thing, but in connection with a woman he had been involved with. Yet another described an insult he had just received from an old friend. A few thousand dollars would enable him not to depend on that friend for certain things and would thereby enable him to be candid with him, and so forth and so on.

The point I had wanted to make was that money can buy almost anything we want—the problem being that we tend to want only the things that money can buy. Money can solve almost any problem, but the solution never lasts. Money can be a reconciling influence, harmonizing conflicting forces—but from the outside, rather than from within the individual. To depend on money is to depend mainly on a force that comes from outside the initiative and inner depth of the individual. I did not mean to say that the earning of money has this characteristic—on the contrary, there are many conditions in life in which the earning or acquiring of money demands the exercise of something like will. No, I was claiming that the wrong dependence on money to get through difficulties puts something external in the place of an internal, psychological force that needs to be developed and exercised in every normal adult man or woman.

Sitting now at the restaurant, eating the refined cuisine of the people, the Japanese, who now have more money than anyone else, Bill pressed me to explain myself further. As he put it, "That is the whole reason I took this course—to understand what money can and cannot buy."

Contact and Exchange

As he repeated this in a fairly loud and emphatic voice, I noticed that the whole restaurant was quiet. The place was filled with students from the class and they had by now all turned toward us. Some even began pulling their chairs closer to our table.

"I think I understand what he means," said Alyssa, trying to reconnect to Bill. "To know what money is for and what it isn't for is like knowing how to live! A lot of wealthy people use money to soften all the edges of life, to avoid working through difficulties. It's like cotton batting. But not only wealthy people. I've seen this in many of my clients. The rich ones sometimes use money in this way, the not-so-rich ones dream of using it like that. But there is one thing I know. There *are* situations where money really is the answer. It's sometimes just as much fantasy to think money isn't the answer as it is to imagine it is! Don't you think so?''

She directed the question to me.

''You could very well put it that way,'' I answered. ''Money was invented by someone, somewhere. It is such an extraordinary device, it could not have just automatically 'happened' in the way some scholars say. You know how scholars and modern scientists are always claiming that inspired human creations just sort of mechanically happen—like the domestication of animals or Gothic cathedrals or herbal remedies. I don't believe that people were just sort of bartering their crops or livestock and then someone more or less said to himself, 'It's awfully inconvenient carrying these bags of grain or leading these cows around. Eureka! Let's use beads or shells or gold— and, to make it even more convenient, so as to be able to own more things and eat more and save time for having pleasure and sleeping and propitiating our superstitiously invented gods, why not make little units of exchange out of our metals and call them coins?' No, it couldn't have happened in that way.

''Money, I'm convinced, is an inspired invention by people who understood the play of forces in human life. There must have come a moment when something was needed that could facilitate man's material life in an expanding society. It must have been created as a means of recognizing that human beings have individual property rights, but at the same time that no human being or family is self-sufficient. In other words, money was created—by the keepers of the sacred teachings underlying all human societies—to maintain a relationship between man's spiritual needs and his material needs. What I'm trying to say is that money is intrinsically a principle of reconciliation, of the harmonization of disparate elements. No wonder that in ancient Greece, Hermes was both the god of commerce and the god of communication between man and the immortals, the god of the borders, the god of exchanges.

"But where there is relationship, there must be contact between the things related. For exchange to take place there must be contact between the elements in the exchange. A principle of reconciliation allows this contact to take place. Money was invented to allow contact and exchange between fundamental aspects of human life, the material, external life and the internal life, in the sense of man's relationship to God within and above.

THE MONEY DRUG

"It has become my understanding," I went on, "that whatever prevents this contact between the fundamental forces of our nature—only that can rightly be called evil in human life. Man is built to allow this contact at a certain level of awareness not possible in any other creature. Whatever stands in the way of a conscious contact between the spiritual and the material in human life, only that is truly evil. The desire for physical things, family, safety, comfort, sex—none of that is evil. These are all aspects of one of the great forces of the universe in the human animal.

"No, the real evil in our lives is now, and has always been, the cloud of human ignorance and fear which prevents experiential contact between the two levels. That is what alcohol and many other drugs prevent, through acting on the body and the body's emotions in a certain way, when taken excessively or with wrong motivation. Man cannot be or act in accordance with the good unless there is a flow of exchange from the higher toward the lower in him, and this requires, first and foremost, contact between the disparate worlds within his nature. God, or whatever name you wish to give to the higher, can never actually influence our lives unless there is this contact.

"Neurosis is a disease of man's power to see himself. Seeing, in its deepest sense, begins as a confrontation of forces— the forces of consciousness and the forces that move away from consciousness toward inertness. These latter are called demons in the old religions. But the chief demon is that which prevents seeing.

"In the legend of Solomon, Asmodeus, the chief of the demons, has vowed never to drink alcohol and he is captured by Solomon through the ruse of making him drink wine. Yet the story of Solomon is also about wealth and power in the world. Do you see why I bring in this story?"

The restaurant was quiet as a tomb. I was looking at about thirty dumbfounded faces. But the momentum carried me on.

"Money is evil when it acts in us the way alcohol acts in the addict. Don't misunderstand me. In its place, alcohol is good. Properly used, it can even bring a certain strength, a certain initiating support to struggle with difficulties. But wrongly used, it becomes a force that prevents seeing, prevents the confrontation within ourself of contradictions, blocking us from exercising and developing our will.

"It can be the same—almost exactly the same—with money, especially in today's world. Used rightly, money allows us to live, eat, drink, protect ourselves, help our families and friends, maintain our health, accomplish certain aims. This it does by reconciling external conflicts, by allowing relationships and exchanges to exist between elements that are not yet in relationship. It can be an instrument of love, hate, challenge, tenderness—all the normal feelings of a normal human being.

"But used wrongly, money prevents relationship, prevents exchange between certain essential elements of the whole life. As a drug, money can simply substitute an external reconciliation for an internal confrontation of forces. It can *solve problems* where what is needed is the *experiencing of questions.* Like technology—and money is a form of technology—money is good at solving problems; it is bad at opening questions. Like technology, money is used wrongly when it converts inner questions that should be lived into problems to be solved. Money fixes things, but not every difficulty in life should be fixed. There are some difficulties that need to be lived with and experienced more and more consciously. The alcoholic, through a certain diseased relationship between personal emotions and blind instinctual sensations, is prevented from experiencing the confrontation of basic forces within himself. Therefore, he cannot develop *will,* which is the name the great teachings have given to the interior third force in man that relates his two natures. The money addict suffers from the same fundamental pathology.''

Fortunately, Alyssa interrupted me at this point.

"Professor Needleman," she said, "I can't say that I follow everything you're saying. So I can't say whether I agree with you or not. But I can tell you that in my own life I have been forced to sit down and ponder very hard about the place of money. Had I not done so, my life would have become a disaster. I had to ask myself how much I wished to really live like ordinary, normal people, with ordinary, normal things like a decent house, privacy, friends. I had to give up my image of myself as a completely devoted artist. I had to learn marketable skills. I had to decide exactly how much money I needed and how much money I wanted. . . ."

I, in turn, interrupted Alyssa. "But that is exactly what very few people do anymore," I said. "You had an inner life— in your case, it was your art." She had said she was a painter. "You had also an outer life you had to lead. You, like every human being, had to give, let us say, half of your energy to

117

the outer life. No human being can live in the inner life alone. No one can live solely in the world of interior values. Maybe angels do that, if they exist, but as you have probably heard, even the angels have jobs.'' (No one laughed at that, very understandably.)

"For you, money was and is a means of trying to live in two opposing worlds at the same time. . . .''

"I'm not very good at that,'' said Alyssa.

"Neither am I,'' I answered. "Who is? But that is the challenge of our lives as human beings. That's what the way in life is about. This is what the word *will* really means—the power to live and be in two opposing worlds at the same time. . . .''

"I've never heard *will* defined like that,'' piped up someone from another table.

"Maybe not,'' I said. "But I can assure you the power to live in two worlds or at two completely different levels at the same time is what the great wisdom teachings have defined as *will*, of course not in those exact words. But I understand your objection. For us, in our culture, will is understood mainly as the power to do what we want in only one world. But if you really look at what passes for will, you'll see that it is often only one desire dominating the others, no matter how it is dressed up in religious or moral language. It is not the development of a consciousness that harmonizes all the impulses in ourselves.

"In any case,'' I continued, "the original purpose of money—that sacred device meant to help us live in two worlds—has been eroded until today it is completely forgotten. Blame it, in part, on the huge increase in world population and international trading. But whatever the ultimate cause may be, from the economic view which prevails in the modern world, money has value almost exclusively on a material level. Money is no longer a reminder of spiritual, inner values as well. It has become only a social convenience, a social necessity. The making of money has become an end in itself. And exchanges of money, far from being a reminder of our dependence on one another and of a greater common purpose for the human species, are conducted usually in an atmosphere of impatience, negativity, and cunning.''

Somehow, I had managed to eat my lunch even while talking so much. It was definitely time to go back to class. Everyone got up to pay their checks at the cash register. After a moment's hesitation, Bill stood up and shouted, ''I'll pay for everyone's lunch!'' Alyssa gave him a tender look, mixed with pity.

10.

THE KING OF
THE DEMONS

I felt a little guilty toward the students who had not had lunch at the Japanese restaurant and I immediately launched into a continuation of the Solomon legend. In fact, the lunch had brought me more than I had hoped for. I understood Alyssa; I understood William Cordell III and, for the first time in all the years I had been thinking about the question of money, I felt I had reached the germ of my own understanding of money itself in the search for self-knowledge.

"Let me remind you that the title of this course is 'Money and the Meaning of Life,' " I began. "The whole phrase 'meaning of life' has become such a cliché that it has assumed the status of a joke. It is generally assumed that no one knows the meaning of life and anyone who claims to know it is automatically suspect. The reason is clear. To know why I exist, it is first of all necessary to know *that* I exist. And the awareness of one's own existence is not something that we can assume. The thought 'I exist' is not the same thing as the *awareness* of one's own existence. This is the principal error of modern philosophy and modern psychology. Thought is not the same thing as consciousness. All of the ancient teachings warn us against the error of imagining that mere thought lends us being and authentic selfhood. There can be no meaning to human existence until an individual exists. That is why the question of the meaning of life is so laughable. Meaning is a property of conscious life.

"Always and everywhere in the Old Testament we are warned against substituting anything for this conscious life. It is the complete and entire meaning of idolatry in Judaism—and, when you really come down to it, in every other great teaching. What else is idolatry but the substitution of something external or mentally invented for the conscious life? *Thou shalt have no other gods before Me.*

THE POWER OF THE SMALL

"Now here is Solomon. To build the temple, to create the place in which the highest holiness can be contacted—and that great temple is internal, not merely an external edifice, obviously—he must have the help of the *shamir*—something small and hidden, something so active that, as it is said symbolically, it can cut through anything. It can penetrate anything. Without this subtle, fine power, the temple of man cannot contain that to which the Hebrews gave the name Yahweh—that is to say, I AM.

"And this subtle, fine, yet all-penetrating something—this force that can cut through the hardest stone—is kept by Asmodeus, chief of the demons.

"Solomon devises a plan. Asmodeus, he is told, dwells in

the mountains of darkness. There he has a well of water covered with a great stone and sealed with his own seal. 'Go to the mountains of darkness,' Solomon tells his most trusted servant, 'and while Asmodeus is away put wine where there is now clear water in his well.'

"The servant obeys and when Asmodeus returns he thunders with rage to find wine in the well. He knows full well its power to cloud the mind. But thirst overcomes him, he drinks, and falls into a stupor. The servant, armed with chains and the magical ring bearing the great seal of Solomon—the six-pointed star representing the interpenetration of the heavenly and the earthly realms, with the sacred name of God inscribed upon it—subdues the great chief of demons and leads him back to the king.

" 'Why?' Asmodeus asks Solomon. 'Why did you subdue me? Why have you covered me with these chains? Why did you not let me live and do as I do, going to and fro in the earth and heavens, attending and studying at the sacred discussions among the angels in heaven and here among you mortals on earth? Why did you not allow me to have the place assigned to me by God in the two worlds of heaven and earth? Was it not enough for you that you are king and ruler over all else in this world? Could you not have allowed me my place as well?'

" 'It is for the sake of God and only for His sake that I bring you here," Solomon replies. 'I need from you what you alone have in your domain, the *shamir,* to cut the stones for the temple of God. Where may I find the *shamir?*'

" 'The *shamir* is not with me,' Asmodeus answers. 'It has been entrusted to Rahab, ruler of the waters and the seas, who in turn has entrusted it to the most worthy of birds, the hoopoe. And you, great king, must know how the hoopoe is charged to employ the *shamir.*'

" 'Speak!' commands Solomon.

"It is the hoopoe's task, explains Asmodeus, to set the *shamir* upon the barren, lifeless rocks of the earth, which then split beneath its action, after which the hoopoe brings in its beak seeds from every kind of tree, dropping them into the new clefts of the rocks. Little by little the bare and barren rocks are made fruitful with life.

"The *shamir* is that force whose action allows life to flourish where until then it could not enter.

" 'For the sake of God's temple,' says Solomon, 'we will find this hoopoe and take the *shamir* from her.' And so it happens. Warriors and huntsmen are sent into the wilderness. Upon a craggy mountain, they find her nest and cover it with glass. When the hoopoe returns and cannot feed her nestlings, she brings the *shamir* to cut through the glass. Seeing this, the huntsmen hurl a stone at her. The *shamir* falls from her mouth, the huntsmen take it and return with it to Solomon. And so, the temple of God is built.

"But the tale tells us that when the hoopoe saw that she had failed in her trust, she killed herself in remorse.

ASMODEUS UNBOUND

"What is the secret in this story?" I asked the class. "There is something not quite right here. There seems to be a violation. Why? What is this remorse, this suicide? How is it that Solomon must go to the chief of the demons for the power to build the temple of God?

"In fact, it is Solomon's own question. Long after the *shamir* has done its work, Asmodeus is still in chains. 'If it was only for the sake of God that you bound me,' says Asmodeus, 'then why am I still here? Let me be free and do my own work which is no less ordained from Above than yours, O great king!'

"But above all, Solomon wishes understanding, knowledge. This is what sets him apart, this thirst to understand. Few figures in all the literature of the world so powerfully represent the wish for knowledge and understanding. That is why he is incomprehensible to those for whom piety consists mainly in uncritical belief. In our era, however, in which the impulse toward knowing is so predominant, we can perhaps respond to Solomon more than to the conventional saintly symbols. But the knowledge that Solomon seeks is very 'expensive.' It can only be had through an exceptional quality of experience, an exceptional engagement in all the forces of life.

"And so, Solomon seeks to learn from the devil himself.

" 'Tell me,' says Solomon to Asmodeus, 'what is the nature of your power? How is it that you rule so mightily over mankind?'

" 'Unbind me,' answers Asmodeus, 'and let me hold your signet ring for a moment and I will show you the secret of my power.'

"Here we can imagine King Solomon's mind. He will take the risk none other would take. I see him as I see King Odysseus, that other great seeker after risk, that other great symbol of intentional engagement in the whole of life, daring solely for the sake of acquiring the knowledge of Being, that same King Odysseus—whose name means literally 'he who searches for difficulties'—who allows himself to be overcome by Circe, the source of animal dreams of pleasure, Odysseus who risks battle with the Cyclops Polyphemus, representing the devouring power of the sensory world. It is that same Odysseus who verifies from the ghost of Achilles that the truly human life is founded on the struggle for conscious presence, that to be in

Hades, in the land of shadows, is to lose the fullness of self-attention even as one acquires fame and glory in the eyes of the world, even if one is, as Achilles was, the offspring of a 'god.' Odysseus, the man of many ruses—king, warrior, fool, outcast; and Solomon, wise, favored of God, passionate, bold, and strangely all-too-human in his loves. The Hebraic Solomon; the Greek Odysseus; the Sumerian Gilgamesh; the Hindu Arjuna; the North American Coyote; the Arthurian Lancelot—the list is endless of symbols handed down from the immensity of myth and legend that tell us of the way in life.

"Solomon takes the risk. He unbinds Asmodeus and hands him the sacred ring. In a lightning flash, Asmodeus swells to enormous size, one of his wings touching the earth, the other grazing the highest realms of heaven. With his wings touching each of the two worlds, the chief of demons swallows Solomon and spits him out with such force that he hurls Solomon far, far away from holy Jerusalem, the city of God, to a distant and alien country. As for the ring bearing the sacred name of God, Asmodeus flings it into the vastness of the ocean, the realm of Rahab, ruler of the seas, to whom the *shamir* was originally entrusted by God."

KNOWLEDGE AND UNDERSTANDING

The class was transfixed. Not a sound, not a movement. The legend was doing its work. But how to proceed? Should I not briefly summarize the rest of the story and bring the students back to the main idea—namely to explain that there was a way in life taught within the Christian context as the monasteries declined in the late Middle Ages? That what we now call Protestantism with its "worldly asceticism" (as Max Weber termed it) became, at a certain point, a fatally incomplete expression of the way in life which, because of what this version of Protestantism left out, helped spawn our modern obsession with money and worldly capitalism?

Yet the whole point of telling the legend was to be sure the students would feel the power and the scale of the idea of a way in life. Like all sacred art, legends are for the feeling; and it is more important to feel what one knows—even if it is only one thing—than it is to know with the head alone a mass of theories and facts. When modern people assume that we have made so much progress over ancient or nonindustrialized cultures, they forget this point. It is far, far better to understand a central truth with the whole of oneself than it is to know many things only with the mind. When one knows only with the mind, and the feelings are not integrated into the knowing, then the knowledge one has becomes harmful. Technology without ethics is the result of having knowledge without developing the instrument of ethical perception, the feelings. As it was said long ago, "The mind is for seeing what is true; the feelings are for understanding what is good."

I therefore chose to resist being the "proper professor" and decided to risk the students' dissatisfaction at not being given enough information. I went on with the legend. Let them come away feeling, really feeling, both the exalted possibility and the inner difficulty of treating money as an instrument for self-study in the midst of ordinary life! I continued my lecture:

THE SECRET POWER OF ASMODEUS

"Having hurled King Solomon into a distant country, and the sacred ring into the depths of the sea, Asmodeus now steals into the inner chambers of the king. There he dons the royal garments and sets upon his head the royal crown, and there *he changes his face into the face of Solomon!* And he sits on the throne in place of the king and judges the people. And, so the legend tells us, none knew that it was not Solomon ruling over them, but the chief of the demons, Asmodeus!

"Solomon had taken the risk of freeing Asmodeus in order to learn the secret of his power over men. *And this is the secret:* the power of Asmodeus is his ability to take on the face and the function of the true ruler, the true self within! The power of all the other demons derives from this chief power of Asmodeus.

"The chief of the demons, the chief weakness of man is the false sense of I!

"The true king is in exile!

"A usurper has taken the throne!"

A student, I didn't see who, cried out: "Why isn't that said in the Bible?"

"It is said," I answered. "It is said a thousand times. When Moses asks God, 'Who shall I say you are,' God answers, 'Tell the people of Israel I AM sent you.' And who do you think Pharaoh is, but the false king ruling over the people of Israel? No, the problem is not that it isn't said. The problem is that it isn't heard, it isn't felt, it isn't understood as the chief problem of human life, the chief feature that prevents man from living the life he was meant to live."

SOLOMON IN EXILE

I went on:

"And now here is Solomon 'coming to' in a strange and alien land. He doesn't know where he is, or where he is going, or what he is doing. He is hungry and thirsty and stupefied. He stumbles aimlessly through a pathless wood until he comes to a pool of water. Bending down to drink, he sees his reflection in the water and what he sees shatters him. The light of kingship and majesty is gone from his countenance, even to the point that he seems small and bent, no longer possessing the stature of a king. Benumbed with dread, he looks more closely and is stunned anew to see that even the furrow around his head has disappeared, the mark made by the crown of the house of David.

"And Solomon wept. All that day he cried unto God with a loud voice: 'Thou hast turned away thy mercy from me and Thou hast driven away my inheritance!'

"And Solomon slept. Some tellers of the tale say that in his troubled sleep he dreamed three dreams. In the first dream mountains of silver and gold spewed forth blood upon him. In the second dream chariots of wondrous horses without number were swallowed by the earth. And in the third dream the great multitude of his wives and concubines danced around him and vanished into the air like ghosts. It is said that he awoke, trembling, and understood that God had visited his sins upon him—his love of wealth, his love of power, and his love of women.

"But in other versions, the legend is silent about these things, leaving it to us to ponder the deeper meaning of Solomon's exile, its *voluntary* beginning, like the deeply voluntary choice of Odysseus to explore, to search in the midst of all the forces of life. In these quieter versions of the legend, we are told only that Asmodeus, ruling in Solomon's place, committed many excesses and yet was recognized by none among the people of Israel save for Solomon's mother, Bathsheba. It is especially in these quieter versions of the tale that the question arises in the hearer, as it is meant to arise, through the hidden feeling, creeping into the mind like a truth that can only be heard by one who wishes to hear: *who*, then, was king when Solomon ruled? *Who* is king when Asmodeus rules? *Who* lives our lives when we are given to our desires and loves and when even the wisdom of God, which we may wish for with all sincerity, cannot free us? *I* am not king of my own life, my own self. How must I live, what must I experience in order to gain the inheritance destined for the human soul?

"The legend now gives us Solomon waking from his sleep, wandering through the alien land from village to village, house to house, his clothes turning to the rags of the poorest beggar. Day in and day out, he cries out to all who see him: 'I am Solomon! King was I in Jerusalem!' He is taken for a madman. Children mock him and throw stones at him.

THE ANSWER TO CYNICISM

" 'I am Solomon! King was I in Jerusalem!' These words of the exiled king echo through the vastness of the legend as it now unreels the adventures of a man in search of his true being and his true place. According to some tellers of the tale, it was when Solomon awoke from sleep that he composed the strangely moving verses known to us as the Book of Ecclesiastes, the vision of a man who has seen through all that ordinary life has to offer, who has seen that life without his own true *I* can give no meaning, that God's love and favor or, as we might also say, the divine energy, cannot penetrate into the nooks and crannies of human life unless there is *I am* truly and fully in one's presence.

There is an evil which I have seen under the sun, and it is common among men:
A man to whom God hath given riches, wealth, and honor, so that he wanteth nothing for his soul of all that he desireth, yet God giveth him not power to eat thereof,

but a stranger eateth it; this is vanity, and it is an evil disease.

(Ecclesiastes 6:1–2)

"This, I believe, is the secret of the strange Book of Ecclesiastes, which has puzzled theologians for centuries with its apparent cynicism, its constatations that there is no justice or fulfillment 'under the sun.' The point is that the influence of God, the influence of that which is *above the sun,* cannot enter into human life save through the conscious presence of the awakened man, the true king.

I have seen all the works that are done under the sun; and, behold, all is vanity and vexation of spirit.

I . . . saw under the sun, that the race is not to the swift, nor the battle to the strong, neither yet bread to the wise, nor yet riches to men of understanding, nor yet favor to men of skill; but time and chance happeneth to them all.

(Ecclesiastes 1:14 and 9:11)

"This is not cynicism. This is the result of understanding that human life has meaning only when there is *I am* in one's presence."

I looked hard at my students and continued:

"The title of this course has been 'Money and the Meaning of Life.' We now see that it could equally have been called, 'Money and the Search for Myself.' It seems crystal clear to me [I was grasping these things anew as I spoke, for the telling of the legend had moved me perhaps as much as it had moved my students] that if there is not the true King in myself, then it follows that the only meaning my life can have is to search for

130

this King. Not to forget that I, too, am Solomon! King was I in Jerusalem!

"And Solomon never forgets. This is the aspect of his greatness that perhaps can touch us the most. Always and everywhere, he cries out his true identity, an identity that is not confirmed by anything outside of himself.

"No, this is not cynicism. It is the accurate vision that human life without the inpouring of divine energy is without meaning, goes round and round in eternally repeating cycles, that both the 'good' and the 'evil' end their days in the grave, that nothing lasts on this earth, 'under the sun,' that life is a rhythm, a pulse, a play of forces meant to serve the Higher, but that for the Higher to be served—as Solomon discovers— man must open to the true I AM—the true meaning—sleeping within him. What are ideals, 'morality,' so-called 'piety,' unless there is the divine human, the spiritually obedient King, in oneself?

"And, yes, it is in the world of matter that the forces play themselves out. Such a view may look like materialism to the ignorant. It is not. It is only accurate vision. And today, the world of matter is represented by the world of money. Materialism is more and more equated with money. Great forces of the earth play themselves out through the medium of money. The person who understands this understands—unconsciously perhaps—that all dreams of good and evil, all 'great projects,' all fantasies of self-involved 'artists' need to be seen *only* in the light of the bottom line—yes, *only* in that light *unless*—and it is a *big* unless—there is in these activities or projects the real call to be open to the inpouring of the true God."

I stopped to catch my breath. It crossed my mind that I should let the students speak now, ask questions or something. But I couldn't stop. I had to go on.

THE TRUTH OF MATERIALISM

"And now," I continued, "I will make a confession to you, a confession about my childhood and money. I was brought up surrounded by people who thought only in terms of money. I hated the deadness of it, the narrow vision of life, the blindness to ideals of truth and wisdom. Looking back, I can see that, yes, they were insensitive to the higher possibilities of life. They were paralyzingly bourgeois. But, after years of studying the realities of the inner search among contemporary people and in the great traditions of mankind's history, I see that these 'dead' people of my childhood were living and perceiving life in a way that was strangely close to the truth. They smiled at my dreams of changing the world, they shook their heads in puzzlement at my philosophizing, my idealistic goals. I hated the way they turned everything around the question of earning a living, equating success and happiness with money in one of its forms.

"But I must say that they saw things in a way that was amazingly close to the truth. They were amazingly close to that attitude toward life that was called in ancient times the attitude of the *householder,* the man or woman with a gut intuition about what really makes life go round, who smiles at people who think they can *do* anything at all significant in a world governed by overwhelmingly great material forces.

"What they lacked, these money-ridden people of my childhood, was a vision of the other reality, that other reality that can penetrate this material world. They lacked that vision, and therefore they were dead. But had they touched that great vision even if only glancingly, they would have been real, living commonsense human seekers.

"And who am I to say that the wish for this vision was not slumbering in them, unexpressed, unacknowledged by the

society they had to survive in? No, give me an out-and-out materialist haunted by a secret vision of God to all the fantasists, fanatics, dreamers, and overintellectualized vagrants that make our troubled lives like the truly desolate life on a painted carousel where, as Solomon the author of Ecclesiastes tells, we go round and round, changing from one "horse" to another on the merry-go-round of life, dreaming of progress while the nickelodeon plays on, while actually we are moving in circles until the day we die!"

I drank from the cup of water that someone had kindly placed next to the lectern. Was I where I wanted to be in the course? Was I communicating what would be useful to these students? There was no question that, for me, it had all been of great value. I was beginning to *feel* the significance of the money question in human life, rather than only react to it with emotionalism or with the foolish abstract intellectualism of a professional philosopher or economist. And I was sure there were students in the class who were coming to that as well. The money question is so intractable to the seeker after meaning just because one never can grasp and feel its connection to the great questions of life and to the ideas that have been handed down over the centuries by men and women of vision.

Alyssa's voice broke the silence.

"What happened to Solomon?"

I determined now to make a quick end of the story, the telling of which I knew had accomplished my aim.

SOLOMON AWAKES

I continued:

"The legends give us many images of Solomon's years wandering in exile, his degradations and humiliations. But, as

in the fairy tales of our childhood, he falls in love with a princess, Naamah, who miraculously returns his love. The king who is the father of the princess banishes them both and together they must live in abject poverty in a barren wilderness. At this point we see that Solomon has been brought low in every respect—that is to say, in the language of legend, he has experienced his nothingness.

"On a certain day, after three years of exile—and the number three always signifies a completed process—he and his wife have in their poverty been brought to the edge of starvation, which is to say, Solomon had become completely empty, completely open. Seeking some means to provide food for his wife and himself, he wanders far and comes upon human tracks leading him to a place by the sea where fishermen are drawing in their nets. With the very last piece of his money, he buys a fish and brings it to Naamah. Preparing the fish, she splits open its belly and cries out to Solomon, 'Come, see what I have found in the belly of the fish!' Solomon runs to her and there, lying in the gut of the fish, is the sacred ring that Asmodeus had hurled into the depths of the ocean!

"The legend now invites us to imagine Solomon placing upon his finger the ring with the sacred seal and the sacred name of God. Suddenly, he is standing straight in all his former majesty. The radiance of kingship streams from his face, the furrow of the crown returns to his forehead. As it is said, he stood before Naamah like a great and flourishing cedar. Once again, he is King Solomon.

"Naamah watches in wonderment as he falls to his knees and utters to God the prayer of thanksgiving. He is now able to receive within himself the majesty that before had not yet penetrated into his being. Years of exile in conditions not corresponding to his nature, years in which the grace, the energy, of God was far from him, years of experiencing himself as a

wretched, mortal beggar, yet never forgetting his identity as king, years of devising stratagems and methods to go on toward the goal of returning to God, have all made their mark upon his nature and brought him to that authentic kingship of man in which the individual's own *I am* becomes a conscious particle of the I AM of the whole of Creation, the latter being the meaning of the secret name of God. For, as it is written in faint letters and whispered in soft words throughout all the inner traditions of the world, the secret name of God is the secret name of man.

"Naamah sees Solomon on his knees and sees the furrow of the royal crown that has suddenly appeared on his forehead. And Solomon tells her who he is.

THE RETURN OF KING SOLOMON

"Like Odysseus returning to Ithaca, Solomon returns to Jerusalem dressed as a beggar. Gradually, the people of Jerusalem—our lesser selves—and the rabbis of the council of elders recognize him and realize who they have been serving. Solomon breaks into the palace and confronts Asmodeus, the chief of demons, who has taken on Solomon's own face and function as king.

"The legend does not dwell on this encounter. No spiritual poet has been tempted to place into the folktales the drama of Solomon's second encounter with Asmodeus, the inner king's second encounter with the false king, the meeting of *I am* and the false I that rules all the impulses of our fallen nature. All I will ask you to do is to call this scene visually before your mind. The true King Solomon, still in his beggar's clothes, but standing in full majesty, his countenance radiating the light of glory, stands before the king of demons whose face is identical to his own and who wears the royal garments.

"The legend only tells us, with no elaboration whatever, that

Solomon showed Asmodeus the sacred ring and Asmodeus instantly
fled far away, leaving the throne to its rightful occupant. There is
no protracted struggle, there are no words between them, there is,
as we nowadays say, no contest. The false I simply vanishes, instantly and without the slightest opposition, when fully confronted
by the true self. The contest, the struggle has already taken place
over the years. But now, with the true self fully awake, the false
self instantly loses all its power. Our effort, the legend is telling us,
must be to awaken that true self. It will triumph without any other
struggle on our part.

"The legends are wiser than we are. We, perhaps, would write
in a climactic struggle. But there is no climactic struggle. There is
only victory, without violence and without the passage of time,
instantaneous and complete, when *I am* is in our presence.

"But the wisdom of the legend does not stop there. It con-
cludes by telling us that, having assumed his rightful place on the
throne, King Solomon remained in fear of the power of Asmodeus,
his chief weakness. From that time forward, each night Solomon
had his mightiest warriors guard him from Asmodeus while he
slept. No man can assume that he will not be taken by his weakness,
no matter what inner glory he has attained. No matter who or
what we are, we must always be watchful, attentive. We will sleep,
it is in our nature. We will not stay always fully present. As the
words of Solomon tell us in the Song of Songs:

> Behold his bed, which is Solomon's;
> Threescore valiant men are about it,
> Of the valiant of Israel.
> They all hold swords, being expert in war:
> Every man hath his sword upon his thigh
> Because of fear in the night."

(Song of Solomon 3:7–8)

11.

THE RELIGION
OF MONEY

I disappeared from view during the afternoon coffee break. Much as I wanted to speak informally with the students, especially with Alyssa and Bill, I had to get off by myself and plan the remaining hour. The Solomon legend had served my purpose of communicating the scale of the idea of a way in life; but now I had to tie up at least some of the loose ends dangling from my presentation of the Max Weber thesis.

Entering the small faculty office, I leaned for a moment against the door. I hadn't expected the story to make me feel so strongly what we are meant to be and how far we are from it, and what an inconceivable struggle we are called to!

A strange, apparently unrelated thought came to me. I had spent my younger years studying minds like that of Max Weber—I mean the intellectual giants of modern Europe: Freud, Hegel, Nietzsche, Heidegger. For a long time I had understood their attitude toward religion in the way most people have come to understand it. I had taken their negative criticism of religion as a turning away from the spiritual dimension of life. Hadn't they, after all, defined the modern rejection of religious values?

But standing there in the faculty office, with the legend of Solomon reverberating in me, and calling to mind the brilliant theories of Max Weber about the roots of modern capitalism, I felt as an absolute certainty that Weber had been a man with great spiritual feeling. "Spiritual" is not necessarily *religion*. A spiritual impulse draws a man toward inner meaning, toward the intangible, toward the enhancement of consciousness and the search to serve the dignity of mankind.

I was sure that Weber, like Freud, like Nietzsche, had had an extraordinary sensitivity of feeling toward the divinity of man, a deep, metaphysical wonder before the possibilities locked within the human structure. The spiritual sensibility of Freud had been stunned by the suffering, hypocrisy, and self-deception of modern civilization, and he had seen one of the great roots of this suffering in the distortion of man's animal, sexual nature, brought about, in large measure, by repressive social conventions and a religious moralism that had lost all contact with an accurate vision of man's biological nature. Freud was saddened and shocked at what religion had done to man. And surely he was right. Surely, the religion that he saw and knew of had lost its way.

WHAT WEBER SAW

But had it not been the same for Max Weber? Surely he had regarded the civilization he lived in with the same mixture of shock and sorrow that a Freud or a Nietzsche felt—as does any one of us in our more deeply sensitive moments—when looking with open eyes at the life around us. Who is this being crawling over the surface of the planet, gifted with an incomprehensible power called awareness, an incomprehensible sense of free choice, a being built on a wholly other plan than any other on earth, as though sent from another world, who yet lies all the time, kills all the time, suffers all the time from the stupidest, most painful waking nightmares of fear, jealousy, envy, hatred—who lives in hell, driven by internal demons day and night; who is this being—and here, surely, we have Max Weber—who spends all his time and all his private energies, who dreams his dreams and fashions his values and ideals, who, in short, gives all his substance, to *the making of money?* Man! The noblest of God's creations! Man! His life on earth dedicated to—to what? Manufacturing, marketing, investing! Man! Possessed of a power of mind that called him to conceive and think rationally about the whole essence of creation and God's order, who can work to grasp the laws of life and matter, who is called to ponder and participate in the essence of divinity itself and yet who uses his specifically human powers of mind for the ultimate aim of: *gathering money!*

"No," I said to the class, after the break and after sharing these thoughts with them, "neither Weber nor Freud nor Nietzsche, no, not even Marx, could possibly have been within themselves that cool, 'superscientific' egoist puffed up with his own assumption of the superiority of modern man that they present in—I won't even say in their writings, but in our reading of their writings. All they had was science and scholarship in which to express themselves. This scientific rationalism has been the language of our era and most of our visionary minds have been compelled to use it in order to express their intuition of the state of human life on earth.

"Freud saw man writhing in a sexual hell; Marx saw man writhing in a hell of class oppression and meaningless work;

Weber saw man writhing in a hell ruled by the money demon. He must have sensed, perhaps even unconsciously—but I do not think it was so unconscious in him—that the energy and the commitment, the blind passion to acquire money, to submit all his mind to the acquisition of this all-too-palpable phantasm called money, the energy to organize his whole communal life on earth for the sake of the perpetual acquisition of money— Weber saw, I am sure, that this incredible psychic energy could only spring from the one essential need which all specifically human energy must inevitably serve—namely, the search for God. He saw that only religious energy could account for this incredible perversion of man's inner structure.

"What Weber saw was not only capitalism. He knew that 'capitalism' had existed in some form in many cultures, wherever the money device had been invented or discovered. What he saw was capitalism made into a religion, a religion in the service of which man employed all the gifts of his mind and heart. He saw the capitalist religion, and the name he gave it was the *spirit of capitalism*. And this, he argued, came from the leakage into outer life of the inner spirit of a form of the Christian religion known as Protestantism, specifically Calvinistic Protestantism!

"Barely able to conceal his own amazement behind the facade of scientific so-called 'objectivity,' Weber reproduces saying after saying from the writings of Benjamin Franklin as examples of what defines the hell of modern man, what Weber calls 'the philosophy of avarice.' "

POOR RICHARD

I took a sip of lukewarm coffee and reached into my stack of books for *The Protestant Ethic and the Spirit of Capitalism*. I read to the class almost everything that Weber cites from *Poor Richard's Almanac*, such as:

> Remember, that *time* is money. He that can earn ten shillings a day by his labour, and goes abroad, or sits idle, one half of that day, though he spends but sixpence during his diversion or idleness, ought not to reckon *that* the only expense; he has really spent, or rather thrown away, five shillings besides.

and:

> Remember, that money is of the prolific, generating nature. Money can beget money, and its offspring can beget more, and so on. . . . The more there is of it, the more it produces every turning, so that the profits rise quicker and quicker. . . . He that murders a crown, destroys all that it might have produced, even scores of pounds.

and:

> Remember this saying, *The good paymaster is lord of another man's purse.* He that is known to pay punctually and exactly to the time he promises, may at any time, and on any occasion, raise all the money his friends can spare. . . . After industry and frugality, nothing contributes more to the raising of a young man in the world than punctuality and justice in all his dealings; therefore never keep borrowed money an hour beyond the time you promised. . . . The most trifling actions that affect a man's credit are to be regarded. The sound of your hammer at five in the morning, or eight at night, heard by a creditor, makes him easy six months longer. . . . It shows, besides, that you

are mindful of what you owe; it makes you appear a careful as well as an honest man, and that still increases your credit. . . .

(Max Weber, *The Protestant Ethic and the Spirit of Capitalism.* New York: Charles Scribner's Sons, 1958, pp. 48–50)

To these citations from Franklin, I added from my own copy of *Poor Richard,* in order to make clear to the class Weber's claim that the "spirit of capitalism" is not only crude material greed, but contains a strong element of sincere piety—a piety, however, that has now become the fuel for a world driven *only* by money. It was not a crass materialist who wrote:

This Doctrine, my Friends, is *Reason* and *Wisdom;* but after all, do not depend too much upon your own *Industry,* and *Frugality,* and *Prudence,* though Excellent Things, for they may all be blasted without the Blessing of Heaven; and therefore, ask that Blessing humbly, and be not uncharitable to those that at present seem to want it, but comfort and help them.

(*The Way to Wealth and Words of Wisdom from Benjamin Franklin's Poor Richard's Almanack,* ed. Nathan G. Goodman. Philadelphia: The Franklin Institute, 1958, p. 24)

In the writings of Benjamin Franklin and in the entire Protestant ethos which, according to Weber, Franklin epitomizes, we have a teaching that seeks to carry into the whole of man's earthly life the virtues and disciplines that also lead man to the "heaven" within his own self, that inner realm of human consciousness where God can speak and act on earth. That the quest for this heaven became the hell of contemporary civilization is precisely the agonizing paradox that Weber seems to have felt so deeply, and that all of us now must face as we ourselves search for the truth of meaning in our day-to-day lives.

A WORLD WE NEVER MADE

Thus, referring to Franklin, to America, to the whole of the modern world, Weber writes:

> The peculiarity of this philosophy of avarice appears to be the ideal of the honest man of recognized credit, and above all the idea of a duty of the individual toward the increase of his capital, which is assumed as an end in itself. Truly what is here being preached is not simply a means of making one's way in the world, but a peculiar ethic. The infraction of its rules is treated not as foolishness but as forgetfulness of duty. That is the essence of the matter. It is not mere business astuteness, that sort of thing is common enough, it is an ethos. *This* is the quality that interests us. Man is dominated by the making of money, by acquisition as the ultimate purpose of his life. . . . At the same time it expresses a type of feeling which is closely connected with certain religious ideas. . . .
>
> (Weber, pp. 51-53)

Such is the origin of the world of money, the world we are all now born into. It was a world created by religious passion that became confused with the world of material life—a too-enthusiastic turning away from monastic escape. But—and this Weber does not see, nor do his critics—this turning from one-sided "spirituality" to one-sided materiality, from the false heaven of the "monk" to the hell of our modern life, took place at least in part because many of our religiously passionate forebears in the seventeenth and eighteenth centuries skipped a step, a step not easily seen by the ordinary eye. That step is what is contained in the teaching of the way in life. What Weber and others speak of as the "Protestant ethos," as it relates to the spirit of capitalism, is the effort to find God in man's material life without the spiritual methods of the way in life, the scale of which I have tried to speak of through the legend of Solomon, and which is spoken of in whispers in every great spiritual tradition of the world.

We are born into a world created by the mechanical explosion of religious energy. Those who created this world at least felt the vividness of that explosion. We, however, are born into the world already automatically organized by that energy. We no longer even feel the religiousness (misdirected though it may have been) of that original energy.

Thus Weber:

> The capitalistic economy of the present day is an immense cosmos into which the individual is born, and which presents itself to him . . . as an unalterable order of things in which he must live. (p. 54)

Yet, says Weber,

> A man does not "by nature" wish to earn more and more money, but simply to live as he is accustomed to live and to earn as much as is necessary for that purpose. (p. 61)

Therefore, a great force of ideas and communal energy must have been a central cause of the fact that in our society "a man exists for the sake of his business, instead of the reverse" (p. 70). Such a motivational force, in Weber's view, could only originate in religious ideas. Or, as one insightful commentator has put it:

> After all, however blind economists may be to the fact, metaphysical convictions are the only ones which have the power absolutely to dominate men's lives. Economic reasons alone cannot account for the extraordinary power in the western civilization of today which the money-making motive exerts. . . . (T)he mood for work in . . . an "ascetic" Protestantism, although engendered by religious considerations, may easily become diverted to a purely economic interest when once the other-worldly point of view is abandoned.
>
> (Kemper Fullerton, "Calvinism and Capitalism," in Green, Robert W., ed., *Protestantism and Capitalism: The Weber Thesis and its Critics.* Boston: D. C. Heath and Co., 1959, pp 16–17)

In Search of a Central Question

It had taken me an hour to present these conclusions to the students and the time had come to end the class. Some were burning to know what was that school or way in life, that had existed in the transition between the Middle Ages and the beginning of the modern era, and which neither Weber nor other historians were aware of.* They wanted to know what, exactly, Protestantism had left out when it had turned away from the monasteries toward the world. In these students, many of whom were themselves Protestants of one kind or another, there was a certain amount of healthy skepticism as well as a healthy desire to find for themselves a school that taught the way in life.

---

* See Appendix I.

But from the other students, the great majority, there came forth a veritable barrage of questions about putting in practice what I had been speaking about on a general, theoretical level. There were questions about money and sex, money and children, money and self-esteem, money and careers, money and health, money and marriage, money and art; there were questions about money and global questions of war, the environment, drugs, crime; there were questions about money and the organization of one's personal life, about business ethics, about executive leadership, about government and the military, about international finance.

Finally, I waved my hands and asked for silence. Rarely in my life had I wanted more to just go on exchanging with a group of students. We had all felt a sense of the scale from which we could approach the central questions of our lives. We all felt at the same moment two imperatives: the imperative need to reflect upon why we human beings are on earth, why we live and die; and the imperative to find our way intelligently and with honor in the rough-and-tumble of everyday life.

As the class gradually became quiet, I understood what I should do:

"I am very sorry that we have to end the course at this point. As you can see, there is another class scheduled for this room [we could hear them milling in the halls] and also many of you have other commitments. But I would propose the following. I will ask the incoming group and their instructor to wait outside for another fifteen minutes. Those of you who can stay, please do so. Stay and write down the main thing you wish to understand about money. Try to formulate your questions as fully and precisely as you can, taking into account the gist of what we have been speaking about today. Don't just write one or two words. Don't just say something like 'I want to understand about love and money.' Try to bring your best thought into what you ask.

"If you will try in this way, connecting your personal money problem to the metaphysical ideas we have been exploring, then I promise you I will respond. I don't promise to give answers—obviously not; I am just as much baffled by the money question as anyone. But I promise to try to open the question further. I cannot do more and I cannot do less. So now, please try."

About two-thirds of class—fifty people—stayed . . . and stayed. Ah, the silence of grown-up men and women really trying to think and formulate an authentic question! A beautiful silence.

I held back the oncoming class with as much wheedling as I could muster. But after half an hour, I had to call it all to a halt. I collected the papers, slid them into my sack and left the building. Alyssa and Bill Cordell followed after me.

12.

QUESTIONS

I had asked for carefully thought-out questions, but I received something quite different. What came back were cries in the night, questions that have haunted mankind since the beginning of time. In another era, or in another culture, these questions would have been asked in different terms—with reference to death, maybe, or pain, or the suffering of innocents, or the betrayal of trust. That these questions now found expression in terms of the problem of money proved to me that I had been right to focus on this issue that is usually considered tangential to the concerns of academic philosophy.

Here are some of these questions, exactly as they were written:

How much of myself will I have to sell for money in order to be able to live more fully later, and can I regain what I've sold?

There is something very frightening about money. I don't understand it. So, apparently, it is not only a material entity, but is tied to inner psychological forces. What can I do to see clearly what money really means?

Why am I so angry that the distribution of wealth is so polarized? Why does it make me feel so exposed, so helpless?

Why do jobs that seem to contribute most to people seem to pay the least? Must one choose between material well-being and service to humanity?

How can I maintain access to the spiritual in myself while living a life of relative affluence and awful money tensions that leave me feeling at times dead and at times in doleful exile from myself?

How can we reach our own economic and emotional potential without basing it on the destruction of another's?

How can I justify wanting and having money when people are starving?

How can I let go of my fears about money—it totally absorbs my consciousness. I fear I will get old and become a street person.

I work for a nonprofit agency and interact with the poorest of the poor as well as the very rich. I want to help things be more equal without anger at the rich or pity for the poor or guilt toward myself.

I want to feel I deserve to make money, not feel guilty about earning money. I want to keep a balance between the self-respect that money brings me and the search to know who I really am, my inner self. How can I prevent my sense of self-worth from being so dependent on how much money I make?

What is money a substitute for in my essential nature? Why do I attach myself to it as something necessary to my life? What do I confuse it with?

Why do I want more when I have enough?

Why should I feel guilty about having money? Unless I've given, what right have I to receive? Isn't money a social product? If that social product is not distributed fairly, not really parceled out according to work done, isn't all money a representation of suffering—*filthy* in that sense?

Is there really something as real as money, but not materialistic in human life? My moral and spiritual ideals seem pale and weak whenever I have to deal with money matters. Please prove to me that the world of ideas is as strong as the bottom line.

Why does spending money cause me so much pain?

The human potential movement is fostering the concept of "right livelihood" or "Do what you love, the money will follow." My experience is that when I follow my greatest passions—art, music, theater, philosophy—I barely make enough to pay the rent. When I cater to other people's needs for what to me is meaningless, boring production,

then I earn a living. My question is: is it only the lucky few in our society who can earn a living doing what is meaningful? Can we change this? How?

Money seems like an objective reality, one that can be reasoned about in the form of numbers. But I become painfully confused when I encounter the emotional component of it that seems to erode away all its apparent objectivity. Is money real—like stones and trees? And if not, why does money seem so real?

13.

WHY DOES MONEY SEEM SO REAL?

The story of money, like the myth of the Holy Grail, is a tale of the corruption of ancient ideals of virtue by slowly corroding evil. . . . The first form of money was shared food, which for many centuries preceded the evolution of coinage. Coinage . . . had the same significance as the Grail—that of a sacred relic symbolizing a holy meal among a loyal fellowship. . . . Money, in our culture, originated in an identical manner as the Holy Grail, in a ritual communion meal in which the shared food symbolized mutual dedication among the communicants. Our money began as a religious symbol. . . .

Insofar as man's ethical ideals are concerned, and however barbaric and cruel the reality may have been, economic relations in ancient times were to some extent conceived of as religious relations. . . . In this lofty sense, despite the slavery, oppression and warfare . . . money symbolized the loving giving and taking among individuals which gave men the feeling of having emotional roots in their community. The community was a religious congregation, and all members felt themselves to be fellows in a sacred communion. . . . Money originated as a symbol of man's soul.

(William H. Desmonde, *Magic, Myth and Money.* New York: The Free Press, 1962, pp. 20–25)

THE MEANING OF MATERIALISM

Since the beginning of recorded history, man has been haunted by the intimation that he lives in a world of mere appearances. In every teaching and spiritual philosophy of the past we find the idea that whatever happens to us, for good or ill, is brought about by deeper forces behind the world that seems so real to us. We are further told that this real world is not accessible to the senses nor understandable by the ordinary mind.

But, and this is a point that is not usually understood, we live in a world of inner appearances as well. We are not what we perceive ourselves to be. There is another identity, our real self, hidden behind the self that we believe ourselves to be.

It is only through awakening to this deeper self within that we can penetrate behind the veil of appearances and make contact with a truer world outside of ourselves. It is because we live on the surface of *ourselves* that we live on the surface of the greater world, never participating—except in rare moments which do not last and which are not understood—in the wholeness of reality.

It is this all-important second aspect of the ancient wisdom, the aspect that speaks of our inner world, that modern thought has been blind to. And the question about the meaning of life is inextricably linked to the need for contact with the real self beneath the surface of our everyday thoughts, emotions, and sensations.

Without this contact, the external world of appearances assumes for us the proportions of an overwhelmingly compelling force. We cannot see the real world because we are not in contact with the deeper powers of thought and sensing within ourselves that could perceive it. Because of this, it is inevitable that we experience the external world as the strongest force in our lives. This is the meaning and the origin of *materialism.*

The error, or, to use Christian language, the "sin" of materialism has at its root nothing to do with greed or possessiveness. Nor does it involve, at its root, some philosophical view about matter and spirit in their usual meanings. No, the error of materialism is an error of reality perception, based on lack of experiential contact with the inner world. What we know as greed and possessiveness, with their attendant traits of cruelty and human exploitation, are *results* of this ignorance of the inner world. We turn to the superficially perceived outer world for that which can only be obtained through deep access to the inner self. Materialism is not a "sin"; it is a mistake.

But a mistake of immense proportions, and with deadly consequences. It is like searching for water on the surface of the moon to search for meaning in the external world. Like grasping a picture of food and trying to eat it. Not only meaning, but also health, safety, service, love, and power, can be obtained only through turning to reality. The unreal world can never yield these things to man.

THE TWO PURPOSES OF CULTURE

The forms of social and cultural organization founded within the great spiritual traditions of the world have been based on a recognition of the reality of the inner world, and of the higher force that can enter into human life through the inner world. As suggested by the passage cited at the beginning of this chapter, money itself may have originated in this context as a sacred device.

These institutions and forms, such as those involving the family, the gathering and production of food and other practical means necessary for survival—shelter, clothing, treatment of illness—all these patterns of living were originally structured to allow human beings to seek contact with the inner self in the midst of the challenges of the external world.*

These rituals, customs, and manners were created to foster this interior contact not only as a thought in the mind or a momentary emotion, but also organically, in the very sensations of the body. Enduring and deep contact with the higher forces requires the participation of thought, emotion, and physical sensation, because each of these functions is an indispensable instrument of perceiving reality. Without this complete perception, the experience of the inner self is less vivid, and the outer

---

*"(I)n traditional cultures . . . the activities of the individual, even in the most 'profane' intervals of his life, were oriented constantly toward a transhuman reality. . . . As such, every human act had, in addition to its intrinsic utility, a symbolic meaning which transfigured it. For instance, an activity so insignificant, so random, as walking or eating was—and still is today in certain Asiatic cultures—a 'ritual'; that is, an effort at reintegration into a supra-individual, supra-biological reality. . . . This integration is made, in our first example, by walking rhythmically, in conformity with the norm of cosmic rhythms (India, China, Austro-Asiatic cultures). Or, with reference to our other example, eating: by the identification of the organs of the human body with certain 'powers' (gods of the body in India), which transforms man into a microcosm with the same structure and essence as the Great All, the macrocosm." (Mircea Eliade, "Barabudur, the Symbolic Temple," in *Symbolism, the Sacred and the Arts*. New York: Crossroad, 1988, pp. 130–31)

world dominates human life. *The inner world is no longer experienced as vividly as the outer world.* The external world begins to seem more real, more compelling, more exigent. Life in the external world begins to have more apparent *value* to the individual and the society. The ideals of the inner world may remain in the form of religious doctrine, in the thought alone or in the emotions alone or in the automatized ritual patterns of movement and behavior, which are no longer understood. But the organic, experiential contact with a higher force becomes weaker and less compelling and may disappear altogether.

The capacity to live morally, according to mankind's highest ideals, requires sustained experiential contact with the higher forces within. Therefore, as actual contact with the inner world diminishes, the individual and the community suffer more and more disorder.

THE SOURCE OF MORAL POWER

To repeat: moral power, the power to live according to the ideals of the inner world, comes only from direct contact with the higher forces that can pass into the inner self from the deeper recesses of the universal world.

We must bear in mind how strong the demands are that compel men and women to act for survival in the physical and social world. These survival demands are of such magnitude that they easily dominate human life in the absence of our direct contact with the depth of the inner world. The traditional social forms were intended both to ensure human survival and to support the struggle for contact with the inner world.

What, after all, is the point of physical survival without this inner contact? What is the point of eating, sleeping, and reproducing without our being conscious of ourselves? If we wish for merely unconscious survival, it means that we wish to be only animals or computers, beings that eat, reproduce, react, or think without self-awareness.

WHAT WE HAVE LOST

The determining characteristic of our modern era has been the unprecedented extent to which the inner ideals embodied in traditional patterns of human relationship—for example, family duty, care for the well-being and dignity of one's neighbor, and respect for life, with all the subtle refinements of behavior and perception that have been associated with these values over the centuries—no longer seem inwardly intense and vivid. On the contrary, for most modern people, the main experience of inner intensity lies in the realm of instinctual and emotional drives such as hunger, sexual desire, the need for safety, and the avoidance of pain. Because of this, time-honored forms and customs that supported the inner life have been altered and abandoned, new forms and customs invented, the result being that countless subtler, finer aspects of the human psyche have been eclipsed. The patterns of living that once nourished these subtler aspects of human relationships have been regarded as oppressive or outdated, while new communal forms that could support the full range of possible inner experiences have not yet been created and disseminated by men and women of vision.

THE TWO DIRECTIONS

The idea that there are two fundamental aspects of reality, two opposing movements, is a universal teaching ancient beyond imagining, ancient beyond Christianity, beyond Judaism, beyond Buddhism and Hinduism, perhaps even beyond Egypt,

Sumer, and Babylon. There are two movements of all energy and life—toward and away from unity, toward and away from the wholeness of the universal oneness. "Materialism" acknowledges only one of these movements—the movement outward toward multiplicity and diversity.

Traditional patterns of living, on the other hand, operate to open human consciousness to both movements—the movement outward, represented by man's participation in an expanding social and physical world, and the movement inward, toward unity, reflected in his yearning to participate in the intelligence that created the universe and which exists as pure energy, awareness, and joy. Many of the emotions, sensations, and thoughts evoked by these rites and ethical practices were meant to lead human consciousness toward awareness of the universal source in the midst of the rhythms of life.

THE TYRANNY OF THE OUTER

But when that inner contact weakens, then the feelings that could move man toward the higher attach themselves to the other, outer movement. When impulses of love, for example, cease to lead consciousness toward contact with the Source of the universal world, these impulses must inevitably lead consciousness toward the multiplicity of the sensorily perceived world. Putting it in Western religious language, "a man either moves toward God or toward the devil."*

In the culture we live in, our forms of communal life—family, religion, education, art, the pursuit of knowledge—do not lead us toward actual, vivid experience of a higher force.

---

* But we must add, lest we forget where our discussion is ultimately leading us: "a true man consciously suffers both movements within himself." That is the glory and the paradox of Man.

The conditions of modern life bring emotions of many kinds, thoughts of many kinds; but none of this fulfills us deeply because it does not point us to deep contact with the world within ourselves. Our feelings and thoughts about truth and value are pale when compared to the needs and sensations delivered to us by the outer world. *We do not experience the inner world as vividly as the outer world.*

All our vivid emotions are tied to desires and fears dealing with the outer world.* Our feelings for God, for Being, for Truth—whatever we choose to call the ultimate unity of reality—pale when compared to the stimulations that survival and functioning in the outer world evoke. *Money, being the principal means of organizing and ordering survival in the outer world, thus seems the most real thing in our lives.*

We must move toward truth or appearance, being or nonbeing. Nothing "under the sun" stands still. Everything moves—and it moves either upward or downward, inward or outward. If we do not love God, we will inevitably love money; there is, as it were, no other alternative!

THE PRICE OF PROGRESS

What does it mean that against the forces of money, our inner values are almost always so weak and insubstantial? How many times have we not actually experienced that money factors overwhelm considerations of love and friendship, trust, good faith, artistic integrity, mercy, justice, truth? Isn't the obvious reason for this that we do not experience friendship, care for another, artistic beauty, inner truth, respect for life, a

---

* Sometimes these desires and fears originate in childhood, and psychotherapy helps open us to that aspect of the inner world. But this is still only the surface of the inner world, the surface of what lies beyond our awareness.

sense of justice, as vividly and intensely as we experience hunger, or heat and cold, or the cravings and fears associated with these and all the other external elements of our lives?

It is not a question of trying to bring back this or that ancient custom or ritual practice or ethical rule. The point is simply to understand that progress in the modern world has been obtained at the expense of certain kinds of experiences available to us. Customs and rules that seem absurd or superstitious to us may have had purposes that we do not now understand—providing experiences of contact with another level of force within ourselves and within the universe.*

A Man Pays for His Bride

To take one example among many: in almost every tribal culture throughout history the institution of marriage was a response to external biosocial needs—economic survival, survival of the species, the satisfaction of sexual needs—for the individual as well as the community.

At the same time, in almost every case, the spiritual law of marriage ordains a duty of respect between the man and wife. The wife must occupy a spiritual role—with the children (in India she is spoken of as the child's "first guru") and in relation to the husband. Sometimes this role is not made explicit; it is often a "hidden" role—private, unspoken, and sometimes discovered by the man and wife, in its real meaning, well after the wedding, although it may be symbolized in the ceremony or the religious texts. The spiritual relation between the couple permeates, but is never mixed with the social/

---

* No one custom or pattern of behavior probably could have provided this. It would have been the whole system of customs and ethical patterns and laws which we call a culture or a tradition.

survival aspects of the relationship. To anyone who cannot see the spiritual, inner aspect of the relationship, the marriage seems to be only a social/survival custom. But the couple and the tradition know otherwise.

Yet a man *pays* for his bride. He does not pay for her spirit, nor can he. But a man pays for his bride. He must reproduce and physically assist the life of the social whole and, in return, he will receive rewards—material and psychological—which pertain to the external world and the outward-directed experience of a human being. At the same time, something else may begin to take place within him. His payment has bought him the conditions that will enable him to pursue both directions of his life, for only a man who pursues both directions of life— inner and outer—will find his place not only in the social community, but in the cosmic universe. And *all of this* has been symbolized and facilitated with money, money that is an essential instrument both for organizing the social/survival life and for making "space and time" available for man to grow inwardly as well.

Think of money, then, as a device invented for organizing the satisfaction of mankind's outer needs—within a cultural context in which most forms of conduct served the purpose of evoking impressions of the inner self. Money, thus understood, *is intrinsically a contradiction!*

THE BEGINNING OF AN INNER LIFE

Money is intrinsically a contradiction because man is intrinsically a contradiction. It has come to seem so real not only because there are no longer strong enough experiences of the inner world, but also *because there are no longer conscious experiences of the two worlds together*. It is the experience of this contradiction that can become the source of inner intensity in our modern lives. This is the main point toward which our discussion has been leading. We need to examine it closely.

Man must ultimately choose between the inner and the outer world, between God and the devil—yes, it is true, it is what our religious teachers have always told us in unmistakable tones. But what the great traditions only whisper to us—in symbol and legend, indirectly, "secretly"—is the fact, obvious once we have consciously experienced it, that in order to choose, in order to move toward either "good" or "evil," it follows of necessity that man must be aware of both movements, both directions; that he has that within him which can be in contact with God *and* money, good *and* evil, being *and* nonbeing.

14.

FACING THE
CONTRADICTION

In every human life there are
glimpses of the inner world, glimpses that could lead us to the
search for the real inner self. They may be only elementary
experiences and they may be isolated, random, and fleeting, but
they certainly exist. What is not understood about them, however, and what is not experienced—that is to say, not willingly
nor consciously suffered—is the contradiction, the opposition
between the inner movement toward the deep self and the outer
movement toward the external world that is given by the senses
and organized by the logical mind.

Something analogous to the experience of this contradiction
is in fact familiar to all of us. We approach this whenever we
realize that how we act contradicts what we feel to be our
deepest values. But we do not accept these experiences as the
gateway to consciousness of our true nature. Our "morality"
compels us to deny them, to cover them over with justifications

or promises to do better next time. Yet it is just these experiences of the disparity between our values and our behavior which could be felt as vividly as anything the external world has to offer. If we would seek a reality stronger than money, we may find an opening in the cultivation of a new attitude toward these common experiences of inner contradiction.

The ancient rites and customs provided the basis of experiences of the inner world, sometimes very deep experiences, while satisfying the needs of the outer world, the external life in physically perceived nature and human society. But the contradictoriness of the two worlds, the spiritual world and the external world, was generally taught only by the hidden path. The mode of living in two opposing worlds and relating consciously to both of them has always been difficult to discover, just as in our own life it is something that will have to be rediscovered again and again against great odds.

THE INTENSITY OF MONEY

Returning to the question of why money seems so real: the conditions of life in our culture do not support inner experiences, experiences of movement toward a higher part of oneself, that are as vivid as experiences of the outer world and the part of oneself that is drawn to the outer world. And as money has become the principal means for organizing contact with the outer world, there is nothing more vivid—for most of us—than the question of how to have, get, make, accumulate money. No fear greater—for many of us—than the fear of not having money.

It is therefore not a question of getting rid of these desires or fears. What do most of us have to put in their place?—nothing that is as vivid, except perhaps in physical pain or in front of death. Otherwise there is nothing in most of our lives as enduringly intense as the money question. Therefore nothing seems as real. The money question is so strong not because money *is* ultimately real but because our experiences with it have become—for most of us—the most vivid and intense experiences of our lives.

There are many concepts, ideas, habits, conditionings from ideas received in childhood, that support this fundamental illusion about money. But the main and basic point has to do with the intensity of experience.

Therefore, the way to struggle with the tyranny of money's seemingly ultimate reality is, first of all, to search for a quality of inner experience that is at least as vivid and intense as our concerns about money. This is not easy or obvious. It is impossible to achieve by turning to religious ideas or to love or to art or the pursuit of knowledge. And the reason this cannot be done in these ways is that all these activities have already been absorbed by the money problem.

THE REAL CRIME OF OUR CULTURE

This is the real crime of our culture—not that we are selling God or truth or morality; at least not as that accusation is usually meant. The crime is that the buying and selling are more intense and inwardly vivid than anything else. But we must not forget that the main reason we have bought and sold God, truth, and morality is that the forms we have used to relate to these ideals no longer offer us the direct experiences of them that are possible and necessary for man. If a person marries for money rather than love or duty, it is not necessarily because he prefers money to love or duty, but because he has not experienced the real force of love or duty. It is as simple and as profound as that. Love and duty, as examples of facets of the inner world, cannot be truly experienced unless we can contact both currents of energy within ourselves. There is no love in the outer world alone, at least not for human beings. There is no duty in the outer world alone. Nor is there beauty, nor creativity, nor understanding, nor anything else we consider authentically human. The outer world alone, the world ''under the sun'' is, as Solomon tells us, ''vanity, vanity.''

Authentic human existence requires the co-presence of two worlds, the inner and the outer. To exist in one world alone is not to exist at all. This is Sheol, hell, death, the disappearance of the soul, its ultimate impoverishment.

And what has become of money itself reflects the fact that it, like our lives, has become reduced to an instrument functioning in the outer world alone. *Intended originally as a device to help man live in two opposing worlds, money has become only a technology to organize our lives in hell.*

The outer world cannot give meaning to a being made to live in both the inner world and the outer world simultaneously. We are living in an outer world that pretends to be the inner world. The elements of human life that are primally rooted in interiority, service to the higher—that is, the realm of relationships, of love, knowledge, creativity, elements that are reflected in family, community, the refinement and perfection of nature (science and art)—all these elements are now embedded in money. Money seems the most real factor of life because our glimpses of the inner world are immediately swallowed by modes of acting and thinking and feeling that are geared to dealing with money. We will never be free of the money demon through what we now call love, ethics, or science and art. The modes of modern comportment in these realms have been altered to become solely part of the deceiving outer world.

BETWEEN TWO WORLDS

And it will do us no good merely to pursue strong experiences of the inner world unless we are pointed toward equally strong experiences that will enable us to contact both worlds simultaneously. That is, we need to find an awareness that can be in contact with the two worlds. And this awareness appears in the first instance as an acceptance of the incompatibility of these two worlds. We must go through a long period of actively accepting this incompatibility before there can be any question of these two worlds becoming one, harmonizing within ourselves.

It will not help to divide our culture into mystics and men and women of action, spiritual seekers and practical "doers." A dream of mysticism is in itself of no greater value than a dream of action and accomplishment. That is, when a man dreams of God without contacting God, his life is of no more significance than that of a man plunged in the torments of materialist illusion.

When monasticism degenerated in the late Middle Ages, surely it was in part due to the illusion that man can contact God without serving the earth, including the material and social needs of his neighbor, as well. For when an individual experiences a higher force and is not aware of the aspects of himself that push him away from this force, it is inevitable that these aspects become even more veiled from him. It is inevitable, that is, that illusions of one's own virtue and godliness mask the egoism, anger, and fear that coexist with the spiritual wish in human nature. *It is inevitable that religion becomes worldly under the pretext of making the worldly life religious.* Psychologically, the biological drives in man become suppressed and, finally, destructive. Something like a great buffer is formed between the two natures in man and the higher, finer influences which the human organism is meant to contain cannot reach the biosocial side of man, even while the mind that is part of the biosocial self reflects the memory of spiritual experiences. Few things are more tyrannical than aborted mysticism. "Lilies that fester smell far worse than weeds."

In the late Middle Ages, long before the Protestant Reformation, there emerged in Western Europe a doctrine of the "mixed life" intended to correct the failures of monasticism not by doing away with its essential discipline, but by reanimating it in the midst of outer life—in the midst of the impulses and desires that comprise the animal/social nature of man. The notion of the "mixed life" was rooted in the ancient teaching that has already been discussed: the teaching that man must confront both the good and the evil in himself with an intensity of interior acceptance that allows the "evil" (the "demons") to serve the Good. The only true evil is that which prevents this confrontation and its possible reconciliation.

This is Christianity we are speaking of, a Christianity revealed in the deepest experiences of all the great mystics, including, no doubt, the founders and renewers of the Protestant tradition. They show us a glimpse of something unfathomably real: a reconciling energy existing in the innerness of all things; an incomprehensible tenderness and forgiveness, a redeeming embrace that contains the whole of creation.

St. Augustine tells us that "God provides the wind, but man must raise the sails." The point is that man can dispose himself to receive this power of reconciling love only under very specific conditions of outer and inner life. These conditions may include principles of living, of relating to one's neighbor, to one's body, to pleasure and pain, to everything in the material world. Above all, there must be a certain inner attitude of the mind and feelings, and a certain openness of the body. The precise conditions and exact knowledge that are needed for this kind of life define the whole idea of demand and obligation in religion. God is merciful and rigorous. That is, He is severe in prescribing the conditions necessary for the infinite outflowing of His love and mercy. Love and mercy can only flow if they are allowed to flow everywhere. At the heart of religion, rigor is what allows love to flow everywhere and in everything. We may recall the words of St. Paul that Christ came not to destroy the law, but to fulfill it.

Followers of the ''mixed life'' in the late Middle Ages seem to have understood that in order to bring the spiritual into the whole of life, it was necessary to bring the whole of life into the realm of spiritual work, to allow, as it were, everything into the monastery. To allow the disciplined attitude of the true monk to embrace all the impulses and sensations within the human organism.

Moreover, they seem to have understood that one cannot just plunge into life, into material exchanges and biosocial actions, with only a feeling or a thought as a guide, with only a prayer or, what is even less powerful, only a theology, only a belief system. One cannot jump into life only in reaction to a corrupted monasticism or a corrupted system of church administration. This was the error of Protestantism. It is not so simple to make the world one's monastery. It is a magnificent ideal, but it is very, very difficult to practice, far more difficult, and difficult in a far different way than, perhaps, we can imagine. Instead of the world becoming a monastery, which was the ideal of Protestantism, the monastery became the world, which was Max Weber's central insight into the origins of our modern crisis of meaning and value. Capitalism has gone wrong, he saw, because it mixed the spiritual and the worldly in a way that blurred their edges, that failed to keep them separate and related at the same time. It did not only mix the two worlds, it mixed them up!

AN UNEXPECTED CONCLUSION

Interpretations of history aside, the question of why money seems so real, why the bottom line seems to be the most real factor in our lives, comes to this: why have we lost the ability to experience the inner world in as vivid and intense a manner as the outer world? Why do we not experience the love of truth, for example, as vividly as we experience hunger or desire or the impulse to protect our children?

The surprising answer is that the way toward the real inner world is to experience with ever greater intensity of feeling the pulls and impulses that draw us toward the outer world! To experience God as intensely as we experience desire, for example, it is necessary to experience desire more consciously, not turn away from it toward some high, but bloodless and, finally, illusory ideal religious image!

To experience love as intensely as we experience fear, it is necessary to experience the fear more consciously. From the true consciousness of fear, love must inevitably follow as a result. Why? Not because love is close to fear, but *because love is close to consciousness.* Such intensity of self-experience, such intensity of self-knowledge, requires carefully guided conditions of living in the midst of ordinary life; it requires the support and companionship of others; it requires knowledge of the structure of man and his possibilities. In short, it requires an authentic spiritual path, the way in life.

To begin moving toward this way, it follows that an individual must begin to take himself as seriously as he takes money. Money is the principal means by which modern man enters into the intense world of desire, fear, pleasure and pain, achievement and failure, sex, friendship, courage, loyalty, deceit, cunning, philosophizing, knowledge-gathering, manufacturing of goods, arts, fun, entertainment, competition—all the impulses and activities that make up this round of life called the *world* in Western traditions, *samsara* in Eastern traditions. The other world, the world of the spirit, is approached through the increase of attention in oneself, through consciousness of oneself in the midst of hell. The awareness of hell is the escape from hell, or the beginning of the escape.

The first practical step that an individual can take to free himself from the thrall of money is not to turn away from it, but *to take it even more seriously,* to study himself in the very midst of the world of money, but to study himself with such diligence and concern that the very act of self-study becomes as vivid and intense as the desires and fears he is studying. ''The truth shall set you free,'' not because it will give you explanations, but because the conscious experience of the truth, even when the truth is hellish, is itself space and light and contact with a higher world.

And what will the individual feel after he begins this work of studying himself in the world of money? If he persists with diligence and guidance and the support of companions, he will experience a feeling more intense than anything the outer world has to offer. With a force and an authority he has until now hardly ever glimpsed in his life, he will directly experience the unbelievable contradiction within himself between the wish for God and the attraction toward material, outer life. This experience was called in ancient Hebraic tradition *a broken heart* and, later, *the turning point.* In the great monastic communities of the Christians it was called *tears* and *sorrow.* It was what the Solomon of legend experienced in his years of exile. Today, in our present era, we may speak of it, giving the word an entirely new dimension of power, as *conscience.*

It is through conscience that the true self first manifests itself in us. This is the return of the exiled Solomon, who with true authority ascends the steps of the throne in between the wolf and the lamb, the hawk and the sparrow—each of the pairs of animals that symbolize the two contradictory worlds in the midst of which man is called to fulfill his destiny.

This realm between the two opposing worlds is, for as long or as short as the experience of it lasts, the *real,* uniquely human world. And the conditions of living, the principles of ethics and mutual relationship that are offered by a spiritual community are intended to support and lead the individual to this place between the worlds. Only then can a man or woman actually know, for certain, that there is something in life more real than the world that is organized by money.

Our rituals, manner, and customs long ago ceased to fulfill this function. Is it any wonder that so many of us still smile to ourselves when we hear people speak of love and happiness as things that money can't buy?

In fact, the things that money can't buy can be known only in another state of consciousness!

15.

THINGS

New questions kept arriving in the mail, including some poignant statements about possessiveness and the power of material things in our life. I sent these questions to Bill Cordell and Alyssa, suggesting they do library research on the role of material things in other cultures. It had been a long time since I had seen the problem of materialism treated from the perspective of how a more traditional society looks at *things,* although when I was in college, and then again during the sixties, there had been much discussion of crafts in other societies, a considerable interest in how other cultures had related to the material object. I hadn't heard so much about that in recent years.

Among these letters was one—which I found very touching—about: *shopping!* The writer said that not long after taking the seminar, she had had a shocking glimpse of herself in a mall:

I am not exaggerating when I say that I saw a person under the influence of a drug. I saw a hungry animal. I saw a person in a hypnotic trance. It's not that I actually bought so many things—it's the *way* I was. In the class we spoke of hell as absence of being. I saw that this is how I become when I am shopping. I actually disappear! When I came home with a dozen packages and started opening them with my husband there, I was aghast. We began quarreling about the money I had spent on clothes, but even while I was defending myself, I realized an extraordinary thing—I saw that each article of clothing was like a little dream. I felt like someone waking up from sleep. The dresses, the belt, the shoes, even the sweater I had bought for my husband, even the cookbook, were bought in a dream, a little dream. I dreamed the shoes and the dresses. More precisely, they dreamed me. I dreamed the dresses would make me happy, beautiful, sexy. I dreamed the belt would make me dangerous. The sweater would make my husband happy. But here's the most interesting thing about it, at least for me it was the most interesting thing: each little dream was accompanied by physical sensations of pleasure! What should I make of that? In each little dream my body experienced pleasure and I, whoever I was in the dream, felt it as happiness and future happiness! I realized all this in the middle of quarreling with my husband about money—it was the money issue that triggered this realization because of my memory of the seminar and the questioning we all did together.

You have invited us to formulate our question about money. Here is mine: what is the reason we think of happiness as involving material things when our experience shows us every day that they are like a drug? They never bring any lasting happiness. How can we understand what we really *need*—like food, clothes, shelter? Could we escape from the money trap by somehow learning to want less, to get along with less, to desire less? But here is the question that follows from that, and please help me understand this: let us say we learn somehow really to want less, desire less, not to have to indulge our craving for material things—then what will take their place? What will fill the void that inevitably will appear? I gave up cigarettes a year ago. I wound up eating too much. Food took the place of cigarettes. What can take the place of material goods? I hope and trust you are not going to say love or healthy activities or thoughtful conversation or good causes, or things like that. I've heard tapes and talked to people about "doing better with less," living lightly and that sort of thing. Just show me someone who's done it without going into something else as bad or worse to take its place!

ARE WE REALLY MATERIALISTIC?

I heard from Alyssa the very next day and over coffee I explained to her what I had in mind.

"It's not just early coinage that often had religious symbols on one side and temporal symbols on the other side. There are cultures in which every object, even the most mundane, was made in a ritualistic manner and had sacred symbols on it. Every object man used—every utensil, every weapon—was designed to remind him of his two natures and his two worlds. You ate with a bowl. The bowl allowed you to feed your physical body, but the bowl was made and had to be used in a way that helped you remember the inner world as well.

"At the same time," I went on, "in these other cultures there was also much more a sense of the physicalness of things and the physicalness of the body with its needs and capacities.

So, here is an apparent paradox: are we as a culture more or less materialistic than other cultures? Is our problem with money—in some strange way—due to the fact that *we're not materialistic enough?"*

Alyssa gave me a puzzled look, as well she might.

"I mean that if we intentionally *gave* more attention to things, as *things,* they would *steal* less attention away from us."

This did not help Alyssa. I wasn't trying to be obscure. I was trying to think together with her. I needed her capacity of mental independence on the subject of money, a capacity I had not encountered in anyone else.

After a little silence, she said:

"Are you referring to what you quoted in class from John Kenneth Galbraith—that modern capitalism is based on the production of more and more things that answer to no natural human needs? I wasn't the only one who was struck by the idea that our economic system *invents* the desires that it satisfies."

I reflected for a moment. Was there a connection between modern capitalism and the poverty of our relation to the physical world? I suddenly saw the tip of a new idea about our hang-ups with things and possessions. I wasn't sure where it would lead.

MENTALIZING THE WORLD

"Remember," I said, "we spoke about taking money *more* seriously, not less seriously? Don't you think it's the same with things, with the whole world of matter? Money is a mode of organizing our life in the material world; money is an invention, a mental device, very necessary, very ingenious, but, in the end, a product of the mind. The body by itself would never invent or need money. The feelings by themselves have no interest in it. Couldn't we say that our highly developed financial structure represents modern man's overall attempt to mentalize the world around him, to dematerialize it?''

At first Alyssa frowned mightily, but then a light went on in her eyes.

''All the great masters,'' I continued, ''have taught that our automatic mind interferes with the experiences that life brings us. The head gets in the way even of the simplest pleasures and begins labeling, explaining, and trying to arrange things. And to the extent that money has become such a complicated mental invention, then when money dominates our relationship to things, it means that thought is interfering with direct experience.''

''That means,'' said Alyssa, picking up the idea, ''that the way to struggle against materialism is to give more attention to matter!'' She practically laughed out loud at the irony of the thought.

So did I. ''Well, isn't this the truth buried in a thousand clichés about greed and possessiveness? Didn't our mothers or grandmothers always tell us to be satisfied with what we have rather than crave what we don't have?''

''Yes,'' Alyssa answered, ''but they didn't tell us *how* to do that.''

''Exactly,'' I said. ''But didn't the poets show us sometimes what it's like to see beauty and meaning in the smallest things? And weren't there always fairy tales that told us about the beauty of the details of life, no matter what outer circumstances we lived in?''

''But they didn't tell us how, either,'' said Alyssa.

''That's right,'' I said. ''They gave us an ideal, a philosophy. And we interpreted it wrongly. We grew up believing it was somehow purer or more noble to turn away from things and from matter. And so we left the relationship to matter to our uneducated bodies and our automatic mind. Our bodies didn't know any better. They took their pleasures where they found them. Our servile logical mind just followed along trying to organize life in order to repeat or prolong or secure what the unconscious body liked. And our other mental functions were turning away from matter into moral and religious fantasies. We never gave ourselves the task of really attending to the material world. We never understood that conscious attention to the material world is precisely what frees us from it, separates us from it, gives us the space and time we long for.

"At the same time, consciously attending to the material world reveals to man the real qualities of things, of nature, of creation, isn't that so? Isn't that what the poets know—in their way, in their impractical, but beautiful way?"

At this point in the conversation, Alyssa and I started moving in different directions. Or so it seemed at first.

"Can you really say that modern man hasn't given the best of his mind to the material world? What about the whole development of science? I thought the whole problem of modernity was that man gave too much of his attention to the material world, and too little to the inner world."

"Well," I answered, "that's more or less the common criticism of modernity, but I don't believe it goes very deep. *Modernity is mentalism, not materialism.* It's the automatic mind, the computer mind in the thrall of the unconscious body. Look: could capitalism have become such a distortion, such an overwhelming force, if the primary motivation of modern culture had not been to make man physically comfortable in the world? I grant you that science started out as a search for God's truth in the created universe, but science soon became devoted to technology and technology to comfort and safety. Imaginary comfort and paranoiac safety. Mentally conceived pleasure and mentally organized paranoiac safety. Paranoia and self-indulgent pleasure—or rather, avoidance of pain—is what the head organizes for the unconscious, childish body.''

THE DREAMS OF AN UNCONSCIOUS BODY

Suddenly, a torrent of connections began to show themselves to me. I started pouring out words to Alyssa.

I understood why Plato, like the great spiritual masters of the ancient traditions, wrote that the only pleasure that a man can hold comes from the activity of the higher conscious mind, which he termed *nous* in Greek. Why they all taught that unawakened man actually cannot have happiness. I understood more clearly why the body was condemned—that it was not really the body, but the body in a false relationship to the mind that was the problem. The mind, serving a childish body, invented all kinds of devices and techniques that actually brought very little real satisfaction to the body. I understood that, past a certain limit, technology itself was a mentalization of the material world. That our inventions, our technologies, were like the things Mrs. X went shopping for. That, when they go beyond what is necessary, our technologies were the products of a devilishly clever but servile logical mind catering to the dreams of an unconscious body.

THE EXPERIENCE OF CONTRADICTION

"But how does this help Mrs. X?" Alyssa insisted. "People are not writing these letters to you just to get more ideas. They want some practical advice!" She was becoming impatient with me.

"What do you mean—practical?"

Without a moment's hesitation, Alyssa answered, "They

want to be able to do something about their situation, change something.''

"Don't you think it's very practical to find a new understanding of money, a new attitude toward it?''

Alyssa was very firm. ''Only if it leads to some change,'' she said.

"And what do you have against ideas?''

"They're not enough! They're wonderful, but they don't lead anywhere!''

A light went on inside *me*. Not in my head, but in my guts.

"Alyssa, look at what we're saying. Here, right in front of us, is the whole human condition. There is such a thing as the world of ideas—I mean great ideas about the inner world and our reason for living. We're not only drawn to such ideas, but, because of them, we're moved to an experience—if only for a moment—of connection to something beyond our little egos and all our social rules and requirements. . . .''

She nodded.

I continued speaking—for both of us. ''And we see that these ideas and this special movement inside us *makes no change* in our lives! That's not just an idea—it's a fact. It's an experience, an impression. And we can't accept it, we can't swallow it. We want to push it away. But, look: this is just what it means to be between two worlds. If we can't suffer this fact, this unique experience of powerlessness, we will never be able to live in two worlds.

"And, look,'' I said, ''just look at this suffering, notice how it 'tastes': it's not the suffering of hell, it's not the diminishing of our consciousness. On the contrary. It's another quality of suffering and has a strange trace of dignity in it. An element of real self-respect begins to enter. This is the suffering of purgatory, not hell.''

Alyssa said: "Does that mean we just go on being swallowed by greed and possessiveness? Do we just go on being slaves to things, things, and more things? We just do nothing?"

"I didn't say that, exactly. The point is not that, exactly. The point is that we are given here an experience of ourselves, our inner world, that could be even more intense and vital than the pleasures and satisfactions brought by money and material things. Our aim should be to have an experience of truth that is as vital—or even more so—than the experience of gratifying the desires that our childish bodies put into our heads, or that are put into our heads by advertising in all its forms.

"And so, there is plenty to do, there are plenty of things to try. Only the whole aim is now different. It's no longer limited to a question of improving oneself, of obeying some frozen morality. It goes far beyond inventing yet more 'devices'—more rules of behavior. An entirely new morality begins to appear, the morality of the way in life, at least in its beginning stages. I am sure that's what the Brethren of the Common Life understood when they rejected the corrupt hypocrisy of the monasteries.

"Mrs. X writes very wisely about the danger of just giving up our 'things'—of imagining we should suddenly change how we live, give up money or something. That's the error of reformism. Hell is full of reformers, self-improvers, moralizers. She wonders what will take the place of the things we crave."

"And what are you going to tell her?" said Alyssa.

I paused and asked myself that question. I said to myself: our culture is between moralities. We don't believe in nor do we want to go back to blind faith in the old moralism with all its hypocrisy. Yet there is not yet a new authentic power of conscience active within us. What can take the place of real morality within us until the happy day arrives when we can hear and obey the voice of conscience that speaks so strangely and incomprehensibly in man, like the prophets of the Old Testament?

Suddenly, I understood how to answer Mrs. X.

"I'm going to suggest that she study great ideas—I'm pretty good at knowing which books or works of art can evoke in people a strong feeling for the inner world. I'm going to suggest that she evoke that feeling in herself more and more."

Alyssa interrupted. "But how will that help?"

"Hear me out. I'm going to suggest, as a practical measure, that she go on with her shopping, or whatever it is that brings her such questions. And then, privately, quietly, as sincerely as possible, that she call before her mind her state of being when she is in the grip of *things*. And to make that recognition more, rather than less acute, I'm going to suggest that she study books and art that speak of man's higher nature and of ultimate realities."

Alyssa objected. "But this is just another form of puritanism! You want her to feel more guilty, more troubled, more at odds with herself?"

"Please, let me finish what I'm proposing, and then you tell me what you think. This is precisely the opposite of the 'puritanical' attitude! The aim is to have the experience of truth become as interesting as money and things. More interesting! Nothing could be more practical than deepening the experience of truth. She has felt deeply the futility of the myth of self-improvement, the myth of progress, that has become the opiate of our civilization. That is why she asks, very intelligently, about what will take the place of material things if we try to give up our indulgence in them. It's the slavery of attachment that is hell, not the things themselves that we are attached to. It's a grave error to imagine that by giving up the object of our attachment we become free from the force of attachment itself. I am sure this is one of the ways a religious discipline degenerates. People think the body is evil or possessions are evil or money is evil. No, it is absorption in these objects, our deadly fascination with them, that is evil, simply because it takes us away from the other movement toward the higher that we could be aware of in ourselves."

"The love of money is the root of all evil," Alyssa whispered.

"It must be that," I added. "It's not the money, it's the love that is the problem. But the question remains: why? What is it about this love? There lies the point of misunderstanding! So, it is the most practical thing in the world to find conditions of living in which another kind of 'love' can be explored in oneself, a love that doesn't diminish our consciousness, doesn't devour our awareness. And it's the most practical thing in the world to intensify the experience of truth, until it can become as intense and interesting as the experience of ego satisfaction, or the experience of momentary physical pleasure, or the experience of satisfying a desire constructed by the automatism of a mind obeying a childish body."

"Do you really think the experience of our inner contradictions can be as compelling as getting what we desire?"

"I'm sure of it," I said.

"That we don't have to flog ourselves into being moral or religious beings? That, somehow, the whole thing is *easy!?*"

I interrupted. "I'm not saying that. Not at all. It's difficult, this search. Remember Solomon and what he had to suffer for his understanding. I'm saying that the suffering of the search is of another kind entirely from the self-inflicted suffering of the 'puritan.' And the joy of contact with truth is of another kind entirely from the pleasure of the self-indulgent materialist who throws all moralistic restraints to the winds. There is a struggle that is more *interesting* than pleasure or ego satisfaction. I'm saying there is something far more *interesting* than what money can buy.''

16.

HYPNOTIC
REALITIES

When Bill Cordell entered the picture a few days later, it seemed at first that his newfound enthusiasm about money would take us all in a very different direction than what Alyssa and I had begun to explore. But it soon turned out that he brought a precious element into the inquiry that actually made it possible for us to go forward.

It seems that immediately after the workshop, he had gone to the Stanford University library and all but emptied it of every book about money. He had been in a reading frenzy ever since. Apparently, his years at law school had made it possible for him to read great amounts of material with extraordinary speed and with a phenomenally high ratio of retention to understanding. That is, he remembered everything and pondered nothing. The copy of Mrs. X's letter that I sent him caused the huge thunderclouds of scholarly theory and information about money that had gathered in his brain to burst forth upon us in a muddy tide of secondhand knowledge. Yet it was just this that allowed us all to take the next step in understanding the money question.

The three of us met at my home one evening after dinner. It took Bill several trips from his car to carry in all his books, journals, and photocopies. After he piled them on the coffee table, I made the "mistake" of asking him what he had discovered in the weeks that had passed since the seminar. The coffee grew very cold in his cup as he leaned into his words, his eyes crisscrossing the ceiling, his large, loose hands sculpting the air in front of him. Here I will reproduce only the gist of his screed and our reactions, leaving out all his interminable digressions, backtrackings, footnotes, and his most rabidly inconsistent moralizing. However, I retain many of his most interesting exaggerations.

"I know it's incredible," he began, "but reading all these academic books about money has produced the most extraordinary emotions in me. I can't believe that I've never actually *thought* about money before! I feel like someone who has been breathing and eating his whole life without giving a single serious thought to the existence and nature of air or food! And I've also discovered *history!* I've been living the whole of my life in the middle of *history!* And what is history? It's forces, forces, forces. There are no people! There are no *things!* There are only forces!"

Here Bill reached for his billfold with one of his giant hands and, at the same moment, grabbed two of the books on the coffee table, knocking several others onto the floor.

Alyssa and I let the books lie there.

Bill hesitated a moment. He abruptly put down the books he was holding in his hand and reached into his wallet for a wad of currency which he then waved in front of us.

"You know what this is? These are articles of faith! Blind faith! Do you know about John Law?"

JOHN LAW

I knew about John Law. In the early eighteenth century, following the death of Louis XIV, when the government of France was at the brink of financial collapse, there appeared in Paris a charming and wildly brilliant Scotsman bearing a plan to rescue the nation from ruin. The son of an Edinburgh goldsmith, Law had fled his native land under indictment for murder (a "love-duel") and had made his way with phenomenal success and panache through the gaming tables and royal courts of Europe and the financial circles of the American colonies and Holland. He developed the idea that lenders of money could back their notes with government land—at its supposed future value—instead of with gold. At the same time, he carried forward the notion, which until then had not been fully explored in Europe, that a financial institution could issue more notes than it had gold with which to back them. This, of course, became the basis of the modern concept of a *bank:* the issuing of notes in excess of the means to redeem them. The French Regent, Orléans, warmly embraced Law's ideas and eventually established the Banque Royale with Law at its head. A few strokes of a pen had transformed France from a poor to a "solvent" nation.

THE CURRENCY OF FAITH

"The government simply invented this money!" Bill sputtered. "The government invented its own wealth! And the people believed it!" Bill knocked over a few more books reaching for Galbraith's *Money: Whence It Came, Where It Went.* He went on:

"Law simply persuaded the French regent that as long as everyone believed their notes were redeemable, they wouldn't try to redeem them. And he was right! It worked like a charm. It *was* a charm. The people wanted to believe you can get something for nothing. Like all con men, the French government needed their victims to believe in fairy tales. It needed them to be greedy, voracious, and fundamentally crooked and immoral . . . and . . . and . . ."

Alyssa coolly broke in: "Come on, Bill. You don't mean to say you didn't know all this!"

"I never knew anything about French history," he protested.

"I'm not talking about history," said Alyssa. "I'm talking about money, money. The money you have, the money we all have or don't have. Are you actually saying that you have never known this about money? You're worth . . . what, sixty million dollars?—and you never knew this about currency and banking? This is elementary!"

Again Bill waved his wad of money at us. "No, I didn't! I mean, I knew it, but I didn't really know it!"

I said: "You knew it, but now you feel it too. This is already a different kind of knowing—or could be if you can calm down a little."

But Bill was not in a mood to calm down and recognize that he was at the threshold of a great secret—not just about money, but about knowledge, about two kinds of knowledge— and I saw that Alyssa was suddenly quite interested in just that. Her glance at me showed that she wanted to hear about *that.*

With his free hand, Bill grabbed a thick black book from the pile on the table, knocking over a few more in the process.

It was *Secrets of the Temple,* William Greider's analysis of the Federal Reserve System. Bill histrionically threw his wad of currency down on the table and excitedly began turning the pages of the book. (I couldn't help making a quick count of the money lying there—about a dozen hundred-dollar bills and some fifties, twenties, and tens, approximately two thousand dollars.) He read aloud:

> But the Federal Reserve did also function in the realm of religion. Its mysterious powers of money creation, inherited from priestly forebears, shielded a complex bundle of social and psychological meanings. . . . Above all, money was a function of faith. It required an implicit and universal social consent that was indeed mysterious. To create money and use it, each one must believe and everyone must believe. Only then did worthless pieces of paper take on value. . . .

Bill looked up at us for a moment and then read Greider's citation of a statement by Henry Ford, Sr.:

> It is well enough that the people of the nation do not understand our banking and monetary system, for if they did, I believe there would be a revolution before tomorrow morning.
>
> (William Greider, *Secrets of the Temple: How the Federal Reserve System Runs the Country.* New York: Simon and Schuster, 1987, pp. 53–55)

Alyssa laughed, her blue eyes sparkling.
"What are you laughing at?" asked Bill, puzzled.
"I'm remembering when I first discovered this," she said.

"Money created by fiat of the government and banks. The government simply pronounces, like God: *Let there be money!* And there is money. And the Fed looked upon its creation and it was good!"

"But this is no joke," Bill said. "It's all a mirage. There's nothing behind our money!" Bill's hand shot into another pile of books and pulled out two paperbacks, *The Triumph of Gold* by Dr. Franz Pick and *How You Can Find Happiness During the Collapse of Western Civilization* by Robert J. Ringer. Two one-hundred-dollar bills fluttered from the table to the floor. Unobtrusively, I picked them up and put them back.

Bill feverishly ran through the pages of these two books and read—seemingly at random—from the Ringer book (dozens of little paper place markers sprinkled down from the books as he handled them):

> In theory, paper money is fine, provided it is given only to people who produce products and services that other people want to buy. So long as the majority of people believe that this is what paper money is used for, they have *faith* in it. Faith is the key to the whole paper-money scheme; it is the key to the stability of *any* kind of money. (p. 164)

> The "money" that comes rolling off the presses isn't really money at all. It's only paper. . . . As more and more people begin to figure this out, they want more and more of the paper—in the form of higher prices—to compensate for its lack of value. Which leads to the ultimate problem: People finally figure out that the paper really has *no* value. . . . (pp. 139–40)

Bill looked up at us for a moment. Alyssa was smiling fondly at him. Then he dove back down:

Though the subtle destruction of paper currency is taking place daily, the official burial is probably still several years off. . . . (p. 140)

"Now comes the part about gold," Alyssa said.

GOLD

"Right!" said Bill, annoyed, but intently turning pages. He went on reading:

Though a paper dollar will buy only about 5% of what it could purchase in 1940, an ounce of gold will still buy about the same amount of products and services that it did forty, fifty or even one hundred years ago. . . . People *know* that gold is money. . . . Gold transcends paper money prices; in fact, it really *measures the value of paper money,* rather than the other way around.

(Ringer, Robert J., *How You Can Find Happiness During the Collapse of Western Civilization.* New York: QED, distributed by Harper & Row, 1983, pp. 162–66)

"We have a goldbug on our hands," said Alyssa.

Although his face was turning red, Bill valiantly tried not to get flustered. "Why do you make fun of me? Maybe you know all this, but it's news to me. Our whole world is based on government officials managing the supply of paper. Gold is a natural substance. It takes great effort to mine it, refine it. It's naturally scarce. Government officials can't just invent it into existence. It's more natural."

"It's God's store of wealth. God meant gold to be money," said Alyssa sarcastically.

"All right, but I trust it more than government officials."

"You trust mankind's fantasy about gold more than you trust their fear of guns?"

Bill was puzzled again. "What do you mean?"

Alyssa slashed away while I began looking for an opening in the exchange.

"By accident," said Alyssa, "gold is a scarce substance, malleable and divisible, pretty and hard to get. You want to base the whole material welfare of mankind on this accident of nature? And let all the rapaciousness and violence and insanity of human nature focus around gold? Besides, that's not even what will happen nowadays. The same government brain—if you want to call it that—which manages paper is going to manage gold. There might be some temporary displacement of power among the nations, but, as Dr. Needleman was saying earlier, it will all still be managed by the mental function— what with modern technology and electronics. People fear guns and trust the mind. That's the basis of money, I believe, I really do believe it's so. . . ."

CYCLES

Bill leaned forward to reach for another book—or so I thought. While he was rummaging in his briefcase, I tried to contribute to the discussion by introducing the idea of cycles in human life. I had read many of the books that Bill had brought with him and it was clear that there never has been, in Western history at least since Hellenic times—there never has been a prolonged period of monetary stability in any major culture! It had become clear to me that the whole idea of monetary stability was a fantasy in itself.

And, I reasoned, if there had never been such a period, then perhaps there never could be such. Hadn't I learned, through years of hard study, intellectual and otherwise, and at great cost to my cherished opinions, that human life on earth can never and will never be stable? Hadn't the great visionaries of the past called our planet the "world of mixed forces"? However, the idea of cycles and rhythms gives one the long view and rescues one from cynicism. Man's life and all of life is a rhythmic and lawful play of forces. The sad thing was only that in the economic sphere it seemed that these forces had to play themselves out by means of human fantasies and dreams—the dream of gold or silver, the dream of mental management, the dream of communistic social altruism, the dream of laissez-faire capitalism.

As I was speaking, Bill took out of his briefcase a shoebox-sized package covered with Scotch tape and tied all around with brown twine. With his head bent forward and with great concentration, he slowly and meticulously proceeded to untie the knots and peel back the tape. I watched him out of the corner of my eye as I went on.

TWO KINDS OF KNOWLEDGE

"Maybe I can speak with some kind of authority," I said, "not about the science of economics, but about knowledge itself. As you both know, I have been an academician in a specialized field for all of my adult life. And I've also had the opportunity and the privilege of studying in other fields, such as medicine and psychiatry, not only as a theoretician but on an experiential level as well. I can tell you this, with complete conviction: academic knowledge alone, knowledge from books and from what we call 'information' is good, but by itself it is only an abstraction. The science of economics is an abstraction, only one tiny aspect of the understanding of man and his nature and destiny. Our science of psychology is also an abstraction, no less than our science of physics and chemistry and anthropology. They are all abstractions. They separate out, they *ab-stract* only one aspect, one tiny piece of the whole of reality.

"But the most important point is that such knowledge would not be evil or misleading if, in acquiring it, a man did not himself become an abstraction. The whole tragedy is that in gathering such knowledge, we ourselves are active in only one part of ourselves, the head. From that mind alone we take our sense of selfhood. But in fact, the whole of us is languishing. All of the rest of us is disintegrating at the very moment that we are gathering both our facts and our sense of identity through being active in the mind alone, aided, of course, by the automatic functioning of the external senses.

"Abstract knowledge, when consciously used by a whole human being, can be and is a real instrument of human power and virtue. But abstract knowledge used by an abstract man, a man living only in the head, is deadly. It is hellish knowledge, what Plato called *opinion,* 'cave-knowledge.' In all these books about economics, with all the information and theory they contain, we need to separate out the few nuggets of concrete knowledge that their authors may have found for themselves, with the whole of themselves."

BILL CORDELL'S SURPRISE

Ironically, as I said the word "nugget," the corner of my eye was invaded by a great light like that of the sun suddenly blazing in a dark sky. Bill had unwrapped his package and was placing on the table a twenty-pound gold bar. Then, reaching again into the dark mahogany box from which the gold bar had come, he proceeded to heap upon the table one handful after another of South African Krugerrands, Canadian Maple Leafs, and Chinese gold Pandas. It was like a scene out of the

Arabian Nights—a mountain of gold rising out of the earth, coins spilling from the heap and rolling on the floor.

As the last gold coin fell resoundingly onto the marble tabletop, the room became utterly silent.

We all listened to some night birds singing outside.

It was obvious no one, including Bill, understood exactly what had happened. I certainly didn't. There had been a moment when all my thoughts stopped—except, I must confess, the process of counting. I had very quickly estimated about five hundred coins which, together with the gold bar, added up to well over a thousand ounces—nearly half a million dollars worth of gold!

A long time passed. No one spoke, no one moved. I felt strangely relaxed.

17.

THE MEANING OF GOLD

A DISTANT MEMORY

With the mountain of gold radiating its power in the stillness of the room, a distant memory drifted into my mind.

Again, I am eight years old. There were thousand-dollar bills in those days, and I am holding one in my hand. I stare at it dumbfoundedly as my mother buttons my heavy winter jacket. Out of the corner of my eye I see the shadowy figure of my uncle. Like a dark specter, like a denizen of Hades, he is standing without moving in his black overcoat at the other end of the living room, next to the dim isinglass lamp that is constantly lit in my grandmother's cold and somber house.

The thousand-dollar bill belongs to him. But it is I who will be carrying it to school, in one stroke outdistancing the efforts of all my third-grade classmates in the great Birney School War Bond Drive of 1942. Fame and glory await me, but even that prospect is eclipsed by the mystery of the green oblong that I am now holding between my thumb and forefinger.

Until then, the largest bill I had ever seen was a twenty, and the biggest I had ever actually held was a one. A lowly penny was meaningful and real to me. A nickel was strong and friendly—I liked the buffalo, I liked the thickness. There were very few desires in life that could not be satisfied with a nickel.

As for dimes, they were beautiful and paradoxical, like a haunting minor chord. How could something smaller than a penny and a nickel be so much more important—something so slight and feminine, like a distant moon glowing with inexplicable light? I was never comfortable with dimes.

Quarters were the limit of what I could grasp. A quarter was *everything:* big, resounding, heavy, masculine, an incredible concentration of power. I remember once stacking ten pennies and three nickels next to a quarter and reflecting with awe and wonder that they were all contained in the quarter, somehow.

And then there was the "half-a-dollar." My favorite uncle (not my uncle Jack now standing like a dark monolith across the room) once actually gave me one of these "half-a-dollars." It was from this favorite uncle, whose name was Benn, that over the course of my childhood and adolescence I learned about the possible existence in human beings of incomprehensible generosity. The experience of this incomprehensible generosity in my uncle Benn exerted a constant pressure on my mental and emotional development which, as I now realize, helped me eventually to be convinced that, despite all other evidence to the contrary, something like God might actually exist in the universe.

I can state in another way what my uncle Benn's half-dollar meant to me by referring to my childhood passion for astronomy. By the tender age of six, I had learned all about the planets, their size and distance from the sun, their temperatures and chemical composition. I also knew a prodigious amount about the sun, the stars, and the galaxies. Astronomy was my religion. The magnitudes and distances sometimes made me deeply quiet inside.

When I first held my uncle Benn's half-dollar in my hand, a light went on inside me. It was like holding the sun in my hands. As soon as I could, I went to my room and put the half-dollar next to the other coins. A quarter was Jupiter. A nickel was the earth. The dime was the moon. And a penny— was *me*. Half-consciously, I fused together Uncle Benn's generosity, the size and value of the half-dollar, the immensity of the sun, and the scientific fact that the sun continuously and incomprehensibly sacrifices vast quantities of its energy for the life of the earth.

Now I am parading toward school, still holding the thousand-dollar bill in my ungloved hand, which is red with cold. The December air is freezing, the bill is fluttering and the sun is obscured by steel-gray clouds. I cautiously negotiate the icy sidewalks trying to imagine I am alone, while ten paces behind me my mother and my uncle Jack silently follow. I can feel his eyes riveted on the bill, I can hear his footsteps crackling in the ice-crusted snow.

Never in my life had my uncle Jack truly given me anything. Probably he has never given anything to anyone. He has never married. He has always lived in my grandmother's big, dark house where I, with my mother and father, have been living for the past six months because we do not have enough money to live anywhere else. My uncle Jack is night to Uncle Benn's day, dead-cold to his radiant warmth.

The thousand-dollar bill comes in and out of focus. In one moment, thinking of it makes me dizzy—its huge value, worth an immensity of pennies, nickels, quarters, an immensity of *half-dollars,* the Milky Way made up of an infinity of infinite suns. In another moment it is only a dead piece of paper, an instrument of a miser's calculated vanity, a paper gift, a meaningless infinity.

GOLD AND THE SACRED

Alyssa's voice brought me back into the present.

"Bill, just what are you trying to prove?" But there was not the old confidence in her voice. The pile of gold had strongly affected her as well.

"That *this,*" he said, pointing to the gold, "is *real money!* This is the *real thing!*"

I was still feeling that strange relaxation and quiet that had come upon me a few moments before. At the same time, my mind was spinning with excitement and it was all I could do to resist plunging my hands into the heap of gold coins.

"Bill," I said, "what you've proved to me is that gold is a *symbol.* I understand now why it has the power it has had over the ages. I think I see why it was chosen by the ancient priests." I then described to them the childhood memory that had just returned to me. "The scholars say," I continued, "that gold symbolized the sun because of its color and they speak about gold's material properties. But what they don't tell us about is the feeling it can evoke of another dimension. Gold is sacred because it evokes the two worlds simultaneously. That's what a sacred symbol does. It's real because it has power, the power of bringing a sense of the two worlds mysteriously together—the earthly and the divine, the incalculable and the calculable. That's exactly what reality *is.* And the force that can experience this two-in-one is consciousness!"

Perhaps it was I who was now talking too much, but what I understood in that moment seemed fundamental to the whole problem of what money is—and still seems so now, as I write. Even now, I can recall that strange juxtaposition of stillness and movement that the gold evoked in me and that great sums of money can evoke, and great magnitudes like the dimensions of the starry world. Stillness and movement: the inner world and the outer world, the invisible and the visible—"That *is* reality!" I repeated, with considerable emphasis. "Take any truly great work of art—its greatness lies in the way it incomprehensibly brings together the two worlds and evokes in us the unique consciousness that for a moment contains these two radically different directions, if only in our feeling."

DEATH OF A SYMBOL

"But that's exactly what Coomaraswamy says about artifacts in early cultures," said Bill, turning away with surprising ease from the pile of gold in front of him, his own gold. "According to him, all things, even money, have the mark of God on them, or something like that."

"Something like that," I answered. "I remember when I was young we used to be forced to go to museums when we studied history and I could never appreciate all these artifacts of ancient civilizations. These poor ancient people taking all that trouble to carve religious symbols on things like spoons and cups, when we modern people could just manufacture everything so easily, so functionally."

"Are you saying," Alyssa asked, "that when money ceased to be symbolic and became just materially functional, it became evil?"

"Yes," I said, "when the spiritual and the material separate too far from each other then all hell breaks loose."

"But you've also been arguing that it's just as bad when the distinction between them is blurred."

"It's the same problem," I said. "They *are* separate, but they have to interact, they have to confront each other. Everything that exists is created by the interaction of these two forces which at the same time remain separate. At the human level, this interaction has to be conscious. Conscious existence is the confrontation within consciousness of these two forces."

"You don't mean," said Bill, "that we should use gold instead of paper for money?"

"I don't think that has anything to do with it," said Alyssa, impatiently.

"Nothing at all," I said. "It's not the gold, it's the consciousness. It's only that gold has some natural, material properties that lend themselves to reminding man of another dimension in life. But no symbol acts automatically past a certain point. If the voluntary struggle for awareness isn't brought to one's dealings with gold, it swallows us just as much as anything else.

"For modern man, gold is now just another metal. Science has moved man past that symbol. That's fine. It's nothing to get upset about. The world is full of symbols. Everything is a symbol if you're seeking Truth. Medieval Christianity had a wonderful symbolic vision of nature. All things the signature of God, and so on. Beautiful. Ancient Egypt had a wonderful symbolic vision also. So did Tibet. The Sufis in eleventh-century Baghdad. Fine. Excellent. Gone now. But it doesn't matter. Mankind moves on. Now we have science and there is an infinity of new symbols waiting to be seen and felt. If there's a search for contact with the higher level in man and a sense of man's nature as embracing the two worlds, the two directions, the entire world that modern science reveals will take on symbolic meanings. The entire world of things will become a world of reminders. Because things are intrinsically symbolic; you simply cannot escape that. Things are the creation of two forces confronting each other under varying conditions of universal nature. And a symbol is just that—the representation of the meeting of two forces under the aegis of a dynamic third force, a mysterious bridge or catalyst.

"So, gold is no longer a valid symbol of the two infinities, the two worlds. Nothing to get upset about. By chance, by luck, I happened to feel the ancient symbolism of gold when you" (I looked at Bill) "piled all that gold on the table. But for me and for all modern people, gold is just another metal, really, scientifically. Forget it. Gold is not really money at the moment—I don't care what the goldbugs say. Even if the world returns to the gold standard, it will only be as an instrument of political and military power—that is, an instrument of desire and fear, an accounting device to reckon the distribution of desire and fear.

"No, our money is now paper notes, or electronic impulses registering what we call credit. Our task is to grasp and feel the symbolism of money and credit. . . ."

PLASTIC

I knew, of course, that I was talking up a storm, but I had no real impulse to stop until Bill started emptying his wallet in what seemed like an endless shower of credit cards—which he defiantly dropped one at a time on the table next to the half million dollars' worth of gold. I saw Visa cards falling, Mastercards, American Express (gold), Diners' (also gold), Chevron, Discover, Shell, Macy's . . . more than thirty cards in all. Each gave off a hollow little click as it hit the gold or the tabletop.

This gesture of Bill's had its effect on me. "Go ahead," the gesture said, "just try to show that these dinky pieces of plastic have as much human meaning as gold!"

WHAT IS GOING ON?

Bill then reached for another book, one of those New Age versions of the old "power of positive thinking" approach. He read aloud:

> The opposite of poverty consciousness is prosperity consciousness: the belief in an abundant universe and your ability to fully partake of it. It involves a trust that there will always be enough money to meet your needs and a confidence that you can easily create more when you need it. In the past, this idea might have been difficult to accept since most prosperity came from personal will applied to the manufacturing and exploiting of a limited amount of natural resources. Today, much prosperity comes from information which is a combination of intelligence, creativity and personal will—all of which are unlimited.
>
> (David Gershon and Gail Straub, *Empowerment: The Art of Creating Your Life as You Want It.* New York: Dell, 1989, pp. 149-50)

When he stopped reading, Bill looked first at me and then at Alyssa. "This *is* nonsense," he said and, after a pause, ". . . isn't it?"

I couldn't help noticing that Alyssa's attitude toward Bill had undergone a big change. It had happened the moment he had dumped out all the gold. The boldness of that gesture seemed to have captivated her. "I believe it is nonsense," she said. "And yet, people do pay me for the information they get from me. But it's not just information; I help them, I do something for them. I provide a service. And it is true that there are more people providing services in our society than producing material goods. Maybe we need to look at information as a service industry."

"Isn't that what credit is—a service?" I said.

Bill sighed and closed the book on his lap. "It's all just too complicated. This passage that I just read is nonsense. I know it and you know it. Poverty consciousness, prosperity consciousness, infinite abundance—it's New Age nonsense . . . isn't it? Gold is real. Scarcity is real. Information, service, credit—none of it's real. Food is real, shelter is real, health and illness are real. What the hell is going on in this stupid world?"

18.

THE CURRENCY
OF ILLUSION

"God's grace is infinite and abundant, matched in its vastness only by the treachery and ignorance of man."

After a few glasses of wine, I tend sometimes to spout aphorisms, usually rather lamely. But this one was not a bad summary of the discussion that then took place. I had gotten up and brought back a bottle of good Côtes du Rhône. While I was out of the room, Alyssa had moved from her chair and was sitting on the couch next to Bill, ostensibly examining some of the books on the coffee table.

As a response to Bill's expostulation about the stupid complexity of modern concepts of money, I sipped some of the wine and launched into one of my own favorite topics, namely, the contemporary idea of knowledge and information. I hadn't forgotten that at the very beginning of the evening, I had opened the question of different kinds and levels of knowledge, especially in relation to all the books Bill had brought with him dealing with economics. Bill was discovering for himself a basic truth about money. A simple truth—perhaps. Elementary. But he was discovering it for himself, in his feelings and instinct. Not all the secondhand knowledge in the world was worth that.

MENTAL INFORMATION AND HUMAN KNOWLEDGE

When a man discovers something for himself, he truly understands it. Nothing can take it away from him. It means that he has discovered a part *of* himself—or, rather, he has been, as it were, "discovered" *by* a part of himself! And this was the whole entire meaning of the money question in modern life. Money enters so deeply into our personality and into our psychophysical organism that the personal exploration of money is necessary for the discovery of oneself, the discovery of those hidden parts of human nature that hold prisoner energies that need to be in relationship to our consciousness.

These energies need to discover us!

But how to express this truth? The "meaning of life"— what a vague formulation! The point is that meaning is an attribute of authentic, full consciousness; an authentic, complete mind relating to itself, aware of itself. Wasn't it Aristotle who said, in his crabbed, abstract way, that God is mind aware of itself? The part of the mind we usually live in is structurally incapable of experiencing meaning—no wonder the whole idea of "the meaning of life" has become almost a joke! There are other aspects of mind within us, of which we are unaware— and they are unaware of us. Why not put my cards on the table and call these other aspects—using the language of Gurd-jieff—not just "aspects," but *minds:* the thinking mind, the feeling mind, and the sensing mind. When a person really begins, even for a moment, to feel what he knows, it means that two of his minds have become aware of each other. And this already produces an entirely new sense of selfhood. Not only does it yield a more objective and complete view of the external world, far more complete and reliable than all the so-called "information" in the world, but it yields an experience of presence-to-oneself that points to the possible appearance in one's life of *I am.* Mythically, metaphysically, it is the escape from hell, the escape from Sheol, defined as the realm of ever-diminishing human being.

Even the faint echo of this state gives an individual a certain aura of balance and weight. Was this what was drawing Alyssa toward Bill?

In any case, with a glass of wine under my belt, I began to offer my views about what is now called *information.* What kind of "commodity" is it? And is it really true, as some observers now claim, that in our contemporary culture information is the real currency, the real basis of wealth?

A lifetime of reading books, teaching about ideas, and trying to maintain a search for myself had given me a rather bleak perspective on what passes for information and knowledge in the world.

"We're awash in information," I said, stating the obvious. "Every hour of every day more information is produced, more data is recorded, more 'facts' are registered, more theories are offered than perhaps were available in the whole lifetime of any previous civilization. There are tons and tons of data and concepts pouring out of our culture. At this very moment, computers all over the planet are printing out a billion times more 'information' than existed, say, in the entire medieval world or in the five thousand years of ancient Egyptian civilization.

"Go into any field of study, any science, any human enterprise, and what will you find? An infinite mass of books, journals, articles, reports which can neither be digested, nor even read, nor even acknowledged by any single human being. In every branch of science—no, every field of specialization, every subspecialization—there are more data and more information than a human mind can acknowledge."

I held up my now empty wineglass. "Look at this glass," I said. "Do you know how much data there is about this object? Its chemical composition? Its history, its relation to other objects, its mathematical properties, its sociological, psychological, technological aspects, the uses to which such objects are put, its manufacture, distribution and sale, the materials from which it is made? There is an infinite amount of data about anything in the world. Data is not knowledge, information is not knowledge, theory is not knowledge. And is all this what people are ready to call the basis of wealth?"

Alyssa filled my glass and smiled at me. I went on:

"And this is so for relatively accurate information—meaningless in itself, but accurate. The situation is far, far worse when you add in all the misleading and false information the world produces—the unsubstantiated data, the information that is carelessly gathered, the hasty opinions that are recorded and accepted as verified observations, the countless books, articles, and reports pasted together from other people's flimsy thoughts and presented as one's own, the arranging and rearranging of flawed information for the purpose of seduction, profit, persuasion—or under the influence of fear, violence, hatred—or simply because of haste and weak attention. All of this gathered into so-called learned texts or in newspapers or in the media.''

I drank, and continued:

''But this is still not the worst of it. Add to it the giant, immense amount of mere speculation and fantasy that passes for serious thought or the reporting of knowledge. Add the propaganda and the lies, some intentional, but most unconscious. And then, add to all this what are called, without remorse of conscience, *ideas* and concepts. Think of what happens when people with well-functioning minds—but unable to sense or truly feel what they know—put together all this information into theories. How many of our concepts are modes of cleverly organizing bad information? Brilliant concepts artistically arranging meaningless data into subjective, flawed meanings. Our concepts—*ha!* How many of them are just clever filing systems for illusory information!''

I knew I was turning an evening discussion into a lecture/seminar and I also watched, with great interest, Bill and Alyssa drawing closer to each other on the couch.

''Of course, I'm aware that service and information are more and more what people want and desire nowadays. More and more people work with thoughts, rather than materials like wood or stone. People sit in front of computers, people deal with words, with logic, systems, proposals, plans, programs rather than wood or stone or metal. Scientists look at printouts far more than they look directly at stars or animals or plants. Our culture is swimming in a sea of mental information. We live and breathe mental information.

''So, yes, let us say that information is the currency of our society. But it is false coin, isn't it? What Galbraith said about industrial capitalism creating the desires it satisfies could now be said in a new way. Informational capitalism creates ever new desires for mental information—illusory information. There's no representation of hell in the traditions that portrays people craving data and proposals and plans. But it is no new insight to realize that men and women crave illusion—that has been said a thousand times over by the sages of the past. It's not that gold is illusory. It's that illusion has taken the place of gold! Illusion is our currency!''

THE MEANING OF CREDIT

I filled Bill and Alyssa's glasses and went out to get another bottle. When I returned, they were waiting with a question.

"How can we escape this situation? How do the ancient teachers see that?'' said Bill.

"I'll tell you what I think,'' I said, picking up a Visa card and a gold Maple Leaf. "What gold represents, what precious metals represent is real experience—solid, authentic experience, contact with nature or even God. People feel gold is real money because it echoes in their minds the ideal of a real, full experience of a real, full reality that exists independently of their own subjective thoughts and impulses.

"Ancient peoples spoke of nature as filled with gods and spirits. This originally meant that for these ancient peoples reality had its own laws and forces that were independent of man's superficial likes and dislikes. When this view turned into superstition, it was corrected by the fathers of modern science who said that the universe obeys impersonal laws. In its origins, science provided the basis for a return to a mature sense of reality by abandoning animism—abandoning the superstitious degeneration of the ancient symbolism. But science became scientism when the element of Godness was taken away from nature—when people began to believe that the universe obeys only the laws understandable by their own mental brains without any contact with the perceptions available to deep feeling and inner sensation.

"Gold symbolizes nature infused with the light of great divinity. Its production cannot be controlled in any complete sense. It is just in nature. It is hard to get. It is rare. It is beautiful. And so on. It is a commodity whose availability does not obey the superficial desires and mentation of man."

"Are you some kind of goldbug, too, after all?" Alyssa asked.

"No, certainly not," I said. "We cannot return to that symbolism in this culture. Gold long ago became as controlled a substance as anything else, as subject to the mental as anything else. But what I'm trying to drive at is the meaning of money in today's world. This gold coin and this credit card . . ."

"One's real and the other's fake," said Bill, finally showing some effects of the wine by semi-intentionally placing his hand on Alyssa's shoulder.

Alyssa stayed cool as ever, but I could see her body accepting Bill's touch.

"No, what he means," she said, looking at Bill and pointing to me, "is that invented, created money has taken the place of gold as a symbol of man's relation to the real material world. And credit is invented money *par excellence*. Is this what you mean?" she asked, turning to look at me. "That, in a way, credit has gone from something you receive when you are in serious need to something you get just to satisfy superficial, invented desires?"

"That's what I mean—fake," Bill said. "These plastic cards give an enormous number of people as much money as they want, but it isn't real."

Alyssa backed off a bit. "It's real enough when you have to pay the bills!"

I jumped in again. "But what do you pay with?"

"What do you mean?" Alyssa asked, and then answered her own question. "Of course. We pay with time."

"And time is our life. We pay with our life," I said. "Just think—what kind of time do we pay with? What kind of hours and days do we pay with?"

Again Alyssa gave me a puzzled look and then immediately answered. "You're referring to the quality of experience—what you spoke about in the seminar, the lack of presence-to-self in our lives?"

Bill interjected: "But that's what everybody's talking about—quality of life."

"No," I said. "We're not talking about quality of life, exactly, in the way it's usually meant. It's quality of experience, not 'quality of life.' You can have everything you desire, everything money can buy, and have an ever-diminishing quality of experience. You can have everything and be nothing. This is poverty. This is hell."

"So the only true wealth is conscious life," said Alyssa.

"I think so," I said. "If *I* am not, then of what value is my life either to myself or to others?"

There was a long silence, not at all uncomfortable, during which I was musing about the symbolism of *long life* in the Old Testament stories and the fairy tales. What God granted men and women who lived righteously was not only length of years in a quantitative sense, but *real* life, full life, meaningful life. Real time.

In lugubrious tones, sounding as though he were at the bottom of a deep well, Bill said, "I still don't see what this has to do with plastic bank cards."

"Or," said Alyssa, "with the hard reality of paying bills.

You can speak of illusion all you want, but when the bills come due, those illusions are mighty real. Or when you try to borrow money, it's all pretty real."

"Certainly," I said. "When an addict craves a drug, it's a very real force. Even though what he craves will never bring him happiness or well-being. Illusion is very strong, or it wouldn't be illusion. Illusion is not just a property of what one desires, it's a property of the force of desire itself. What we come up against when we deal with the world of money is, to a large extent, the force of desire and craving."

Finally, Bill spoke in a startlingly new voice. Somewhere down in that well, it seems, he was bitten by an insight.

"Now I understand what you're driving at!" He lustily quaffed some wine. "Plastic credit cards, masses of debt, enormous rates of interest, equaling massive inflation in personal finances, continuous production of ever-new items of superficial information exactly like the continuous production of new consumer products that satisfy artificially created needs, easy credit, borrowing debt, borrowing notes, electronic transfers of millions of what, *billions* of whatever—all on the surface of life. And all very strong at the same time. It all hangs together. It all moves very fast. . . ." He slumped back on the couch. His eyes roved the ceiling. "I understand what happened now when I inherited my money! I wasn't allowed to give. My friends came to me with deals, with demands. I wanted to give. I still want to give. . . ."

It was surely now the wine speaking in Bill. But it was speaking the truth. Tears started in his eyes.

"Everyone has money passing through them now," he went on. "The poor demand welfare, the rich demand interest or tax write-offs or ego satisfaction. Nobody begs, nobody gives, the government does everything. It's impossible to give. It's impossible to ask from the heart, from need. Nobody owes gratitude, they just owe money. Nobody gives without getting something. . . ."

Bill lapsed into drowsy inaudible mumbling and Alyssa gently took the half-full wineglass from his large hand. She had only been drinking water, but she took a sip of wine from Bill's glass and placed the glass on the table next to the pile of gold.

THIRTY-FIVE POUNDS OF GOLD

As Bill slept, softly snoring, Alyssa and I neatly stacked up all the gold, credit cards, and currency. I began fitting the gold into the mahogany box while she inserted the credit cards and currency into Bill's wallet. Then she bent down and picked up the coins that had rolled onto the carpet. Sitting on the floor, she hefted them in her hand and gave them to me to put into the box.

I sat there with thirty-five pounds—about half a million dollars—weighing heavily on my lap. I'm sure Alyssa was having the same sort of thoughts I was having. This compact, immensely heavy box filled with human illusion and craving. The answer to all my problems. If this were mine, it would bring me time to work and create, freedom from care. I could buy the house I was renting. I could travel, I could help my father, my children. . . .

Why not keep a few of these gold coins? Bill wouldn't even notice they were missing. Shocking thought! Trying to stay true to my own principles of search, I allowed the temptation to exist in front of me. I didn't try to push it away or become fascinated by self-condemnation. Perhaps because of the wine and perhaps because over the past months my body had tended to be in an increasingly relaxed state, free of gross tensions, the thought of stealing a little of Bill's gold did not pass into my body, did not form itself into an impulse to do anything. The thoughts just quietly faded away back to wherever in myself they came from. I didn't feel at all "virtuous." I hadn't "done" anything. I hadn't *overcome* anything. I had tried, with the support of a quiet body, simply to watch and study. How extraordinarily interesting! In that moment, at least, I had verified what I had been speaking about: in that moment, at least, the wish to study myself had simply been more interesting than the desire for money. "Morality" had been a *result,* not an effort.

19.

A GUIDE FOR
THE PERPLEXED

Against the background of
Bill's gentle, childlike snoring, Alyssa and I now started gathering the books and papers that were strewn around and upon the coffee table. It was immediately apparent, however, that this task would take a long time as Alyssa and I took turns opening various books and reading to each other from them. Alyssa went to the passages that Bill had marked and I to the passages that I knew about from my own research.

THE EVILS WE BRING UPON OURSELVES
Some of the books that Bill had brought surprised me—pleasantly. I was intrigued to see among them *The Guide for the Perplexed* by the greatest of Judaic thinkers, Moses Maimonides. I started the round of reading aloud by locating the chapter where Maimonides speaks with startling common sense

about the cause of the evils and sufferings that befall mankind.
He divides these causes into three kinds—the first being those
evils brought about by the simple fact that man is subject to
birth and death and has a body, the second being the evils
which people cause to each other, and the third being those
evils which we bring upon ourselves by our own actions. This
third class, says Maimonides, is by far the largest, and almost
everything that human beings complain of when they bewail
their "fate" actually belongs to this third category. The suffering we attribute to external factors is actually brought about
by ourselves. And here Maimonides cites King Solomon:

> "Lo, this only have I found, that God hath made man
> upright, but they have thought out many inventions"
> (Eccles. vii:29) and these inventions bring the evils upon
> him. (pp. 269–70)

"Do you think Solomon is speaking about the production
of unnecessary and superficial goods, services, and information?" asked Alyssa, with a twinkle in her eye.

I laughed, but then read on quite seriously:

> This class of evils originates in man's vices, such as exces-
> sive desire for eating, drinking and love. . . . This course
> brings diseases and afflictions upon body and soul alike. The
> sufferings of the body in consequence of these evils are well
> known; those of the soul are twofold:—First, such evils of
> the soul as are the necessary consequence of changes in the
> body, in so far as the soul is a force residing in the body;
> it has therefore been said that the properties of the soul
> depend on the condition of the body. Secondly, the soul,
> when accustomed to superfluous things, acquires a strong
> habit of desiring things which are neither necessary for the

preservation of the individual nor for that of the species. (p. 270)

LIMITLESS DESIRE

It had been years since I had read these passages of Maimonides. I hadn't remembered how clearly he portrayed what I had come to see as the effects on the mind and emotions caused by the desires in our childish bodies. I continued reading as Alyssa listened with keen attention:

> This desire is without a limit, whilst things which are necessary are few in number and restricted within certain limits; but what is superfluous is without end—for example, you desire to have your vessels of silver, but golden vessels are still better: others have even vessels of sapphire, or perhaps they can be made of emerald or rubies . . . those who are ignorant and perverse in their thought are constantly in trouble and pain, because they cannot get as much of superfluous things as a certain other person possesses. They as a rule expose themselves to great dangers, for example, by sea-voyage, or service of kings, all this for the purpose of obtaining that which is superfluous and not necessary. When they thus meet with the consequences of the course which they adopt . . . (p. 270)

Alyssa interrupted: "He means when people are thwarted or suffer trying to get what is unnecessary." I nodded yes, my sense of wonder growing at the precision of Maimonides' diagnosis. How unafraid a great thinker truly is to state simply and directly that man's only essential aim in life must be to serve God! I continued reading the passage:

COMPLAINTS

When they thus meet with the consequences of the course which they adopt, they complain of the decrees and judgments of God; they begin to blame the time . . .

Alyssa: "The time?"
Me: "The time, the culture, the world, external factors, rulers, Japan, the Middle East, the economy, politicians, you name it."

. . . they begin to blame the time, and wonder at the want of justice in its changes; that it has not enabled them to acquire great riches, with which they could buy large quantities of wine for the purpose of making themselves drunk, and numerous concubines . . . for the purpose of driving themselves to voluptuousness beyond their capacities, as if the whole Universe existed exclusively for the purpose of giving pleasure to these low people. The error of the ignorant goes so far as to say that God's power is insufficient, because He has given to this Universe the properties which they imagine cause these great evils, and which do not help all evil-disposed persons to obtain the evil which they seek, and to bring their evil souls to the aim of their desires, though these, as we have shown, are really without limit. . . .

Alyssa: "Whew! What's going on here?"

THE DEVOURING WORLD

In fact, I hadn't remembered Maimonides as being quite this strong. "It's just what we've been speaking about all along," I said. "Without contact with another force within ourselves, man's desires are limitless, that is, all-devouring, like the demons of hell who eat human beings. The outer world is created to take from us whatever it can by continually evoking these desires. The world will never just get enough and then pause and politely say to us, 'Thank you, sir or madam, I have had a good meal and now I give you leave to quietly and peacefully find the inner meaning of your life—perhaps in a friendly little cave under a gentle flowering tree.' No, this is not the nature of the outer world of human life on earth. It was built to take, take, take. It can't help it. There are stories and legends all over the world that speak of this. The outer world can't help it, and really, it would rather not suck us dry. It would rather have something else from us, something of another quality. But if it can't receive from us a specifically human quality of energy, it will make up in quantity what it lacks in quality. It will take, take, take. And it will make it very easy for us to spin our wheels incessantly pouring out our psyche into its engines. . . ."

"Why do you say 'it's not its fault'?"

"Who do you think put the serpent in paradise?"

Alyssa paused. "Why, God, of course."

"God creates both the evil and the good. That's the paradox every era and every man has to resolve in his life. Who created the demons in the legends? God, of course. You know, the Judaic legends speak of two kinds of demons—and until now, I always took this as a sort of joke, but it isn't: the legends and the folklore speak of two kinds of demons—one type are called 'Jewish demons,' these are the demons who also study the Torah and worship God and do His work. And, by the way, the king of these demons was . . ."

"Asmodeus?" asked Alyssa.

"Asmodeus," I answered, myself amazed. But before

Alyssa could ask about the other demons, I went back to reading Maimonides:

> The virtuous and wise, however, see and comprehend the wisdom of God displayed in the universe. . . . For those who observe the nature of the Universe and the commandments of the Law, and know their purpose, see clearly God's mercy and truth in everything; they seek, therefore, that which the Creator intended to be the aim of man. . . .
> (p. 270)

WHAT IS NECESSARY?

As I was about to read the last word of this sentence, I caught my breath: *"comprehension."* I looked at Alyssa and then read the phrase again: "they seek, therefore, that which the Creator intended to be the aim of man—comprehension." I was tempted to pause and discuss the notion that the central aim of human life is to comprehend, to understand. But I was even more strongly drawn to go on reading, to see (or rather, remember) how Maimonides developed this vision of the aim of human life in relation to man's material needs and existence. Speaking of those who grasp the aim of human life, Maimonides writes:

> Forced by the claims of the body, they seek also that which is necessary for the preservation of the body, "bread to eat and garment to clothe," and this is very little; but they seek nothing superfluous; with very slight exertion man can obtain it, so long as he is contented with that which is indispensable. All the difficulties and troubles we meet in this respect are due to the desire for superfluous things; when we seek unnecessary things, we have diffi-

culty in finding that which is indispensable. For the more we desire to have that which is superfluous, the more we meet with difficulties; our strength (is) spent in unnecessary things, and (is) wanting when required for that which is necessary. (pp. 270–71)

GOD THE PROVIDER

Once again, I paused. It was impossible just to read on with these extraordinary ideas coming one after the other pulling together every question I had about money and the meaning of life. The aim of human life was understanding. Man needs to live in the material world and for this need, he easily has sufficient strength, that is, energy. Beyond what is necessary for his obvious physical needs, his energy must be devoted to gaining understanding—the understanding of himself and his relationship to the Higher, or God. And this understanding does not come just from books and reading, but from studying oneself in the midst of life. And for this total aim, man has and will receive energy from the Universe itself!

Many are the religious writers—Jewish, Christian, Moslem, Hindu—who have spoken of superfluity and necessity in the conduct of man's material life, but few have spoken with the impartial, scientific clarity of this great physician, philosopher, and mystic of medieval Judaism. And fewer still have shown how nature and the material universe itself are built to nourish and provide for the man who strives for conscious understanding and service to the Higher:

Observe how Nature proves the correctness of this assertion. The more necessary a thing is for living beings, the more easily it is found and the cheaper it is; the less necessary it is, the rarer and dearer it is. For example, air,

water, and food are indispensable to man: air is most necessary, for if man is without air a short time he dies; whilst
he can be without water a day or two. Air is also undoubt-
edly found more easily and cheaper than water. Water is
more necessary than food; for some people can be four or
five days without food, provided they have water; water
also exists in every country in larger quantities than food,
and is also cheaper. The same proportion can be noticed in
the different kinds of food; that which is more necessary in
a certain place exists there in larger quantities and is cheaper
than that which is less necessary. . . .

(Moses Maimonides, *The Guide for the Perplexed,* trans.
M. Friedländer. New York: Dover Publications, 1956, p. 271)

Having written this, Maimonides then presents in great
philosophical detail, and from a hundred different angles, his
vision of how God provides what is for man the most necessary
thing of all—the means for a life of understanding, precisely
the aim in the heart of King Solomon. Seen in the context of
what is necessary and what is superfluous for human life on
earth, the whole idea of what God provides—the whole idea
of *providence*—takes on a completely new and startling meaning,
completely free of the sentimental and superstitious accretions
that have surrounded it over the centuries.

Maimonides presents his idea in the scientific language of
his day—the language of Aristotelian philosophy, infused with
the mythic language of the Old Testament—a fusion of the
language of the intellect and the language of the heart. It is
this fusion of two fundamental sources of perception that marks
the greatness of the medieval mind. God, he says, acting
through His creation, Nature, provides for the species—for
plants and animals and for *man's biological nature,* man's physical
survival. But, unlike all other biological species, man has an

individual soul. This individual soul needs to grow and develop; it, too, needs its nourishment. And this nourishment, this "food" of the soul is provided by God directly, not through Nature, but through the Intellect in the form of a guiding teaching and actual events and experiences in man's personal and collective history. *God acts in history:* that is, God provides ideas, methods, and *experiences* intended to bring comprehension to man, an understanding heart, a conscious life.

God thus provides for both parts of human nature. For man's biological part, God provides as He provides for all of the natural world, the world of mutual feeding and exchange—food, water, air, and the physical necessities. In this aspect, man is a species among species. In this aspect he is "earth"—the Hebrew word for earth being *Adam.*

But insofar as man is also a *soul,* a potential conscious individual, God provides another nourishment, another "food"—His Law and the means by which to experience life with ever-increasing consciousness, namely, the practices of the inner tradition with all its rites, rituals, customs, and commandments. God's providence extends to both "halves" of human nature—but these two "foods" are entirely different "substances," and cannot and must not be confused or mixed up. The Judaic laws prescribing the separation of foods and materials—and many other laws dealing with separation of human activities into clean and unclean, just like the creatures on either side of the steps of Solomon's throne—are remnants and expressions of the fundamental teaching concerning man's two natures.

WHAT MAN MUST PROVIDE

But there is something which God does not provide, which man alone must provide for himself and from himself. And what this is, is something entirely mysterious, unfathomable, uniquely human, something which distinguishes man not only from the animals, but, we are told, also from the angels. What is this "something"? It is none other than the mysterious power which we call "freedom of the will." This all-too-familiar phrase in fact designates something entirely incomprehensible and invisible to us in our everyday mode of thinking. Philosophers and psychologists and theologians have squabbled and argued about it for centuries—to no avail, and for the simple reason that it is a power we cannot really comprehend, which has its source in conscious man's capacity to experience the contradictory forces of universal creation and, *from himself,* to open himself to the ultimate reconciling force called, in Christianity, the Holy Spirit.

While I was speaking about this, Alyssa interrupted to ask why man is considered higher than the angels.

"Potentially higher," I said.

"How so? I never heard that in Sunday school."

I put down my wineglass and recited from memory an extraordinary passage from the Koran where Allah informs the angels of his intention to create man:

Behold, thy Lord said to the angels: "I will create a viceregent on earth." They said, "Wilt Thou place therein one who will make mischief and shed blood? —whilst we do celebrate thy praise and glorify Thy holy name?"

To this question of the angels, Allah simply answers:

"I know what ye know not."

(*The Holy Quran,* Sūra II:30, trans. Abdullah Ysuf Ali.
Lahore, Pakistan: Sh. Muhammad Ashraf, 1969, p. 24)

THE FOOD OF EXPERIENCE

Several centuries later, from within the esoteric circle of the Islamic tradition, a community following the way in life wrote down the tale of a disillusioned worshiper who sees himself being pulled apart by conflicting "masters," all equally embedded in nature and all equally valid in their own right. He cries out: "Oh God, Thou hast brought together contradictory elements, mutually pulling and repelling forces! I know no more what to do or how, lost as I am between them!" God responds at first by reminding the worshiper of the blessings He has bestowed on man, especially the faculties with which He has endowed man and which are capable of steering him on an ethical "middle" course.

But this does not appease the man. God then reminds him that He has also sent down the moral laws to keep man from error. This, too, does not appease him. Finally, God gently reassures him that the deepest contradictions of human life are not there to be solved but to be lived in full consciousness of their contradictoriness. (Al-Faruqi, Isma'il, "On the Ethics of the Brethren of Purity," *Muslim World,* Vol. 50, July 1960, p. 196.)

"What is most necessary for man," I said, "and what is given him in great abundance, are experiences, especially experiences of the forces within him. This is his most essential food, his most essential wealth. If man consciously receives all this abundance, the universe will pour into him what is called *life* in Judaism, *spirit* in Christianity, *light* in Islam, *power* in Taoism. . . ."

My hand was reaching again for the wine. Alyssa filled my glass.

"And so," I concluded, "If I had to say what I think the role of money is in human life, I would take my stand on these teachings of the masters. I would say that one needs money to live and survive in the outer world, to fulfill one's obligations to the community and to nature, but that above and beyond this, the role of money is to serve as the instrument for getting understanding. We come to the bottom of civilization if, instead of understanding, we are going after 'information.' Information is the plastic version of understanding. Just as bank cards stand to gold, just as easy and deadly credit stands to honest need, obligation, and giving . . ."

20.

THE GIFT

The moment I pronounced the word "giving" Bill made a strange loud noise in his sleep. Alyssa and I looked at him to see if he was going to reappear, but he immediately resumed his gentle, childlike snoring. Was it only coincidence that Alyssa was holding in her hand Lewis Hyde's scintillating essay called *The Gift?*

There were dozens of Bill's markers in the book. Alyssa read from the first place that he had underlined, where the author strongly expresses his vision about the two forces in human history which he calls *the gift* and *the commodity.* "A gift," he writes, "is a thing we do not get by our own efforts. We cannot buy it; we cannot acquire it through an act of will. It is bestowed upon us." In modern times it is in the realm of art, according to Hyde, that the gift is encountered. The gift obeys entirely different laws than the laws of the marketplace. Alyssa read:

It is the assumption of this book that a work of art is a
gift, not a commodity. Or, to state the modern case with
more precision, that works of art exist simultaneously in
two "economies," a market economy and a gift economy.
Only one of these is essential, however: a work of art can
survive without the market, but where there is no gift
there is no art. (p. xi)

Here Hyde is speaking of artistic gifts not only as a quality
of individual talent and the creative act. He extends the term
to what happens to the work of art after it has left its maker's
hands. "That art that matters to us," he writes:

—which moves the heart, or revives the soul, or delights
the senses, or offers courage for living, however we choose
to describe the experience—that work is received by us as
a gift is received. Even if we have paid a fee at the door of
the museum or concert hall, when we are touched by a
work of art something comes to us which has nothing to
do with the price. . . . The work appeals, as Joseph Conrad
says, to a part of our being which is itself a gift and not
an acquisition. (p. xii)

Alyssa read on:

. . . religions often prohibit the sale of sacred objects, the
implication being that their sanctity is lost if they are
bought and sold. A work of art seems to be a hardier breed;
it can be sold in the market and still emerge as a work of
art. But if it is true that in the essential commerce of art a
gift is carried by the work from the artist to his audience,
if I am right to say that where there is no gift there is no

229

art, then it may be possible to destroy a work of art by converting it into a pure commodity. (p. xiii)

THE TWO ECONOMIES

From the outset, Hyde makes it clear that he is speaking not only about the merchandising of art in our society. He is speaking about the two natures of man and about two forms of communal life that reflect them. He is like a contemporary St. Augustine writing about the city of God and the city of Man. What makes his book important is how he portrays this distinction in strictly contemporary terms relevant to the experience all of us have in facing the conflict between the money question and the question of our own inner reality.

Alyssa, with her extraordinary sensitivity and keenness of mind, detected immediately that what Hyde was calling artistic creativity was what the traditions speak of as the divine in man, that in us which is unconditioned, given by God, our essential nature. She interrupted her own reading by remarking, "Why should we feel this way only with a work of art? I experience the same thing sometimes when I look at a tree or a child or even a stone." Then she turned to Bill's next marker and read what Hyde writes about the gift in the culture of the American Indian. The hallmark of a gift, as opposed to a commodity, is that the gift must be reciprocated or given away to someone else. It cannot stand still; it cannot be hoarded or accumulated or stored up as capital wealth. Whole civilizations, Hyde reminds us, have been founded on the "economy of the gift," rather than the economy of the market exchange.

The Indian giver (or the original one, at any rate) understood a cardinal property of the gift: whatever we have been given is supposed to be given away again, not kept.

230

Or, if it is kept, something of similar value should move on in its stead, the way a billiard ball may stop when it sends another scurrying across the felt, its momentum transferred. You may keep your Christmas present, but it ceases to be a gift in the true sense unless you have given something else away. As it is passed along, the gift may be given back to the original donor, but this is not essential. . . . The only essential is this: *the gift must always move.* There are other forms of property that stand still, that mark a boundary or resist momentum, but the gift keeps going. (p. 4)

With a slightly puzzled look on her face, Alyssa read the next passage Bill had marked:

Another way to describe the motion of the gift is to say that a gift must always be used up, consumed, eaten. *The gift is property that perishes.* . . . Food is one of the most common images of the gift because it is so obviously consumed. Even when the gift is not food, when it is something we would think of as a durable good, it is often referred to as a thing to be eaten. Shell necklaces and arm-bands are the ritual gifts in the Trobriand Islands, and when they are passed from one group to the next, protocol demands that the man who gives them away toss them on the ground and say, "Here, some food we could not eat." Or, again, a man in another tribe . . . says, in speaking of the money he was given at the marriage of his daughter, that he will pass it on rather than spend it on himself. Only, he puts it this way: "If I receive money for the children God has given me, I cannot eat it. I must give it to others." (pp. 8–9)

Her puzzlement increasing, Alyssa read aloud Hyde's recounting and interpretation of the Grimm fairy tale, "The Ungrateful Son":

Once a man and his wife were sitting outside the front door with a roast chicken before them which they were going to eat between them. Then the man saw his old father coming along and quickly took the chicken and hid it, for he begrudged him any of it. The old man came, had a drink, and went away.

Now the son was about to put the roast chicken back on the table, but when he reached for it, it had turned into a big toad that jumped in his face and stayed there and didn't go away again.

And if anybody tried to take it away, it would give them a poisonous look, as if about to jump in their faces, so that no one dared touch it. And the ungrateful son had to feed the toad every day, otherwise it would eat part of his face. And thus he went ceaselessly hither and yon in the world.

Concerning this story, Hyde comments:

This toad is the hunger that appears when the gift stops moving, whenever one man's gift becomes another man's capital. To the degree that we desire the fruits of the gift, teeth appear when it is hidden away. When property is hoarded, thieves and beggars begin to be born to rich men's wives. A story like this says that there is a force seeking to keep the gift in motion. (pp. 10–11)

THE TRUE GIFT

When Alyssa saw what the next marked passages of Hyde's book were, her puzzlement turned to irritation. Having distinguished the realm of buying and selling from the realm of the gift, Hyde had offered examples of cultures based on the mysterious laws of giving and receiving rather than on the laws of the marketplace. This both Alyssa and I found interesting and provocative. Puzzlement had set in for both of us when Hyde had identified the making and distribution of art as the modern equivalent of the gift. Was Hyde pointing to artistic creativity as a realm where contemporary men and women could search for an experience of the inner world of the spirit, or was he only romanticizing the work of painters, writers, and other artists in our society? Was he dividing the two worlds along right lines or was he only speaking about two aspects of the ordinary, outer world and romanticizing one of those aspects— as has happened throughout the history of mankind? Was he merely overestimating what artists do and say about what they do?

What Alyssa found irritating was Hyde's citation from the sermons of Meister Eckhart, one of the greatest masters of inwardness of the Christian Middle Ages. It offended her that anyone would try to lump together true interior spirituality and what she considered the egoistic self-indulgence of the modern artist.

Hyde cites one of the many sermons and tracts in which Eckhart speaks of how the soul, in deep contemplation, receives the gift of divine energy which God freely pours into it:

That man should receive God in himself is good, and by this reception he is a virgin. But that God should become fruitful in him is better; for the fruitfulness of a gift is the only gratitude for the gift. (p. 54)

"Eckhart," the author writes, "is speaking his own particular language here. To understand what he means we need to know, first, that according to his theology, 'God's endeavor is to give himself to us entirely.' The Lord pours himself into the world, not on a whim or even by choice, but by nature. . . .

"For Eckhart," Hyde writes, "we are not really alive until we have borne the gift back into the Godhead. Whatever has proceeded from God comes to life, or receives its being, only at the moment when it 'gazes back' toward Him. The circuit must be completed. 'Man ought to be flowing out into whatever can receive him.'

"We come alive," says the author, "when we give away what has been received. In Eckhart the passage is purely spiritual. He tells us not to pray to God for things, because things are nothing; we should simply pray to be closer to the Godhead. The final fruit of gratitude toward God is to be drowned in Him.

> In the abstract Godhead there is no activity: the soul is not perfectly beatified until she casts herself into the desolate Deity where neither act nor form exists and there, merged in the void, loses herself: as self she perishes, and has no more to do with things than she had when she was not. Now, dead to self, she is alive in God." (p. 55)

Concluding his reference to Meister Eckhart, Hyde writes, "The labor of gratitude accomplishes the transformation that a gift promises. . . . For Eckhart, the child born in the soul is itself a god: whoever gratefully returns all that God has bestowed will, by that act of donation, enter the Godhead" (Lewis Hyde, *The Gift: Imagination and the Erotic Life of Property*. New York: Vintage Books, 1979, p. 55).

The Overestimation of Art and the Underestimation of Money

I was struck by how much these references to Eckhart troubled Alyssa and I asked her about it.

"I don't know much about spirituality," she said, "but I do know something about being an artist. I told you that before becoming an accountant, I tried to make my way as a painter. I remember how I used to think of myself before I entered the world of the marketplace. And it was the same for every other artist I knew. We all gave absurd names, such as 'inspiration,' 'gift,' 'creative intuition,' to the fantasies that bubbled up automatically from our unconscious minds. We all imagined we were a sort of elite and that the world had an obligation to praise us and support us.

"Maybe what this author is saying about other cultures is right, I don't know, I've never studied anthropology. Maybe there have existed worlds without money, without the marketplace. I know there is that fascinating ritual of potlatch—a kind of contest of gift-giving among the Northwest Coast Indians. Maybe there have been societies whose economy is not based on buying and selling. But my own experience tells me that it's a very healthy thing for an artist to have to sell his work. . . ."

"Of course, that can go too far," I said.

"Of course, it can. But which is better?—the artist romanticizing his poverty and expecting others to take care of him, or the artist selling out just to make money by pleasing the crowd? In any case, I can tell you that what went on inside me when I was painting was not what Meister Eckhart is describing, not by any stretch of the imagination."

"Then you do know something about spirituality," I said. Alyssa grew very serious. "I've tried things," she whispered.

"And so have I," I said.

Neither of us said anything more about the subject. The world of interior spiritual search is a world that is terribly real. Even to speak about it requires extraordinary conditions of mutual trust and a background of exact language and knowledge. Perhaps all one can say is that the interior search takes place under universal laws as rigorous as those governing the external world, and that in the inner world what can be given to man is of such immensity that it dwarfs any concept or image we may have of it, and that it requires of us an effort or a sacrifice of such unimaginable quality that the only representation of this exchange between God and man that has endured in our civilization has been, as the great masters such as Eckhart show us, the event of a God-infused man voluntarily dying on the cross.

After a pause, Alyssa said, "I think that what we call the marketplace has always existed. Art and money are both part of the same world."

"So," I replied, "the problem is that we tend to be inaccurate and sentimental when we try to draw the line between the two worlds of man. This is what I've been saying all along."

WHAT MONEY CANNOT BUY

"You mean there's nothing that money cannot buy?" This was Bill speaking. I didn't realize he had stopped snoring and was listening to us. Both Alyssa and I took his reentry in stride.

"What I think we're saying," I answered, looking at Bill, "is that in the world we live in now, money represents everything that man can actually *do*. Everything he can achieve through his mind and body as they function uninfluenced by a higher energy or power. There are strong unconscious influences that act on us under certain conditions, but these influences are not necessarily the higher forces. Art, science, ethics, even certain forms of religion, even many things we call love, are all things we can cultivate and perfect by our own efforts. Therefore they can be and in fact have become part of the marketplace. Thank God! It's all much clearer that way. By studying money, by understanding money, we can begin to understand all the things that are within our power and only then, after we have really understood that, after we have really mastered the world of money, can we begin to grasp what it is that money cannot buy.''

Bill was surprisingly lucid. ''That seems just plain wrong,'' he said. ''We can't control life and death, we can't control our passions, we can't buy artistic inspiration. I don't see how you can say that!''

''I'm not saying that, exactly. I'm saying that there is and always has been a danger of attributing to God, or whatever we call the higher reality, that which is really within the world of human ego. Just because the intellect cannot grasp something, or cannot control it, that doesn't mean it comes directly from God or the spirit. We're speaking about what the ancient Hebrews called idolatry—attributing to God that which is an aspect of the human ego. Money is the present-day name for the world of the human ego. Money dictates how we deal with everything—material, intellectual, and emotional things.''

''You can't buy love! You can't buy happiness! You can't buy truth! You can't buy loyalty. . . .''

Alyssa interrupted, looking at me quizzically. ''You're not claiming that, are you?''

"No," I said. "You *can* buy love, you *can* buy happiness and you *can* buy truth and loyalty! But there is a love you cannot buy and a truth, a loyalty, and a happiness you cannot buy. But we will never know what they are until we've understood the love, the truth, and the happiness we *can* buy. We can do many things to find love and truth and happiness and, finally, to position ourselves so that we can receive as a gift the love and truth and happiness that do not depend on our efforts. We are meant to live in two worlds. It's very hard to swallow that, I tell you! Money is an instrument of what we can do: that is what money means. It wasn't always so in other cultures. There have been other sorts of instruments—weapons, tools, all sorts of things that represented and served as the key to what man can do by his own efforts. Today, it's money. Health, war and peace, justice, pleasure and pain—they are all decided on the basis of cost. And we will stop deceiving ourselves about love, truth, and happiness only when we have seen exactly the kind of love and truth money *can* buy, the kind we can work for and achieve.

"We are disappointed in the world because we expect the world to be God. I mean the world of the human ego, I don't mean the world of raw nature. We become disappointed with love when we expect the love that money can buy—I mean the love that we can work for by our own efforts—to be like the love that money can't buy. When we expect the justice that money can buy to be like God's justice. We continually make wrong divisions between the two worlds and then are disappointed when the world we thought was spiritual behaves just like the world of the human ego. We call a piece of stone God, dress it to look like a god, and then are disappointed when it behaves like a stone. That's idolatry. We call art spiritual, art that comes from ordinary, talented people, but people like you and me, and then we are disappointed when the artist acts just like anyone else. It's the same with ethics, with all human relationships. There's plenty we can do, by our own lights and the knowledge we all have, and the normal goodwill we all have, to care for each other, to be fair, to be intelligent, but all that will not lead to ultimate happiness and meaning. Nor is it to be despised."

"I don't get it," Bill cried out, "what can money buy?"

"Money can buy everything," I said, not being inclined to mitigate the paradox of human life on earth. "Money can buy everything. The only thing it cannot buy is meaning. The ultimate source of every human activity, every human function, is something, some force, beyond the ego. Money can't touch that, but it touches everything else."

MONEY AND SAMSARA

It may have been the wine that kept me from trying to put everything into logical form. I certainly wasn't trying to upset anyone. "Don't you see," I said, "how much mischief is caused by the wrong division of the two worlds?" I pointed to the piles of books Bill had brought. "When people only imagine they are choosing the spirit, it only causes the animal in us to grow in strength while taking on the mask of the spirit, like Asmodeus took on the face of King Solomon. How many of those books that have words like 'ethics' in the title are like that? Love of country? Care for the planet? Concern for equal rights, housing, medical care, the drug problem? Money can buy any of them, but if you set one of them so apart from the others as to make it sound like what is highest in human life, if you create such a wrong division between normal individual needs on the one hand and concerns for the survival of the human family on the other hand, then you have fashioned an idol. The need to care for the well-being of my family, environment, or countrymen is all part of the same movement as the need to care for myself. As Maimonides says, God provides for that as long as we grasp what is necessary and act on it. Such action, ordinary, normal, sane, human action in the world is nowadays to be carried out in the world of money transactions. Money is our instrument of doing things. You can't love your neighbor unless you take money into consideration.''

Not even Alyssa could accept this.

"That's not Christian love!" she said. "That's not the love of the heart!"

"Who's speaking of Christian love?" I replied. "I'm not speaking of Christian love. That kind of love is something else. That kind of love, which I hope to experience at least once or twice more in my life, comes from nowhere and goes nowhere. That love is love of everything, reconciliation of all forces, love of every human being. It is pure gift. It sees and understands and transforms. But when I speak of money, I am speaking of everything, everything connected with what the human mind can grasp and choose and do. That's what money means now. It's part of everything in our lives—that is, our mind and thought and emotions in their untransformed state are all involved with money. Money touches what we know of as love: care for children, care for our planet, care for our bodies, our health, our safety, our art, our science. Money is the name we now have for the whole world of samsara. . . .''

Bill grunted: "What's samsara?"

There was no question about it, I had had one glass too many. I started laughing and I was glad to see that both Bill and Alyssa were laughing with me.

"Samsara?" I said, "samsara is the Buddhist word for

everything, what the Christians call the *world,* what the Hebrews called *heaven and earth . . .*"

"I thought God lives in heaven," said Bill.

As suddenly as I had started laughing, I stopped. It was not the wine that had made me laugh, I saw that; and it was not the wine that had stopped me cold in front of what Bill had just said—without much weight in his words.

After a moment's silence, I said, "God dwells in heaven, yes, but God is not the same thing as heaven."

After another pause, Alyssa spoke, putting down the book she was holding, and quoting from the prophet Isaiah: "For the heavens shall vanish away like smoke, and the earth shall wax old like a garment, and they that dwell therein shall die, but my salvation shall be forever."

"You know the Bible very well," I said.

Bill started looking unhappy. I think he was suddenly feeling like an outsider, or maybe there was just too much religion for him, too much Bible. Or, if not that, perhaps too strange a use of the Bible. I began looking for a way to put the point we had come to in another language, a more scientific, psychological language, like that of Buddhism, for example.

Always, it is a daunting challenge to speak adequately about the way in life, to feel the scale of the teaching that opens man to conscious experience of the whole of human life, that rejects the false divisions and dualisms that have brought so much suffering and confusion to the world under the names of "good and evil," "soul and body," "heaven and earth," "spirit and matter"—in order to sense, feel, and know the real division between the movement inward and the movement outward and in order to grasp the immensity of the task that man is created for, the task of consciously experiencing these two movements everywhere and in everything—in love, in hate, in times of pleasure and in times of suffering, with our children, our friends, our enemies—in science and in art, in religion; in winning, losing and in "breaking even." In *everything,* everything *under the sun.*

AN UNEXPECTED EVENT

Whatever the cause of Bill's sudden unhappiness, he stood up and wobbled for a moment on his feet. Alyssa anxiously followed him with her eyes as he picked up a big stack of books and headed for the door.

"What are you doing?" I asked.

"I'm going home."

We watched him awkwardly open the door and heard him going down the outside steps to his car.

"Why is he doing this?" asked Alyssa.

"I don't know."

Bill returned and stuffed some papers in his briefcase. He picked up another stack of books and started again toward the door, books under one arm and briefcase in his other hand. Alyssa made a move to go after him, but remained in her place.

When he returned for the second time I saw that he was in an unusual emotional state.

"Bill, what is it, what's wrong?" said Alyssa. As for me, I was simply interested, very interested. What was going on in him? I remembered how he was when I first met him at the seminar and how quickly I had turned him from his dark mood by inviting him to lunch. I didn't want to try that again and, anyhow, in my guts I felt there was something else going on, something I wanted to understand and, even more important, something that Bill wanted to understand. He was unhappy, to be sure, but there was something else in him.

Yes, I began to see a little what it was. He was *trying* something, some inner exploration. There was something else in him alongside his bad mood. Why not honor that "something else," which was certainly more fragile and more important a part of him than the unhappy mood. And so, when I noticed that Alyssa was about to get up to soothe him, I gave her a barely perceptible little look that said "please let him be!"

What happened next neither I nor, almost certainly, Bill could have anticipated. Due in part, perhaps, to the fact that neither Alyssa nor I were overly solicitous toward him, his dark mood had grown in intensity to the point that his eyes were glistening with tears. At the same time, it was clear that he was passionately interested in the ideas we had been discussing with such an unusual attempt at impartiality and with such trust in each other's wish for truth. It thus became clear to me, just a moment before the event I am about to describe, that Bill himself was *in between* two opposing qualities of feeling: on the one hand, self-pity triggered by who-knows-what old childhood associations and, on the other hand, the wish for understanding. And although such a psychological state is not the same thing as being in between the two forces, it is certainly a foretaste of it, a glimpse of that purgatorial suffering we will all have to accept on the way to self-knowledge.

With a stiffening of his spine and with a bizarre smile playing on his lips, Bill picked up the mahogany box full of gold and handed it to me.

"This is for you," he said, his voice crackling.

"What do you mean?" I said, genuinely puzzled, although at the same time it was as though a great eagle had soared into my chest with the knowledge of what he was doing.

"It's a gift," he said.

Inside my chest, I calmly and instantly understood everything; I even understood, without any words, how to respond, how to feel. I sensed a quiet light and warmth coming down into me like the light of the sun. But in my mind there was pure chaos and bewilderment, and the muscles in my shoulders were suddenly filled with devils, tensions of every kind. I don't know what moved me to open the box, but I can remember my thoughts just before I saw the gold. Somehow, my head was telling me that I could coolly look at the gold and politely acknowledge it, as though I were being offered nothing more than a pound of chocolates.

The radiance of the gold blazed into my brain and a powerful bolt of electricity snaked down the length of my torso igniting everything in its path, especially in the region of the solar plexus and genitals. My legs started trembling as though filled with nervous little sparrows. My breathing became rough and coarse like the panting of a hungry wolf.

Who Am I?

Yes, it is one thing to speak about the state of being in between the two natures, but it is quite another thing to experience it at any level and in any conditions. I can give a rough picture of that state now, but while it was happening there was nothing in myself that could stand aside and comment on what was happening to me. On the one side there was this calm light moving as though in the fine interstices of my body, calling me gently. *It*—I should really speak of it as *I,* yet it was not I, not my personal self—*it* did not care one way or another about the gold; it neither wanted it, nor did it not want it. It wished only to be, to exist in me, to perceive. And it wanted from me only my attention so that it could enter me. Truly, it was gentle as a lamb.

Ah, but there on the other side, on the battlefield of hell, I was being torn apart by warring, all-consuming impulses. Had I not been seated, I would have fallen to the floor, so giddy and light-headed was I. "Take it! Take the gold!" a strong, euphoric voice urged me. "A half million dollars! And to him it's nothing! He's worth sixty-five million! He wants you to have it. He appreciates you. Accept the gift! Don't be a fool. Think of the good things you can do . . . etc. All your problems are over . . . etc. You owe it to him to accept it . . . etc. You deserve it . . . etc. and etc." I started fingering the gold coins like some comic-strip miser and my body thrilled to the feel and weight of them.

At the same time, a stern voice was shouting at me, "You must not! You haven't earned it! It's not yours! He's drunk! He's neurotic! You must not take advantage of him. And besides, Alyssa is watching. What will she think of you? Word will get out. What will people think of you? Don't do it! It's immoral, it's only money. Don't sell yourself!"

There were devils dressed as angels and devils dressed as devils warring within me. I call them both devils because the effect of this struggle was to pull my attention away from the fine, calm light circulating throughout my being. And there was this overwhelming sense that *I* had to make a choice—instantly and wisely.

I? Who was this *I* that had to rule and decide whether to do the "good" thing or the "bad" thing? Was this not the real chief of the demons, Asmodeus, taking on my face and lineaments? Wasn't this Iblis himself who refused to bow down to man when Allah created man? And he was right, this angel-turned-devil. It was not the True Man whom he refused to serve; his enmity was not directed toward the perfected man, but solely toward the deep ego, the deep lie that lives at the root of all the thousand other lies and illusions by which the energy of human consciousness is devoured. His task, this chief of demons, is to destroy the illusion of goodness and morality that causes the unperfected man to imagine he is close to God.

THE COIN OF GREATEST VALUE

This is the secret that Satan shares with God, and with no other. And under the dynamics of this secret—as it is said in the hidden recesses of all the great spiritual teachings of history—Satan, or Asmodeus, or Iblis, or the Trickster, or whatever he may be called, this "fallen angel" serves God with total, unswerving love and devotion!

But of course no such abstract thoughts could find their way into my consciousness at that moment. I remember looking directly into Bill's eyes and saying, in a deep voice that I hardly recognized as my own, "I can't accept this, Bill." At the very moment I uttered these words, that fine, calm light that had all but flickered out, suddenly grew very strong for a second, no more. But in that brief second there was *I am* in my presence. And I saw with unmistakable clarity where money resided in my being—I saw how deep down it was, deep down in my body, not so far from where the impulses of sex and survival lived.

I will not try to describe this moment further. I will not try to describe the extraordinary sense of joy and freedom that filled me. I will only say that I directly verified what I had suspected about the place that money occupies in the lives of many of us. I saw, at least in myself, that the passions and drives that surround the money question have been formed in us at the very roots of our personality and that there can be no such thing as authentic morality until we confront this fact in all its immensity. And until we do, we must live as we live, obeying the moral rules handed down to us, knowing that these rules do not speak to us from our own authentic conscience and that our chief aim must be to search in the midst of our lives for the conditions and companionship that can evoke in us the inner state in which conscience, which is the voice of *I am,* can be heard. The intellectual, social and psychophysical conditions that are necessary for this search, and the companions who can support it, comprise—in part, at least—what is meant by the way in life.

I closed the mahogany box and stood up on steady feet. I held it out for Bill to take. "Thank you," I said.

Bill took the box and, looking over to Alyssa, put it back on the table. He, too, was now calm and balanced. Instead of leaving, he sat down again on the couch. Alyssa quietly went into the kitchen to make coffee.

PART III

THE

INDEFINABLE

SOMETHING

THAT

ENTERS

INTO

EVERYTHING

21.

THE HIDDEN KEY

When I began this book, I had intended to limit my study to our lives as individuals and all the dilemmas and difficulties that each of us faces more or less on our own—in our family life, on our jobs, tangled in our technologies, burdened by our possessions, straining after self-respect and a sense of personal worth. I had not intended to speak on the scale of nations and the peoples of the world. And if I now offer some thoughts along such lines, it is only because, when I started this book, I did not appreciate the extent to which our attitude toward money serves as the key to understanding every aspect of our present lives and concerns. I thought I already knew how deeply and intimately money enters into areas that we might have imagined as essentially independent of it—areas of human life which economists and anthropologists refer to as "non-monetized," such as kinship, creative thought and expression, or religious belief. But only a few days ago I discovered again, with new and startling clarity, not only how true this thesis is, but what it entails on a global and planetary scale.

An Encounter in Pacific Heights

The scene is a mansion in Pacific Heights, San Francisco's most elegant neighborhood. I am seated with twenty men and women at a large dining table laid with Belgian lace, layers of Coalport china, and a forest of multicolored crystal stemware. Through the panoramic window, San Francisco Bay gleams in the sunlight below us, studded with white sails and ornamented by the Golden Gate Bridge, with thousands of sparkling automobiles streaming across it in both directions.

Across from me is Jerry Brown, former Governor of California; two places over from him is the distinguished sociologist Robert Bellah and two places in the other direction is Michael Murphy, president of Esalen Institute. Two places to my right is Mary Metz, then president of Mills College, and to her right is Jay Ogilvy, a philosopher and business executive. Others at the table include Don Johnson, noted for his bodywork and spirituality workshops, and James Garrison, head of a Soviet-American trade organization. At the end of the table is our host, Rupert Hills, owner of one of San Francisco's business empires (Hills Brothers Coffee); and at the far end sits the guest of honor whom I am here to meet. He is none other than Ivan Timofeyevich Frolov, Editor-in-Chief of *Pravda,* a close confidant of Mikhail Gorbachev and one of the principal agents in the creation of the Russia that is now struggling to be born.

Under Michael and Dulce Murphy's leadership, Esalen Institute has for some years been working to open a channel of communication between the United States and the Soviet

Union, based not on military and political considerations, but on the exchange of ideas about man—ideas which, for better or worse, are now lumped under the sobriquet of "the human potential movement."

This is meant to be more than a social luncheon. After the meal, each of the invited experts is obliged to give a brief presentation about his work, to which Mr. Frolov will reply. I've been brought here by my old friend Mike Murphy because of the book I'm writing about the philosophy of money and because the new Russia is suddenly facing the money question with a vengeance—a vast nation seeking to shake off its totalitarian chains and trying to step forward into the global marketplace with very little to sell that the world wants; a nation that would pass abruptly from basing its power on fear to basing its power on desire.

Mr. Frolov was sitting too far away for me to hear his conversation during the meal, but I kept watching him and exchanging smiles with him. I had never met a Soviet official before, far less someone so close to the leadership of what only yesterday had been for us in the West the most feared political and military force in the world. Hadn't we all grown up under the same nightmare of the atomic bomb, the same images of death and total destruction at the hands of the Russians? Was I supposed to just set that aside? And who was this young Russian sitting next to me who spoke no English? Was he perhaps carrying a gun?

WHAT IS RUSSIA?

I tried looking intently at Frolov without appearing rude. His was not a harsh face—quite the contrary. He was about my age—brownish-gray hair, stocky build, soft gray eyes behind professorial rimless eyeglasses. He seemed relaxed and genial, especially as compared to ex-Governor Brown, who was aggressively pushing several conversations at once across from me. Frolov was probably as close as I would ever come to directly experiencing this archetype called "Russian" that had terrorized a part of my mind almost all the years of my life. I alternated between trying to discern something ruthless behind the surface of Mr. Frolov's face, and trying to see a warm fellow human. Maybe it was due to my own Russian ancestry, but I couldn't call up the fear—much, strange to say, as I wanted to. I eventually let it all go and started simply enjoying the lunch, forgetting that for me (and for many of us) the Russian character is a grippingly incomprehensible factor determining the very fate of the earth.

As the meal ended, the more structured part of the program began. Robert Bellah led off with an eloquent and insightful commentary about the threatened traditions of individual expression in the United States and, speaking through a simultaneous interpreter, Frolov unhurriedly replied that the same issues were now in the forefront in the Soviet Union. Stalinism, he said, had been a falsification of the Marxist vision, resulting in an authoritarian bureaucracy that suppressed individual expression.

My ears pricked up when he spoke of the importance in his own education of the writings of the nineteenth-century mystical theologian Vladimir Solovyev and the writings of Dostoyevsky, especially the figure of Father Zossima in *The Brothers Karamazov*. Solovyev and the character of Zossima point to the spirituality of Eastern Orthodox Christianity which, in certain of its forms, expresses the very deepest vision of man's search for the inner world of the soul. How, I wondered, does a leading Marxist theoretician reconcile Communism with a vision of human nature that places all economic and political considerations in a strictly secondary position? Is there some typically Russian religious fantasy at work here?—comparable in its way to the Western Calvinistic fantasy that bred the distortions of capitalism? Again the question: what is Russia?

DEMOCRACY AND MONEY

Ex-Governor Jerry Brown then took the floor a few paces away from the table. I knew that for the past year or so, he had been exerting his considerable political talents in an effort to rebuild the California Democratic Party, and I was afraid his remarks now might be only the self-serving rhetoric of the typical American politician. But, in fact, what he brought was extremely interesting.

The essence of politics, he said, is communication. In today's world, however, the ability to communicate requires access to mass media and this costs millions and millions of dollars. In politics, he said, the problem is not so much *what* you communicate, but where you get the money that is needed in order to communicate. Those who can provide the money inevitably stand for special interests that do not correspond to the needs of the people as a whole. When a very small minority controls access to the means of communication, the politician is obliged to please one or another of these small groups—banks, for example, or large business interests of various kinds. So today, more than ever, the problem of democracy is how to save the people if they don't or won't pay to be saved. The laws that now restrict the amount of money politicians can get are of no help as long as there are no laws that restrict the cost of television time. In sum, he concluded, democracy in America depends upon bribery. The term "bribery" describes three-quarters of the activities of all politicians in the United States. "Democracy depends on control of money."

AMERICAN REALISM

As Frolov was preparing to reply to this, I was able to exchange a few words with the person sitting to my right. He was disgusted by what he had just heard. "How could he say such things?" he whispered, while the former governor remained standing near the window. From his accent, I guessed—rightly as I later discovered—that he was German. "But what he said is very accurate," I said. "In a way, it's refreshingly honest." The German gave me a politely contemptuous look. It was then that I began to wonder if the way different nationalities regarded money might be a key to understanding them as people. I recalled some frustrating dealings I had had in the past with European publishers, frustrating as compared to what I had learned to appreciate in the way American publishers candidly based their decisions on "the bottom line," although this obviously can go too far. After outgrowing my adolescent "artist's fantasy" that whatever I wrote deserved to be published, I began to understand the business aspect of publishing as representing a precious and real factor in my relationship to my fellow man. I had experienced much more frustration with some European editors who professed a high idealism but who had to be businessmen as well. They were compelled to cover it over, as though considering the money factor to be something dirty.

WHO IS THIS RUSSIAN?

These thoughts made me all the more interested in how the Russian, Frolov, would respond to the former governor's candid, and very American, comments. Frolov—with continuing intelligence and good humor—spoke from a historical point of view about the need for more than one party in the Soviet Union and of the accompanying danger of having too many political parties. He talked for a fairly long time and then stopped without ever once mentioning the money question that had been the main point of Jerry Brown's remarks. This intrigued me. Was this omission due only to the precarious financial structure of present-day Russia—to the fact that, from an international perspective, the Soviet Union actually had practically no money, the ruble being one of the world's most internally overvalued and unstable currencies? Or was something deeper at issue, something more revealing of the Russian character?

The discussion moved into the salon. On the way, I was informed that I would be the last one to speak and I was asked to summarize briefly my research about the role of money in contemporary life. "Remember," I was told, "Frolov is a trained philosopher. He loves to explore ideas and he wants to hear from American philosophers."

In the intimacy of the salon, I was seated in a soft leather armchair directly across from Frolov, practically within arm's reach. He seemed surprisingly happy sunk into the lush, floral upholstery of a decorator sofa in a millionaire's drawing room. But the rugged planes of his face, the rimless eyeglasses, and the dense volumes of his body reminded me that this was not his natural environment. I couldn't help thinking of the scenes from Tolstoy's *War and Peace* which portrayed the Russian intelligentsia and upper classes straining to be more French than the French. And I remembered even more sharply G. I. Gurdjieff's portrait of the Russian character in *Beelzebub's Tales to His Grandson*. In that book, the "Russian" is presented as a joining of two completely disparate elements: the healthy essence of the tribal Asiatic overlaid by the persona of a hyper-cultivated European.

At the same time, Jerry Brown's observations about the relationship of democracy and money still rang in my mind. Democracy depends on the control of money, he had said. Was it not also partly true that—as someone else had once cuttingly observed—the mission of America in the modern world had been "to make the world safe for money"? But, even more striking to me—seeing this strong Russian presence before me within the very moneyed environment the Communist system was once pledged to overcome—was the sobering possibility that money itself had become the new basis and meaning of democracy. After all, wasn't the new global financial interdependency of the world's nations finally bringing the world together? Weren't money and money concerns the one thing we all had in common, the one area where we all understood each other, the realm, the concern to which all other human concerns were being reduced?

The passage from barter to money was a movement toward the quantification of life, reducing the qualitative differences inherent in the world around us to a single uniform measure. From being a convenience, money had become a determiner, a definer of worth and value. And this had also happened among people in their relations. Yet although people began to share the same kind of money problems, this newly arisen common factor in our experience had not lessened our conflicts and our differences; it had only linked them inextricably with money.

To know ourselves and to know each other, it had now become necessary to understand how each of us as individuals deals with money. Our relationship to money had become a key to our individual personalities and natures. Was the same thing true now among the nations of the world as they all entered into the one global marketplace? With this in mind, I asked myself: who is this *"Russian"* that I had feared for so long, and to whom I had also felt this deep attraction in his darkly beautiful emotionalism and spirituality?

First to speak in the salon was Don Johnson. He asked Frolov about the rising interest in Russia in esoteric and mystical spirituality, meditation, myth, bodywork, spiritual healing methods, out-of-body experiences—in short, all the things that some people in America regard as comprising a "spiritual revolution," and which others condemn as the new narcissism and which still others—myself included—view as a phenomenon offering our culture a bewildering mixture of real hope and false dreams.

Frolov's reply only heightened my wish to understand "Russianness." He began by saying there was considerable interest in such things in the Soviet Union and that the Institute of Man, of which he was Director, was engaged in studying them. I was a little startled by this admission—I still get surprised whenever I see the "New Age" being taken seriously in other parts of the world. Surprised—and disappointed. I would like to hope that there exist big forces of common sense in the world, a skepticism, and even a certain honest narrowness that can help to separate out the fantasy element in the "spiritual revolution" so that, little by little, what is authentically revolutionary can be heard by whoever has ears to hear. Truth is always revolutionary, always a shock. But when truth becomes mixed with fantasies, associated with subjective interpretations, it becomes comfortable. Surely, Soviet Marxism could not easily accept the whole package of "New Age" spirituality!

I was somewhat relieved when Frolov explained further that the subjects being studied were psychic phenomena of various kinds, as manifestations of the riddle of human nature. That was fine. The attitude he communicated was that of a good old-fashioned scientific materialist trying to be open to whatever phenomena appeared. It was not really a turning away from enlightened materialism toward acceptance of ancient teachings about consciousness that, taken seriously, completely undermined Marxist materialist philosophy.

However, the way Frolov spoke of "scientific investigation" intrigued me further. Was it possible that the Russian vision of science was itself a sort of religious fantasy, a sort of idealistic fantasy as out of touch with the real laws of universal reality as any California dream? I had long since been struck by how rare it now is to find deeply sensitive but equally tough-minded scientists and businessmen in Western society. Was I about to be equally disillusioned about the rest of the world? Were Marxist materialists who saw clearly the overwhelming power of bodily needs and material forces, who exposed the hypocrisy and secondariness of most so-called religion and morality—were they disappearing as well? Was there no one left to put an honest challenge to the metaphysical worldview to keep it from slipping into dreams?

No wonder King Solomon was interested in Asmodeus! Without him, how would he have ever found the real resistance to the deceptions of his so-called piety and wealth? And without confronting that resistance, how would he have ever become emptied of identification with the ego?

The way Frolov then spoke seemed to confirm my suspicions that a quasi-religious passion was somewhere at the root of Russian materialism. Smiling benignly at us, he spoke of his mother as a devoutly religious woman and revealed that his grandmother had been a "sorceress." It was believed that she, his grandmother, would at times fly up through the chimney into the sky!

With a more serious countenance, he reported how in his village women would bring their colicky babies to his grandmother, who would quiet them by saying some special words. As Frolov spoke of these things, it was clear by his attitude that he wished to convey a warm, scientific objectivity toward all and any aspects of human nature, without implying that he believed in anything supernatural. As though to make sure we grasped this attitude, he cited Tolstoy's remarkable confession, written at the peak of his success, that the question of the meaning of life had become more urgent to him than living itself, a passage that I myself had long carried in my mind as the quintessential expression of the upsurge in man of the spiritual search. When I interrupted by completing the passage from Tolstoy, Frolov seemed happily surprised. Our eyes met for an instant, rather strongly.

THE GLOBAL MARKETPLACE

Jay Ogilvy then spoke, a trained philosopher now involved in global business networking. "We are moving toward a marketplace world," said Ogilvy, "in which mankind is becoming free of the sort of idealistic or nationalistic goals and aims that have characterized civilizations in the past. We are moving toward planetary *goal-lessness.*" By this term "goal-lessness," Ogilvy meant something positive and benign—not at all what is usually characterized by "aimlessness." He felt that the vast international scale on which money was now being exchanged had itself become a force which would bring the world together without one nation being able to impose its "goals" on others. The complex checks and balances of a world marketplace where getting and spending money is the common motivation would free mankind to "just live." It sounded to me like the old raw, capitalistic faith in the forces of the marketplace not only to establish price, but to establish true human values as well.

THE INVISIBLE HAND

I wondered if Frolov was hearing the same sort of thing I was hearing. Wasn't this Adam Smith's Invisible Hand applied now to the whole world, the idea that the interaction of the forces of human self-interest is actually the instrument of the Divine Will? Wasn't this precisely the philosophy that Marx and Lenin saw as underlying the injustices of unrestrained capitalism and which it was their mission to destroy? And wasn't there something indelibly *American* about it—as expressed, for example, in the nineteenth century by Ralph Waldo Emerson even more articulately than by Benjamin Franklin, who also raised it to a metaphysical and psychospiritual principle. "The laws of nature," wrote Emerson, "play through trade, as a toy-battery exhibits the effects of electricity. The level of the sea is not more surely kept, than is the equilibrium of value in a society, by the demand and supply. . . . The counting-room maxims liberally expounded are laws of the universe. . . ."*

Emerson was certainly the quintessential American when he argued both that the laws of the universe are spiritual rather than mechanistic, and that these laws play themselves out most clearly and exactingly in an economic system where the virtues of self-reliance, common sense, and hard work bring material wealth. "Do not legislate," he writes. "Give no bounties: make equal laws: secure life and property, and you need not give alms. Open the doors of opportunity to talent and virtue, and they will do themselves justice, and property will not be in bad hands. In a free and just commonwealth, property rushes from the idle and imbecile, to the industrious, brave, and persevering."

And it is surely an expression of the American vision, the

---

* These and the following citations are from Emerson's essay "Wealth."

American *type,* to conclude by defining wealth in interior terms: "Wealth is mental; wealth is moral," says Emerson. *"Man is born to be rich."* Wealth consists in the expression and cultivation of man's intrinsic power to be in active relationship to the whole of reality, the whole of nature. To be rich, for Emerson, is to exercise man's unique capacity for knowledge and love as ends in themselves. Material prosperity and, therefore, money, are but means to the development of man's inner capacities for consciousness and compassion.

If Max Weber had found in Benjamin Franklin the sacralization of man's material life, how much more might he have found it in Ralph Waldo Emerson! And here was a contemporary American philosopher, Jay Ogilvy, standing on California's metaphysical soil, engaged not in academic pursuits, but in global financial consulting—here was an American philosopher proposing to globalize this American-ness to a leading representative of a nation that until now had been the principal counterforce to everything American in the world!

RUSSIA AND MONEY

Frolov's reply went to the heart of the matter. "In Russia," he said, "there is no memory of a marketplace. We have no history of the marketplace. In the Russian psyche there is no mythology of the marketplace." His deliberate repetition of the word "marketplace" lifted it out of its ordinary associations for me, and in fact gave it a sort of mythic dimension. It was *our* myth, my myth, my metaphysical category. "You have to understand the Russian attitude toward work," he went on. "Lenin knew this and wrote about it. For the Russian, work, labor, is a punishment. It has been that from which the Russian seeks to be free. The Russian bears a long, long history of serfdom as a form of slavery. . . ."

In a flash, I grasped—that is to say, I felt—why the tide of communism swept through Russia on the issue of work and labor. But Frolov went on:

"The Russians want the things you have in America. But they don't understand how much you have had to work to get these things. They don't want to work so hard."

In Russia, money does not mean enough! I honestly don't remember whether I only thought these words to myself or whether I said them out loud. I only remember that suddenly all eyes were on me. It was my turn to speak. I was told that Frolov had another appointment. I had only a few moments to put my question.

Despite the pressure of time, I took a moment to gather my thoughts. Then I looked directly at Frolov. Again, there was a strong, wordless sense of exchange between us.

"I'm a professor of philosophy and comparative religion," I said. I heard the deep voice of the interpreter as though from a distance. There was only Frolov for me. "I study the ancient teachings of all cultures, the teachings that have guided man's life on earth everywhere and at all times. But my special interest, my own passion, has been to see how these sacred ideas— these great *metaphysical* ideas—" (I corrected myself and Frolov nodded in assent when I changed the word "sacred" to "metaphysical") "—can help us to understand and live now and here in the conditions of modern society. I'm not an antiquarian. . . ."

Aha! A serious silence was now in the drawing room. It had to do not so much with the words, but with the seriousness of intent—or, yes, with the fact that I was talking directly to the man, not to the official. At the same time, the words were important.

I continued: "I want to understand what, precisely, it is

in ourselves that prevents great truth from penetrating into our lives and which therefore prevents us from acting ethically in the only real sense of the word. Ethically means acting and being in the service of what is the true greatness of oneself as man. I've studied many aspects of our culture from this perspective—science, education, medicine, religion. But now I see that in our society, in our world, it is our relation to money that needs to be understood. If great truth does not enter into our relation to money, it cannot enter into our lives."

Frolov looked at me with simplicity and directness. "It is the most important thing," he said.

I detected in the room a little nervousness from the Americans about Frolov's schedule; some watches were being looked at. But not from the Russians. Their emotions were touched. They were Russians. We were Americans. We were concerned about schedules. They were not.

But how to go on? I had to say more. Perhaps I should have let the silence continue. Perhaps a genuinely miraculous exchange would have developed. But I gave in to the sense of time pressure.

"In my class at the university," I said, "I told my students I would be meeting you. I asked them what they would like me to speak to you about. They told me to ask you about the younger generation in Russia."

Frolov seemed both relieved and, perhaps, a little disappointed at this question. He became genial again. But obviously the rich atmosphere of self-inquiry had dissipated.

"Ah," he said, smiling paternally, "we simply do not understand our young people." Everyone laughed together at this, the common problem, and suddenly everyone felt free to move and chatter. The Russians rose from their places, friendly good-byes were exchanged, and the meeting was over.

THE HIDDEN KEY

I stayed in my place and reflected. It was clear—we Americans were about to find our relation to the Russians on the basis of money. And I, for my part, understood something about them now in a way that I never had before. They did not take money seriously enough—they did not wish to give all their energy to money, working for money. I know that trait quite well; it is in me, too.

But do the Russians really want their young people to value money like we do? Why should the Russians work like the Americans? Are we going to have a world of American capitalists, Russian capitalists, Japanese capitalists, German capitalists—for God's sake, Navajo capitalists, Tibetan capitalists? Wasn't it enough to have all of America and Europe homogenized under the sway of the money game?

Is this the unity of the family of man?

I walked back toward my car alone and in a turmoil of conflicting thoughts and moods. I was elated that the meeting with the Russian had confirmed my sense that the study of our relationship to money is the hidden key to seeing ourselves as we really are.

But I couldn't help feeling sobered by *what* we all were. I thought of how Gurdjieff had seen the nations of the world—America, France, Russia, England; how he had seen the patterns by which the nations each fell away from their essence, their organic inner uniqueness.

In *Beelzebub's Tales to His Grandson* Gurdjieff speaks with warmth of America's inner possibilities, but observes that one of the chief factors that have already all but destroyed these possibilities is how we teach our children to behave with money.

And, surely, it is true. Weren't most of us sternly admonished at a very tender age to save our money, to be so very careful with it—to such an extent that we grew up feeling, if not consciously thinking, that our relationship to money was the source of our virtue and worthiness as a human being? For many of us, money was the most real thing in life, and therefore the most sacred thing.

Since what is real is the same as what is sacred, in our guts—in our "unconscious"—reality had the contours of the merely mental, that which we can control by calculation, "saving." This is no longer even the "spirit of capitalism" that Max Weber had identified, no longer even the deterioration and degradation of a religious passion. This "saving money" is already the bourgeois ego, the ant-mind. Give me a Benjamin Franklin to that anytime! Give me the early American struggling, however blindly and pseudo-monkishly, to overcome desire, to the insectlike calculation of the child's savings account! It is a corruption of a corruption! No, it is not that we modern Americans are "greedy materialists"—it is that we locate our sense of self in the automatic, logical mind. It is not simply that we prefer money to God, it is that our sense of self gravitates to a part of ourselves that cannot experience God. That is what we do when we insist on, in Gurdjieff's language, "dollar savings banks" for children.

Each nation has its own way of turning away from Truth and Being, but all nations and all peoples are in each one of us as well. In a large, overall sense, Americans are Americans— we have our dominant coloration, we are a historical "type"; but I have a Russian inside me, too, and an Englishman, an Arab, and a Japanese. I have a "Russian" who would rather "drink vodka"—that is, whose body likes pleasant dreams and whose mind passively submits to all sorts of alien "European" complications; I have an "Englishman" who is hypnotized by form, a "Japanese" in the thrall of authority, a "German" inventor, an "Arab" believer, and so on through all the peoples of the world with their typical formations by which the inner movement toward openness to Being is obstructed in them. And in the world we now live in, all of these typicalities will be expressed through varying relationships to the invention called money. We cannot study ourselves, as we are, nor therefore can we understand our neighbor, without calmly observing our own selves in the thick of the money game.

WHAT DO WE TEACH OUR CHILDREN?

Let us therefore try to consider what we are teaching our children to be when we teach them about money! How we ourselves behave toward money—and how we teach them to behave toward money—has momentous consequences for their further inner development, as it has for our own relationship to life. In the world they will grow into (our present society), money factors will, for most of them, be what tests or proves their values and authenticity. It will be the main arena where they can take risks and confront the vagaries of life, the shocks and satisfactions that are meted out to every human being.

At the same time, this monetized world that they will enter is not the great world of nature and nature's laws. It is a mixed world where cosmic laws of nature are in many ways covered over and obscured by mental invention, the mental technology of finance. Our children will, at least unconsciously, sense that how a person behaves toward money is a true test of authenticity—but can we help them also to sense that a man or woman ought to be tested by much wider challenges than can be found in the monetized world of contemporary life? *That money is where most of us are tested says precisely as much about the weakness of man as it does about the power of money.*

How can we convey this to our children? How can we convey to them—and to the developing being within ourselves—that in order to obtain the most serious good of life, it is necessary to give exactly the right amount of attention to the aspect of life represented by money? Can we and they grow to be attentive to what is secondary in human life while being deeply attentive to what is primary? For, if we do not give sufficient attention to what is secondary in life, then, sooner or later, what is secondary will take all our attention and leave us no energy or time to pursue what is most essential. We must give the devil his due—no more, but also no less. "Render unto Caesar that which is Caesar's." We are not angels. We are human beings. We are built to occupy two worlds simultaneously and in so doing to build within ourselves what has been called "the third world of man."

What, then, can we do for our children? First, of course, we must realize that they are watching us very carefully. With them, it is not only what we say about money, but what we do, how we *are* when money is at issue. They will see quite clearly what areas of human life we convert to a money question, what we associate with money. It is imperative that in our relationships with each other and with the world, we show them there is something that is independent of money and that this something is of first importance. Here, no pretense is possible. It must be true for us or it will not be true for them. There must be something in our lives that we really and tangibly take more seriously than money—and it must be something that really and tangibly, metaphysically, *is* more serious than money.

What could that something be? It cannot be what we usually call "morality" or "spirituality." The whole burden of this book has been to show that in the conditions of modern life the perennial values that we would represent by such words have been contaminated by egoistic desires or, at best, alienated from the essential aspects of ourselves. For most of us, the only thing that can actually be more important than money, and that actually is connected to what is objectively higher in ourselves than all our other parts, is the search for the truth about ourselves as we are.

In practice, this can only mean that we respect truth more than anything, even if that truth be unpleasant or unflattering. It is how we are toward the truth about ourselves that will be the most significant influence on our children—not only in what we say, but how we actually are.

The question of how to be toward our children therefore leads us back to the central question of how to be toward ourselves in the midst of the monetized world we live in. Can we find a new attitude toward the problems of life in this monetized world, an attitude that faithfully reflects the great teachings of the past? Can we translate the ideas in these teachings into terms that are applicable to our life as it is—now and here?

MEANINGFUL WORK

Take, for example, the question of "selling out." It is more and more a source of suffering for modern people who feel they must compromise what they consider sacred or morally obligatory in order to satisfy their material needs, and are thus prevented from respecting themselves. There are relatively few people nowadays for whom the making of money is in itself considered honorable or noble in any way. Earlier generations in America placed considerable moral value on an individual's ability to "make his own way," to "stand on his own feet," almost without regard to what sort of work one did. But now more and more people yearn for work that is in itself "meaningful." They feel unable to bear the psychological stress (the "hell") of a job—especially in an office—when the reward is "only" money.

People want to serve some greater good, some immediate human need—*and* get paid for it. They find it impossible to respect themselves if they are giving most· of their time to helping to produce and sell products or services that do not correspond to deeper human values. Yet earn money one must, and this usually translates into becoming enmeshed in the tense, complex network of forces that characterize the money game upon which the current social order is based.

It is, of course, an age-old problem. It is Faust selling his soul to the devil. Isn't it obvious that it is nobler to assist the poor, to teach children, to help save the environment, than it is to write advertising copy, say, for a high-tech electronics firm, or to plot marketing strategies for a new line of soft drinks, or to manage investment portfolios for the rich?

But in the light of all that has been said in this book, the question of self-respect cannot be posed so simply or naively. The wheel of samsara, the hell in Buddhist imagery, can show us scenes of all kinds, including men and women "doing good." One can "do good" with such agitation, violence, and hidden egoism, or with such dreaming self-satisfaction, that in certain essential aspects one's life proceeds no differently than that of an individual caught up in the most degrading or trivial of activities. How much of the gross evil in the world is due, in its origin, to people "doing good" in such a way that their actions almost have—sooner or later—the effects of an intentionally villainous act?

This is not cynicism, nor is it a palliative justification to keep us turning the wheels of a corrupt society. It is an obvious fact of world and individual history. Who does more good—a man or woman with inner freedom selling a pair of shoes, or a madly self-righteous prophet blind to all the humanly destructive effects of his "good deeds"? The question of self-respect cannot be separated from the inner state of man. What is there to respect in ourselves when we are not only devoured by our activity, but also regard this condition of inner slavery as a mark of our superiority?

TWO KINDS OF SELF-RESPECT

Our question becomes: what do we respect when we respect our *self*? It is very difficult to answer this question in a world where traditional inner values are so penetrated by the money factor. We see quite clearly that most of us cannot help but respect people with money. Theoretically, when we are alone in our rooms, we may acknowledge that it is foolish to defer to a person just because he is rich, but in fact when we are with that person we cannot help ourselves. And it is a fact that our culture generally expresses its appreciation of people by the amount of money it pays them.

To accept this as a fact about ourselves is, I think, the beginning of real self-respect. The point is that we are two-natured beings, and the road to real self-respect starts from understanding that there are two kinds of self-respect, two selves in us, each of which needs to be valued in the manner and to the degree appropriate to it. Money is, at the present moment in history, the principal means by which we attain respect from others and is therefore the principal means of social self-respect. The question is—how to identify in our being that other self, that other inner consciousness which has nothing to do with the opinion that the world has of us?

The hard truth is that this higher self can no longer automatically be identified with such things as artistic creativity, scientific study, altruistic action, or family relationships—so enmeshed has everything become with money, and what is associated with money. The artist starving in his garret no longer even symbolizes the pursuit of values higher than what the social world recognizes. Today's artist must be a businessman, even in his own eyes. If he turns away from the question of selling his art, he is turning away from part of his own reality as a human being. Every human being needs to be appreciated.

Then where to find the seed of the inner self? What can allow us to respect ourselves independently of money? It is the thesis of this book that the effort of seeing the truth, no matter what that truth is, is the real seed of the higher self; and this effort we can make—no matter what life hands us.

The effort to see the truth can and must be an effort independent of everything else, and when a man or woman makes this effort and persists in it, a certain self-respect begins to appear that has a remarkably different "taste" than the social self-respect we all crave so much.

One cannot "sell out" ideals that are already compromised in one's thinking and conditioning. It is surely not "selling out" when one is compelled to give one's time and energy to material obligations. But in principle nothing, no force on earth, can compel a man or woman to be less than sincere with himself or herself. Sincerity is, in its origin, a power of the mind that can exist under any conditions of life. All that is needed is a basic discrimination between what is actually within one's power and what is not.

Modern man has become a deeply and unnecessarily lonely being. Our moral ideals, our sense of inner worth, have been radically and unnecessarily ripped away from all the forces in the universe that draw conscious beings upward and toward each other. Human beings are built to be in intentional relation to each other not only as biosocial mechanisms, but as creatures within whom there exists the seed of an openness toward the source of all Being. This openness to Being begins as a direction of the attention that is completely other than all the biosocial impulses within us which, taken together, make up our usual sense of selfhood, the biosocial self, or "ego." Authentically human self-respect, an authentically human sense of self-worth, can never come from the ego alone, from the outward movement alone. Self-respect in its authentic form is based on awareness of something within ourselves that is completely independent of the ego and the body.

THE MEANING OF INDEPENDENCE

The only independent element in our selves is the attention of our mind—not our passing thoughts, but the force of attention that is obscurely linked with our thoughts. This is why all great spiritual disciplines are rooted in the understanding of the attention factor in human life and seek always to develop in man a stronger and more enduring quality of independent attention. The ancient philosophers, such as the Stoics, based their whole teaching on the cultivation of independent attention; and there has been no more articulate philosophy than Stoicism on the subject of authentic self-respect.*

Two of the greatest exponents of this view of self-respect were Marcus Aurelius and Epictetus. The former was the Emperor of Rome, the wealthiest and most powerful man on earth,

---

* In modern times, the great American philosopher and psychologist William James spoke of the power of attention as the only aspect of human nature for which we are truly responsible. Like the ancient Stoics, he suggested that all morality, all ethics, is founded on how human beings direct their attention. It is the only aspect of our being which is unconditioned by social or biological influences. See Chapter XXVI, "Will," in James' *Psychology, Briefer Course*.

and the latter was a Roman slave. Both the emperor and the
slave saw self-respect in the same way:

> If thou wilt separate, I say, from thy ruling faculty the
> things which are attached to it by the impressions of sense,
> and the things of time to come and of time that is past
> . . . and if thou shalt strive to live only what is really thy
> life, that is, the present—then thou wilt be able to pass
> that portion of life which remains for thee up to the time
> of thy death free from perturbations, nobly and obedient
> to the god that is within thee.
>
> (The Thoughts of the Emperor Marcus Aurelius Antoninus,
> Book II, #3, trans. George Long. Philadelphia: Henry
> Altemus, p. 291)

As was fitting, therefore, the gods have put under our
control only the most excellent faculty of all and that which
dominates the rest, namely, the power to make correct use
of external impressions, but all the others they have not
put under our control. Was it indeed because they would
not? I for one think that had they been able they would
have entrusted us with the others also; but they were quite
unable to do that. For since we are on earth and trammeled
by an earthy body and by earthy associates, how was it
possible that, in respect of them, we should not be hampered by external things?

But what says Zeus? "Epictetus, had it been possible I
should have made both this paltry body and this small estate
of thine free and unhampered. But as it is—let it not escape
thee—this body is not thine own, but only clay cunningly
compounded. Yet since I could not give thee this, we have
given thee a certain portion of ourself, this faculty of choice
and refusal, of desire and aversion, or, in a word, the faculty which makes use of external impressions; if thou care

for this and place all that thou hast therein, thou shalt never be thwarted, never hampered, shall not groan, shall not blame, shall not flatter any man."

(*Epictetus,* trans. W. A. Oldfather. Cambridge, Mass.: Harvard University Press, Vol. I, pp. 10–11)

Therefore, to the question, "How can I know when I am 'selling out'?" the only reply is to begin the search for an independent attention in oneself that is not ruled by the ego. It means that inwardly one becomes an "intentional slave"— that is, a human being intentionally aware of all the contradictions and compromises that actually make up our social self, or ego. That in us which can accept these facts about ourselves— *that* fleeting and fragile independent attention of the mind and heart is precisely the seed of what can develop into the authentic self. The only true "selling out" is when we turn away from truth. We are at present powerless to make significant changes in the moral and metaphysical quality of our lives, but we have the power to try to be sincere, to try to see ourselves as we are. It is that power in ourselves which we can respect.

MONEY AS AN INSTRUMENT FOR EXERCISING SINCERITY

It is a power that can grow. And there is no aspect of human life better suited than money to provide occasions for us to begin exercising that power. Seen in this context, money can be treated as an instrument for exercising our sincerity. Thus, from being an instrument of the "devil," money becomes an instrument of the search for truth. In this way one escapes from "hell" and enters "purgatory." In this way, a life crowded with demands and anxiety suddenly has a margin of space and moments of human time.

And now one begins to see the whole human condition in a way that is acutely understandable to the modern mind. Almost all that the philosophers and spiritual teachers of the past have said about man's life on earth now is translated into aspects of the money question. When, for example, St. Paul cries out, "The good that I would do, that I do not; and that which I hate, that I do," he is expressing the fundamental human dilemma that we do not act according to what we inwardly know is good. In modern life, this human condition needs to be studied and faced in the realm of our dealings with money. Not changed—but seen, faced, studied with sincerity.

And when the sages of old say that the world of the senses, the physical world around us which we believe in so implicitly, is not the real world, when they speak of a reality beyond the world we ordinarily perceive, we can translate it into the idea of a reality not subject to the forces of money. This is not to trivialize the ancient doctrine of an invisible reality; it is only to make this idea practical in our actual lives. Theoretically, philosophically, I may be quite willing to accept that there is a higher reality, even to accept that the physical objects in the world are in some sense illusory, to accept that even my sensations of pleasure and pain are fundamentally deceptive.

But when it comes to money—ah, that is usually quite a different matter. When I must pay the mortgage, or respond to a request for a loan, it is not so simple to treat it as "unreal." No, we are obliged, compelled by the emotions related to money. Everywhere it is still understood, often even more forcefully than in matters of illness and death, as representing the "real world"—the "bottom line."

22.

CONCLUSION:

PERSONAL GAIN
AND THE
GIFT OF EXISTENCE

We come to the conclusion that money is so central in our lives because it now embodies most clearly the central problem of man's life on earth—the dominance of the principle of personal gain. The great teachers of the world have always spoken of this as man's main weakness. The ancient and timeless doctrines tell us that we human beings are meant to serve something greater than ourselves—in that alone consists our happiness and our well-being on earth and beyond the earth. But through some profound misperception or inner weakness—what the East calls illusion, or what the West calls sin—mankind continually lives to favor only the biosocial aspects of his nature. He has been given ideas that convince him he is meant for something greater, but in fact he lives in opposition to that conviction. Man is not aware that the principle of personal gain is much subtler, much more powerful than he imagines. He is not aware that it concerns far more than outer behavior alone. He is not aware that what he wrongly identifies as his ruling principle, his ordinary mind, is not the real instrument of service to the Higher.

I remember as a child how strange the idea of sacrifice and service always seemed to me. It seemed against nature, illogical. Perhaps it lies in the essential nature of a small child that one sees and feels everything in terms of one's own personal wants and needs, just as in the Buddhist idea of the "animal hell" all creatures strive only for their own satisfaction and survival. As I grew up and was exposed to religious and ethical ideals of self-sacrifice, and began to appreciate them, I was depressed by what I sensed as the hypocrisy of people professing these ideals. In any case, although surrounded by self-sacrificing actions in my childhood, I was unable to relate them to my own aims in life.

THE GIFT AND THE PAYMENT

I can therefore say that neither as a child nor as a young adult did I ever fully appreciate the fruits of someone else's sacrifice. I never *gave* nor *accepted* in any way even approaching the interior meaning of these words, the meaning they have in the ancient teachings. Consider now these ancient, perennial teachings in the light of all that has been said about our monetized world. Consider that man may be defined as a being who is constructed to receive a gift of unfathomable immensity and is, at the same time, obliged to pay for that gift with unfathomable commitment and service. Consider a new way of understanding the paradox that is man: the being who must pay for what he is freely given! This is not only what might be termed "lost Christianity"; this is "lost Judaism" as well.

In fact, it is an understanding and a paradox that is always being lost.

I was not an especially deprived child—neither psychologically nor materially. I am not speaking of myself as a special case or as a member of a special social or economic class. I am speaking about something deeply metaphysical—our very conception of existence itself, human existence and the existence of the universe. Our culture's concept of reality does not contain or allow us to perceive the gift-nature of existence. Yet this idea forms the nucleus of every teaching—including some of the most intellectually sophisticated—that has been handed down to us from the past about the nature of reality. And when society or human communities grew to such an extent, when material needs developed in a certain way, laws and customs, symbols, practices, inventions, were created by inwardly developed people to allow material and biological needs to be met while at the same time allowing human beings to feel the gift-nature of existence. Money was one of these inventions.

Personal gain is not excluded from a spiritual life. On the contrary. But the aim of personal gain is clearly defined: one gains something in order to give. This is the essence not only of human life, but of existence itself.

This word, *existence,* and, even more so, the word *being*—these are strange words. They conjure up very little in our minds. As philosophers, we ask: what is existence? What does it mean to *be?* Or even, why does anything exist at all? For us, existence, being, reality just *is.* The universe just *is.* When something comes into being it is a complete mystery. All the more, when a human being is born or dies, it is absolutely inconceivable. And the mystery is most intense when it is I, myself, who exist and who will someday cease existing. But if we can break out of this mindset, we come upon a view that is expressed in every mythic, philosophical, and religious teaching of the past, that there is no such thing as just existing. Everything is in service to everything else. Existence is giving and receiving. A stone gives and receives no less than a saint.

The modern worldview cannot comprehend this notion of existence as a gift. It sounds romantic or sentimental. We tend to experience reality as harsh and demanding. We are educated to take, not to give, but this says more about our minds than about nature or reality. The animals give and take without consciousness of themselves. Our minds are educated to be animal minds. But man is the being who gives and receives consciously. Consciousness is a gift that man was built to receive and it requires a payment that he is built to give. Perhaps this sounds too "mystical," perhaps it sounds absurdly far removed from something as mundane and pragmatic as the question of money in our lives. But remember, we are trying to understand something very difficult—the whole entire root of the attitude of personal gain that underlies our modern culture.

WHY IS MAN ON EARTH?

Consider these lines, dark, rich, and luminous, written by Rainer Maria Rilke, perhaps the greatest poet of the twentieth century:

> Why, if this interval of being can be spent serenely
> in the form of a laurel, slightly darker than all
> other green, with tiny waves on the edges
> of every leaf (like the smile of a breeze)—: why then
> have to be human . . . ?

Why are we here? Why is man on earth? The poem continues:

> Oh *not* because happiness *exists,*
> that too-hasty profit snatched from approaching loss.

Not out of curiosity, not as practice for the heart, which
would exist in the laurel too. . . .

Rilke is one of those authentic poets in whose work
language re-creates itself in the midst of the language we
already have, the language of men and women who do not
sense and feel what is at the heart of reality. The poet—the
artist—always strives for a new language in the midst of hell.
A language that emanates from a consciousness of hell, the
world of meaningless gain and loss, the world we live in.
The poem continues:

But because *truly* being here is so much; because
    everything here
apparently needs us, this fleeting world, which in some
    strange way
keeps calling to us. Us, the most fleeting of all.
Once for each thing. Just once; no more. And we too,
just once. And never again. But to have been
this once, completely, even if only once:
to have been at one with the earth, seems beyond undoing.

This is not the language of escape. The poet opens to another world and finds that in that other world, he is more fully
and consciously in *this* world. The poem continues:

And so we keep pressing on, trying to achieve it,
trying to hold it firmly in our simple hands,
in our overcrowded gaze, in our speechless heart.
Trying to become it.—Whom can we give it to? We
    would
hold on to it all, forever. . . .

What can we give? What are we meant to give? Now, consider the heart of the poem:

> For when the traveler returns from the mountain-slopes
>   into the valley,
> he brings, not a handful of earth, unsayable to others,
>   but instead
> some word he has gained, some pure word, the yellow and
>   blue
> gentian. Perhaps we are *here* in order to say: house,
> bridge, fountain, gate, pitcher, fruit-tree, window—
> at most: column, tower . . . But to *say* them, you must
>   understand,
> oh to say them *more* intensely than the Things themselves
> ever dreamed of existing. Isn't the secret intent
> of this taciturn earth, when it forces lovers together,
> that inside their boundless emotion all things may
>   shudder with joy?

For the poet, what the lovers are given and what they give represents the most intense passion of the human heart and mind. But it is not neurotic intensity, it is not the intensity of ego. It is the intensity of love, the intensity of giving, rather than doing; of receiving, rather than taking. There is something that only man can give. What is that? The poet answers: consciousness. Consciousness that is suffused with feeling and sensing of *this world* in all its variety and particularity:

> Praise this world to the angel, not the unsayable one,
> you can't impress *him* with glorious emotion; in the
>   universe
> where he feels more powerfully, you are a novice. So
>   show him

something simple which, formed over generations,
lives as our own, near our hand and within our gaze.
Tell him of Things. He will stand astonished; as *you*
    stood
by the rope-maker in Rome or the potter along the Nile.
Show him how happy a Thing can be, how innocent and
    ours,
how even lamenting grief purely decides to take form,
serves as a Thing, or dies into a Thing. . . .

Things, the poet tells us, are not only external objects, but
all that is and takes form within ourselves, our own inner
Things, our *own* inner earth. This earth, this world, is all our
thoughts and feelings and sensations, all our impulses to act
and move. It is this world which we are meant to see and love
with the impartial passion that knows each thing, as Adam
named the creatures under God's gift to him. Under the radiance of this power of man, all inner and outer things take their
unique and proper place, none stealing or gaining from the
other. It is in the inner world that one must overcome the
principle of gain, of ego. Fallen man is not an "ego," but a
thousand egos. In fallen man, each function and part seeks to
take more than what it needs. . . .

                                And these Things,
    which live by perishing, know you are praising them;
        transient,
    they look to us for deliverance: us, the most
        transient of all.
    They want us to change them, utterly, in our invisible
        heart,
    within—oh endlessly—within us! Whoever we may be at
        last.

Earth, isn't this what you want: to arise within us,
invisible? Isn't it your dream
to be wholly invisible someday?—O Earth: invisible!
What, if not transformation, is your urgent command?

(Rilke, "Ninth Duino Elegy," from *The Selected Poetry of Rainer Maria Rilke,* ed. and trans. Stephen Mitchell. New York: Random House, 1982)

THE MESSAGE OF ZEUS

In one of Plato's later works, *Critias,* of which only a fragment has survived, there exists a remarkable passage. In this work, which many scholars treat as little more than a curiosity, Plato describes the fabled island of Atlantis and the kingdom that once flourished there—a land blessed with natural riches, a people of unparalleled scientific and technological prowess, a society governed by wise laws and a people in whom the divine spirit ruled the baser parts of their human nature. But the passage of time saw the decay of their inner virtue and the start of a mighty war that presaged their ultimate destruction.

Such was the vast power which the god settled in the lost island of Atlantis. . . . For many generations, as long as the divine nature lasted in them, they were obedient to the laws, and well-affectioned towards the god, whose seed they were; for they possessed true and in every way great spirits, uniting gentleness with wisdom in the various chances of life, and in their intercourse with one another. They despised everything but virtue, caring little for their present state of life, and thinking lightly of the possession of gold and other property, which seemed only a burden

285

to them; neither were they intoxicated by luxury; nor did wealth deprive them of their self-control; but they were sober and saw clearly that all these goods are increased by virtue and friendship with one another, whereas by too great regard and respect for them, they are lost and friendship with them. By such reflections and by the continuance in them of a divine nature, the qualities which we have described grew and increased among them; but when the divine portion began to fade away, and became diluted too often and too much with the mortal admixture, and the human nature got the upper hand, they then, being unable to bear their fortune, behaved unseemly, and to him who had an eye to see, grew visibly debased, for they were losing the fairest of their precious gifts; but to those who had no eye to see their true happiness, they appeared glorious and blessed at the very time when they were full of avarice and unrighteous power. Zeus, the god of gods, who rules according to law, and is able to see into such things, perceiving that an honorable race was in a woeful plight, and wanting to inflict punishment on them, that they might be chastened and improve, collected all the gods into their most holy habitation, which, being placed at the center of the world, beholds all created things. And when he had called them together, he spake as follows:—

(Critias 121, Jowett trans.)

Here the passage, and the fragment, ends. We do not know what words the great philosopher meant to put into the mouth of Zeus. Who are these "gods" summoned to the center in order to hear the message of their king? And what is this *center,* which in the Greek evokes the ancient Pythagorean idea of a quiet central fire that illumines and vitalizes the whole of creation? Are these "gods" within ourselves, as are the "demons" of the Solomonic legend?

We know only that, in Plato's concept, Zeus was to order a great war, a great struggle for the purpose of chastening and purifying a noble race on the brink of decay. If the legends are timeless, as they all are, then we need to ask: what is the war that is coming? And if the legends speak of the inner world, as they all do, then we need to see very clearly the real nature of the inner struggle that we are called to.

It remains only to be said, perhaps, that the name Zeus is the same word as *theos,* God, and that this word may derive from the root *thein,* which means, simply and purely, to *see,* to *watch,* to *observe.* Perhaps Plato never intended to say anything more.

A Message from the Center

What I have tried to do in this book is to call for the inclusion of the money problem in the search for a consciously regenerate life. This means to include in our search all that we usually judge as evil, selfish, violent, and harsh. The other world, the "higher" world, is, as Rilke tells us, *this* world consciously experienced.

The following is the gist of another conversation I had with the businessman I spoke of in the Introduction.

"Tell me," I asked him. "You yourself have been in business all your life. What's your secret? I don't mean the secret of making a lot of money, but how have you managed to make being in business something that's really what you call 'interesting'? What does it mean to you, when you say that making money is *interesting?* I'm sure you mean more than piling up material things or having people envy you."

He reached on his desk for a book. I was a little surprised to see that it was one of the new translations of the poems of Jalalludin Rumi, perhaps the greatest of the mystic poets of Islam. He leafed through the slender volume and handed it to me opened to a poem which the translator had entitled, "Why Organize a Universe This Way."

"Read this," he said.

I took the book and read aloud:

What does not exist looks so handsome.
What does exist, where is it?
An ocean is hidden. All we see is foam,
shapes of dust, spinning, tall as minarets, but I want wind.
Dust can't rise up without wind, I know, but can't I
    understand this
by some way other than induction?

Invisible ocean, wind. Visible foam and dust: This is speech.
Why can't we hear *thought?*
These eyes were born asleep.
Why organize a universe this way?

With the merchant close by a magician measures out
five hundred ells of linen moonlight.
It takes all his money, but the merchant buys the lot.
Suddenly there's no linen, and of course there's no money,
which was his life spent wrongly, and yours.
Say, *Save me, Thou One,* from witches who tie knots
and blow on them. They're tying them again.
Prayers are not enough. You must do something.

Three companions for you: Number one,
what you own. He won't even leave the house

for some danger you might be in. He stays inside.
Number two, your good friend. He at least comes to the
  funeral.
He stands and talks at the gravesite. No further.

The third companion, what you do, your work,
goes down into death to be there with you,
to help. Take deep refuge
with that companion, beforehand.

(John Moyne and Coleman Barks, *Open Secret: Versions of Rumi.* Putney, Vermont: Threshold Books, 1984, p. 79)

Taking in this beautiful poem, I immediately sensed why he had asked me to read it. But I wanted to hear him say it.

"Very well," I said, "the only reality is work. But this kind of work is not what people usually mean. What has this got to do with working to make money?"

He handed me another Rumi volume and said again, "Read this." Again, I opened the book and read aloud:

A friend remarks to the Prophet, "Why is it
I get screwed in business deals?
It's like a spell. I become distracted
by business talk and make wrong decisions."

Muhammad replies, "Stipulate with every transaction
that you need three days to make sure."

Deliberation is one of the qualities of God.
Throw a dog a bit of something.
He sniffs to see if he wants it.

Be that careful

Sniff with your wisdom-nose.
Get clear. Then decide.

The universe came into being gradually
over six days. God could have just commanded,
Be!
Little by little a person reaches forty and fifty and
    sixty,
and feels more complete. God could have thrown
    full-blown prophets
flying through the cosmos in an instant.

Jesus said one word, and a dead man sat up,
but Creation usually unfolds,
like calm breakers.

Constant, slow movement teaches us to keep working
like a small creek that stays clear,
that doesn't stagnate, but finds a way
through numerous details, deliberately.

Deliberation is born of joy,
like a bird from an egg.

                        Birds don't resemble eggs!
Think how different the hatching out is.
A white-leathery snake egg, a sparrow's egg;
a quince seed, an apple seed: Very different things
look similar at one stage.

These leaves, our bodily personalities, seem identical,
but the globe of soul-fruit
we make,

each is elaborately
unique.

(Rumi: *We Are Three,* trans. Coleman Barks. Athens, GA:
Maypop Books, 1987, pp. 28–29)

"I don't mean to be cryptic," he said, when I had finished
reading, "but the point is that outer life can support the inner
work when the demands of life are taken as a challenge to one's
attention, as a reminder that one needs to cultivate the question
of who I am and what in this moment is devouring my attention, taking more of me than I need to give it. In this world
we live in, nothing brings that challenge more often and more
dependably than the adventure of money."

A long silence followed, which we both gladly allowed.

I then spoke to him about my plans for writing this book.
He listened to me with a calm attention that made me feel I
was being weighed in a balance scale.

"The problem of writing about living," he said, "or even
speaking about living, is that it makes it sound too easy."

Slowly and semiautomatically, I nodded yes, only dimly
perceiving what he meant.

After another silence, I made a movement to end the conversation, but he did not reciprocate. Perhaps, I thought, he
was just being polite. He was, after all, a busy executive, the
president of a corporation. Yet he did not seem the slightest
bit driven to get back to his business.

Feeling increasingly uncomfortable, I stood up to go, gathering my papers. Still, he made no move. I reached out to shake
his hand and thank him for his time, but he did not rise from
his place or put out his hand. He simply went on looking at
me with the same even, calm attention.

I said something about it being time for me to go—
although the truth was I had no other appointments.

"Of course," he said, quietly. But still he did not move. I held out my hand again and, still seated, he slowly held out his hand. The handshake struck me like lightning. I found myself gripping a powerful, muscular hand that gave back no pressure at all. It was a hand that could easily have crushed my own, yet it was completely without tension. In any other man, such a handshake would have given the impression of weakness, but in this case it was I who felt weak. I sensed the contraction of my own hand as falsehood.

The shock of that soft handshake remained in my body as I walked to the door. It was only much later that I understood what was then proceeding in me. I was a man who had studied the great ideas of philosophy and religious tradition. I had a fairly well-trained mind which, over the years, had been capable of receiving the shock of awakening ideas. Mentally, I was capable of submitting to teachings that undercut our usual assumptions about reality and the self. Intellectually, and to some extent emotionally, I was able to accept the relativity of the ego and the idea that man must surrender his self-will to another force. But this handshake, strange as it may sound to put it this way, brought this idea to me through sensation. It undercut deeply conditioned habits of the personality that were fixed in the very muscles of my body.

Such observations were very far from me at the time, but as I was turning the doorknob, I said to myself, "What am I doing? Why am I leaving the presence of this person who embodies something that I am searching for? Do I really want to return to the street—to crowds of people, shops with Christmas windows, hotel lobbies, cafés, restaurants, bookstores, and magazine stands? But wait—weren't there some important calls I needed to make—to my editor? Or my agent? Shouldn't I call my wife to see if everything is all right at home?"

I stood in front of the door and was surprised to see my hand pulling it open. The reception room lay in front of me with the secretary busy at her desk and several important-looking businessmen waiting to keep their appointment. I felt my body filling up with its usual tension, overlaying the echoes of the soft handshake that were still reverberating in me. I felt "myself" coming back, my usual "self." I reached for my cigarettes. But I did not step over the threshold.

All of this did not last more than a few seconds, but in those few seconds time had assumed a new dimension.

I stayed where I was, gently but resolutely closing the door in front of me. Then I turned and went back to where I had just been. I sat down.

The man behind the desk showed no surprise at my behavior—quite the contrary. It was as though I had naturally just joined him in another world, a world where the only important thing was to experience truth.

"Of course," he said, "as you know, the subject of your book interests me very much. Because the money question is the only thing that wakes people up these days. You remember the conference you invited me to in Wisconsin some years ago—what was it called?"

" 'Money, Power, and the Human Spirit,' " I said.

"Yes; money, power, and the human spirit. By coincidence, one of the people who was at that conference wrote to me last month. You probably wouldn't remember him—he wasn't one of the speakers. He was in the circle of spectators and he didn't participate much. It seems that something I said touched him and stayed with him all these years."

"What was that?" I asked.

"Well, do you remember when that young woman who

had worked in Central America mentioned the fairy tale about the fisherman's wife?''*

"I remember it very well," I said. "She was using it as a symbol of American capitalism and you finally lost patience with her characterization of all wealthy people as greedy and selfish."

"Apparently, what touched this man was my interpretation of the fairy tale."

"Not only him," I said. "It struck me, too. You interpreted it as a story about the need to know what one wishes from life. You said, if I remember correctly, that greed is inevitable in the absence of an inner aim. You said that greed in one form or another tends to usurp the place of the inner wish to understand, and that almost every vice in human life represents a lower function trying to imitate the work of an undeveloped higher capacity within man."

"You have a good memory," he said.

"Not good enough," I replied. "I remember ideas, but in the midst of a life situation, especially when money is involved, ideas don't help, they're not there, I forget."

"Because," he said, "the inner wish is not an idea. It's a force."

I took that in.

"Is that what you meant when you said that speaking or writing about these things makes them sound too easy?"

Another silence.

"I agree," he said, "with your main thesis—that in modern society money enters into every aspect of human life. That means that it enters into every aspect of ourselves, yes? Every

*See Appendix II.

294

impulse, every perception within ourselves is related to the money factor—or, to be more exact, the principle of personal gain. That follows from your thesis, doesn't it? Personal gain, or the ego principle, is expressed through money in this society—I think that is what you're writing about, isn't it?"

I nodded yes. He went on:

"When you say that in other cultures money was not as pervasive as in this society, you're surely not saying that in those societies men and women were less dominated by egoism, are you? You are saying, as I see it, that it's through money that the ego manifests itself most centrally in our culture. And that the ego is more, far more, than just vanity in its obvious forms. It's the belief in one's power to do, to be safe, happy, and fulfilled by one's own efforts—without the help of a higher influence, yes?"

Again, I nodded. "But the question," I replied, "is, how to remember in the midst of a money situation that there are higher purposes and forces within ourselves?"

"No, you go too fast. If you put it that way, you are lost. To put it that way only brings the whole spiritual quest into the realm of the ego. Of course, you can speak like that, you can even write books like that. But the fact is one forgets, yes? There is no *method* that works. Money is just too powerful, life is just too powerful. I will be very interested to read any book you write about this, if you ever actually write it, but I am sure that after people put down your book, they will still be devoured by money situations. It will be good if you can help people come to a new attitude toward money; it is indispensable as a first step. But the question you are now bringing goes beyond change of attitude."

This conversation took place long before my encounter with Bill Cordell and his gold, and so what was then said to me made an impression only on my mind. But now, as I reach the conclusion of this book, I actually feel and sense the truth of it:

"The fact is," he said, "it is only through forgetting that you can remember. Or, rather, that you are remembered, if you see what I mean."

"I don't understand," I said.

"The point is," he continued, "that money is modern man's instrument of the personality, the instrument of his emotions, his adaptive thought, his action. Falling man is continually reinventing himself and modern man reinvents himself through the technology of money. Evolving man is discovered by himself; falling man invents himself. It's like that, isn't it?"

"Please explain."

"What more can I say? Remembering the true self is not an act of the mind or the emotions or the physical body. The evolving self does not care for money or sex or time. But the ego invents itself out of money, sex, and linear time. If you can find conditions and companions among whom you can study how the ego continually invents itself, imagines itself, you'll understand what I mean. You've studied ancient traditions, but no book can give you the direct experience of how the ego invents itself, how it uses material things and ideas and energies continually to imagine itself."

He paused for a moment, and then continued:

"There is in man a wish that does not come from the ego. There is a wish that is not invented by the ego. It is an energy, a movement that exists outside of linear time. Only when you are ready to experience the complete breakdown of the ego without the slightest impulse to reestablish it again, only then will you experience the wish of the evolving self. It is a certain kind of suffering that is mixed with joy of quite a special taste.

Money and linear time and sex all enter into everything that is of the ego and so one needs to have a very specific study of money, sex, and time.

"I say *study,* because truly to study oneself introduces into life an element completely alien to the ego, yet which the ego can accept. The ego has to become gradually convinced that what it wants—safety, happiness, existence—cannot be obtained through mechanical thinking, personal emotion, or instinctive action. The mind has to become convinced that the only source of its well-being is consciousness. The work of studying oneself introduces a motivation that is free of personal gain, egoistic gain. Study, without the impulse to change anything, motiveless study, choiceless awareness is like the breath of the true wish, the true aim of evolving man. Do you follow?"

Without waiting for my response, he went on:

"The fisherman's wife is the desire of the ego, life in the absence of the wish for being. You know how the fairy tale ends. . . ."

"The man and the wife are put back in their lowly shack. . . ."

"And they live happily ever after?"

"I don't believe the fairy tale says that."

"Well," he said, "it should. All fairy tales end with 'happily ever after'—which is fairy-tale language for the state of inner freedom, freedom from the illusions of ego.

"In any case," he went on, "and fairy tales aside, one needs to discover a wish that is stronger than the ego, and to which the ego can assent. And when you are willing to see how you compromise everything of real value because of the force of money, then it is possible to be remembered by the higher forces within. The point is that, since money has entered

297

so deeply into the formation of the contemporary ego, then it is necessary for us to play the money game with our best abilities, but with a new intention.''

"How would you describe that intention?" I asked.

He paused before replying. I suddenly felt as though I were in a cathedral.

"There is an action, an allowing, a surrender within, that has always been the birthright of every man or woman. The ego experiences it as a kind of stoppage. It is a special quality of silence. In that moment, you *know* why you are on earth and you know that as you are you cannot serve. You know you must change your life and that this can only happen by searching for companions and conditions that will support the appearance of this moment of opening. On the basis of that moment, a new intention enters into one's life, a new morality. It is the morality of the search. Whatever supports that search is good; whatever hinders it is evil. One begins to understand that it is only through that opening that one can love as one wishes to love and as we have heard of love in the teachings of the masters. Then, truly, the world and life in this world, with all its pleasures and pains, with all its obligations and difficulties—just this world that you and I live in now—this world becomes my monastery."

APPENDIX I

THE BROTHERHOOD OF THE COMMON LIFE

There exists considerable historical material concerning the beliefs and practices of the spiritual community that called itself the Brotherhood of the Common Life and which took form in northern Europe around the figure of Gerard Groote (1340–84). Scholars generally consider the Brotherhood part of the broad current of reformist mystical Christianity that flowed through western Europe between the thirteenth century and the Protestant Reformation and which included numerous communities and spiritual schools of varying importance and influence.

But although the Brotherhood has received careful academic study, the surviving evidence concerning this community has only recently been gathered together in a manner that illuminates its extraordinary importance to what might be termed the "hidden" history of Christianity. It is to be hoped that the numerous other communities of this period will receive similar attention on the part of investigators who have both the scholarly erudition and the spiritual sensitivity that are necessary for such a task.

The following excerpts are offered mainly to encourage further research. They are from an unpublished manuscript by the British historian Ross Anthony Fuller and can give only a hint of the rich material contained in this massively researched and deeply insightful study. I have arranged these excerpts topically according to their relevance to issues discussed in the present book. Some books providing information about the Brotherhood are listed in the bibliography.

All citations are from Fuller, Ross Anthony, *The Brotherhood of the Common Life,* unpublished manuscript, London, 1986, 477 pp.

THE WAY IN LIFE:

Monasticism was (and is) one of the fundamental Ways by which men have sought a direct relationship with higher truth and meaning—God—from early days. The subject of this thesis is simply the means adopted at a certain period for intensifying this movement: the emergence and the renewal, during the later middle ages, of a religious way in life, which did not contradict the real monastic path yet which was not based on formal withdrawal from the world, and the transmission of monastic spiritual exercises to laymen, designed to make this way possible and which, largely unremarked by historians, was the other face of the laicisation and declericalisation of the medieval church. This was the "mixed life," uniting action and contemplation in the midst of daily activity. . . . (p. 19)

The "vita apostolica" or "mixed life" was the aspiration of the military orders and permeated the symbolic literature of the Grail quest, it inspired the lay guilds, informed the rise of the Mendicant Orders and was expressed in the lives of remarkable contemplatives like Bernard of Clairvaux, Hugh of Avalon and, later, Jean Gerson, who played active parts in the events of their times. In the later middle ages, the teaching of the New Devotion and the "imitatio Christi" became its chief vehicle. (p. 31)

The phrase "new devotion" was used to describe the results of the attitude, values, exercises and aim communicated by Gerard, called "the great" (Groote, latinised as Gerardus Magnus), 1340–1384, and his pupil Florence Radewijns, 1350–1400. These men and their companions became the nucleus of the Brothers of the Common Life, and, after Gerard's death, of a house of Augustinian canons at Windesheim, whose life was based on the same newly understood principles. . . . The "new devotion" *(devotio moderna)* denoted a "modern" adjustment, a new or renewed impulse in religious endeavour [designed to help men and women] find the necessary intermediate stage between"the world" and active religious commitment. (p. 167)

RELATION TO PROTESTANTISM

Without a practical approach to [its] inner dimension, the mixed life became only another ideal, of as little significance and force as the monastic in its decadence. If the Brethren's particular struggle for genuine religious feeling prepared the ground for the fundamental Jesuit experience of undergoing the *Spiritual Exercises,* which was to generate such a current in the next century, it also entered into the specific Protestant experience of moral dilemma and separation from God when an ideal somewhat like the mixed life supplanted the monastic as the framework for a reformed Christianity based "in the world": the influence becomes mixed entering life.

The desire for freedom, "the great glory of the Christian religion," was the issue of the Reformation. . . . The New Devotionalists often spoke of freedom, not as a revolutionary slogan, nor even as an aim, properly speaking, but as the lawful result of an inward state of service, that is, right order. Gerard Groote wrote of "that freedom of the spirit which is the principal good of the spiritual life. For the affections are fettered by many things and, having been fettered, they are controlled. Such affections, infecting the soul *(anima)* resist the peace of the heart and the quiet of the mind, which is very often defiled and disturbed by the cares connected with them."* . . . The freedom valued by Gerard was to be found as much within the tasks of everyday life as at prayer, not surely without great discipline, search and, in a sense, violence, but without doing violence to one's true nature; while . . . the freedom which tended to become the goal of the reformers was a freedom from various external "injustices," from papal control of the church, the monastic rules or ecclesiastical convention, a freedom it was hoped would inevitably result if these "causes" were abolished. When it was drawn into the turbulent stream of life, this is what the desire for freedom became. . . . (pp. 219–20)

---

* Thomas à Kempis, *Opera Omnia,* ed. E. Sommalius, S.J., Vol. 3, p. 28.

The ideal of the mixed life was able to influence sixteenth-century devotion because of its assimilation to the Protestant notion of the godly vocation, but they were ideas of different orders. Those admitted to the Brethren sought their truth in life through the guided practice of "recollection" and exercises of prayer but they accepted religious forms and never spoke of the unconditional godliness of life work and position. . . . The New Devotion, which remained a small-scale movement, stood for the existence of different levels of Christianity. The godly vocation in the thought of Protestantism, which quickly became a large-scale popular movement, was connected with the idea of "the priesthood of all believers" and that all men are equal, and equally poor, before God. In reaction to the hypocrisy of otherworldly piety and appalled at the reality it masked, the sixteenth-century reformers asserted the rightness of the objective social order: within that "common life," rather than in monastic separation, a man might more honestly and morally find his religious duty. The mixed life represented a balancing of the forces of outer and inner life, "action" and "contemplation" and was the expression of a practical discipline leading, it was believed, to the threshold of a religious way, in the traditional sense. The Brother's daily struggle was his work and this work, to recollect himself in the midst of the disorder of his energies, was his preparation to face the call of Christianity. The significance of Protestantism, which aspired to bring the individual into confrontation with the power and mercy of God without intermediary, lay in its releasing and channeling the energies of half Europe at a time of vigorous expansion and growing national assurance, energies that had been blocked and dissipated among the impossibilities of late medieval religious culture. Here the godliness of work had another sense. (pp. 372–73)

By 1500, the Brethren appear to have been deflected by influences exterior to their work, their attitudes and practices drawn into the intellectual, religious and even social life around them, their independent force diminished. Christian ideas, which had been precise, practical instruments within an accepted discipline, took on subjective meanings as they became mixed with material or other qualities: these ideas, as their field of action moved toward the external, became random, imprecise and negative in their influence. Both the radical-libertarian and the social-revolutionary wings of the Reformation then drew force from them. (p. 300)

SPIRITUAL DISCIPLINE

Note: the essence of spiritual discipline goes far beyond anything that can be described in terms of exercises, attitudes, or emotions. The following passages from Mr. Fuller's book are offered merely as hints of an authentic and precise practical discipline which the Brethren may have pursued. In general, however, any estimation of the depth or authenticity of any spiritual community is beyond the power of an external observer, especially when what we are dealing with are fragmentary written documents. At the same time, Mr. Fuller's citations and remarks are extremely helpful in supporting the idea of a spiritual discipline in life that must be contrasted with what often, among certain Protestant and other religious followers, became only a religious attitude, however sincerely held and nobly professed.

Although there remains a gulf between us and the experiences being referred to, although the instruction begins at too high a level as if the first, practical step has been taken for granted, nevertheless we can recognize the description of a different way of working and the states to which it may give rise: prayer at the same moment as outward activity rather than before or afterwards, a simultaneous inner and outer engagement in work. The Brethren were instructed to stop before they began a task, to pray briefly and then to carry a meditation into their work, to "digest inwardly" *(ruminare, interius ruminandum),* whilst working. Any man may pray and then work: it can signify much or little, depending upon how he prays and how he works. The alternation of activities in time is comprehensible, anyway, but what does their simultaneity mean? It must, surely, be connected with a movement towards that unity of body, soul and spirit, which, as we have seen, the Brethren did not ascribe to themselves as they were. They speak, unmistakably, of their work as a separation in the moment, of "exercising yourself in love and fear," for example, while, (or rather "beneath," *infra*) outwardly acting. This way of working had been "the rule of our holy fathers," said Zerbolt. If the kernel of this question lies in the religious aphorism "laborare est orare," what is meant by "work"? (p. 265)

These endeavours correspond to the remarkable Biblical injunctions to "watch" and "pray without ceasing," to which frequent reference is, indeed, made in New Devotional writings. Gerard, when reflecting upon his former academic habits and the harmfulness of unnecessary talking, says, "it is evident that everything must be ordered in praise of God, if it is to have always a good purpose, that is to say, one must pray always." Florence says the same when speaking of the way in which we take food, for then the Devil will lie in wait for us, "therefore let us always watch and pray." So important was this "watching," that upon it depended the whole progress of a man in the spiritual life, according to the *Tractatus de Cotidiano Holocausto:* many stay where they are, it says, "because they do not see behind the parts they play nor watch themselves." (pp. 276–77)

The records of these practical men indicate again and again that, in this inner movement attention is being renewed and strengthened. A little later, when speaking of the "opus dei" and the way in which the Devil particularly molests all who seek to praise God, the Harderwijk writer says: "Therefore attend, little by little and as completely as you are able to and read the hours according to the words of Augustine: what is brought forth in the mouth depends upon the heart. But because your heart easily gives way to empty things, for that reason you are bound to always recall your attention to the purpose."

The manuscript combines the imperatives "Attende!" and "Collige te!" with examples of the thoughts and feelings to be aroused at corresponding parts of the mass. The writer's intention is surely to help himself to live the "new devotion," to find a practical way to participate more deeply and with more of himself in the ancient sequence of liturgical experience and to support this self-reminding for the future by writing it down. He is transcribing part of a method for his own use. If ritual, prayer, meditation and music had once served as a bridge between men and the fullness of Christian teaching, then their means of using what remains of this bridge lies still at hand: in this manuscript, as in the Bridgettine material to be examined later, it is implied that the key to these means lies in the development of the power of attention. John Mombaer's *Rosetum Spiritualium Exercitiorum,* contemporary with the manuscript, has as its stated purpose the fostering of the inner life, understood in the same practical sense. In this vast, encoded summary of tradition, considered by the scholars who have penetrated it to be a formulation of much of the practice and method of the New Devotion, Mombaer describes "three beds" in a "garden of roses," praying the hours, meditation and communion, which could be tended only by the practice of containing attention, by not allowing it to wander.

In the belief that we already know what attention is and that we possess it as of right, we are likely to find this emphasis of the Brethren upon working for it shortsighted and naive, if not dishonest, confirming entrenched modern prejudices about the irrelevancy and superstition of medieval religion. But who amongst us has looked into this question deeply? What is the difference between attention and concentration? Is that attention, which a man thinks he can command, really free, mobile and at his disposal? Is it not constantly drawn? If his attention is unfree, where is he then and how can he know? If there is only one, already known, quality of attention, what is the meaning of the sleep of men and their possibility to awaken, spoken of in the religious traditions? The question of attention relates not only to thought and the "mind," but to the virtually autonomous worlds of emotion, sensation and instinct. Altogether, there is everything to be understood here, practically and experientially, rather than intellectually and theoretically: even a glimmer of this understanding will enable us to be more just towards the Brethren, for we will be putting ourselves in their position.

Consider the words of another contemporary of the Harderwijk Brother, who had pondered the ancient records of spirituality:

". . . holy men tell us of divers kinds of attention during the Divine Office. But because men in these days are dull of understanding and but little skilled in things divine, few are able to catch the spiritual meaning of what these holy men tell us." (pp. 284-85)

Our subject became densely interwoven at the turn of the century. During the 1490's Cisneros [Garcia Cisneros, abbot of Montserrat] had visited Paris and returned with copies of works by Zerbolt, Radewijns, Kempis and Mombaer. The latter's *Rosetum exercitiorum spiritualium* (1494) states in the prologue: "Exercitabam et scopebam a Hierusale et in Hiericho de lapsum originali iusticia, dignitate, puritate spoliatum resculpere, reformare atque in priorem restituere gradum opere precium erit purgativis primum exercitiis exemplo clarissimi prophete David a viciis et corruptis affectibus eundem spiritum scopere, purgare, castigare." Cisneros may well have met Mombaer, who was known to have been in Paris in 1496 attempting, with the help of John Standonck, to introduce the discipline of Windesheim to certain Augustinian houses. Cisneros' *Directorium horarium canonicarum* and *Ejercitatorio de la Vide Espirituel* outline a system of meditations and exercises intended to strengthen the attention during the performance of the horarium and the celebration of the mass and speak of re-establishing internal order and balance in the spirit of the New Devotion.

All our material concerns, in one way or another, the practical relationship between religious ideas and method. On the one hand, there is the ancient teaching of the microcosm, that the lower was created in the image of the higher, the idea of a universal but hidden order in all worlds, and on the other, there is man himself, in the wrong place: and there is, or has been, religion. Let us remember "the possibility that all genuinely religious ideas have an empirical basis, and are embedded in a method by means of which a man may obtain the experience necessary to verify and use them.'' It may be difficult to define practicality, the key to living understanding of these ideas, because of the relative coarseness and superficiality of the evidence of religious culture and our own inexperience, but the records of the New Devotion hint at its possibility and the Brethren certainly believed that they had a method. The meaning of method must relate to a known way of opening us to the action of genuine religious ideas. Therefore the New Devotion emphasized the growth of the attention of the heart through self-knowledge.

Subsequently, Reformation thought rejected many of the traditional ideas of order in reaction to the theoretical elaborations of late scholasticism, leaving the Platonists of the Renaissance to re-interpret the old categories, and tended to concentrate upon an order conceived, like its freedom, externally, as a matter of organisation. (pp. 234–35)

APPENDIX II

THE FISHERMAN
AND HIS WIFE

There was once a fisherman who lived with his wife in a ditch, close by the seaside. The fisherman used to go out all day a-fishing; and one day, as he sat on the shore with his rod, looking at the shining water and watching his line, all of a sudden his float was dragged away deep under the sea, and in drawing it up he pulled a great fish out of the water. The fish said to him, "Pray let me live: I am not a real fish; I am an enchanted prince. Put me in the water again, and let me go." "Oh!" said the man, "you need not make so many words about the matter; I wish to have nothing to do with a fish that can talk; so swim away as soon as you please." Then he put him back into the water, and the fish darted straight down to the bottom, and left a long streak of blood behind him.

When the fisherman went home to his wife in the ditch, he told her how he had caught a great fish, and how it had told him it was an enchanted prince, and that on hearing it speak he had let it go again. "Did you not ask it for any-thing?" said the wife. "No," said the man, "what should I ask for?" "Ah!" said the wife, "we live very wretchedly here in this nasty stinking ditch; do go back, and tell the fish we want a little cottage."

The fisherman did not much like the business; however, he went to the sea, and when he came there the water looked all yellow and green. And he stood at the water's edge, and said,

> *"O man of the sea!*
> *Come listen to me,*
> *For Alice my wife,*
> *The plague of my life,*
> *Has sent me to beg a boon of thee!"*

Then the fish came swimming to him, and said, "Well, what does she want?" "Ah!" answered the fisherman, "my wife says that when I had caught you, I ought to have asked you for something before I let you go again; she does not like living any longer in the ditch, and wants a little cottage." "Go home, then," said the fish, "she is in the cottage already." So the man went home, and saw his wife standing at the door of a cottage. "Come in, come in," said she; "is not this much better than the ditch?" And there was a parlor, and a bed chamber, and a kitchen; and behind the cottage there was a little garden with all sorts of flowers and fruits, and a courtyard full of ducks and chickens. "Ah!" said the fisherman, "how happily we shall live!" "We will try to do so at least," said his wife.

Everything went right for a week or two, and then Dame Alice said, "Husband, there is not room enough in this cottage, the courtyard and garden are a great deal too small; I should like to have a large stone castle to live in; so go to the fish again, and tell him to give us a castle." "Wife," said the fisherman, "I don't like to go to him again, for perhaps he will be angry; we ought to be content with the cottage." "Nonsense!" said the wife. "He will do it very willingly; go along, and try."

The fisherman went, but his heart was very heavy; and when he came to the sea, it looked blue and gloomy, though it was quite calm, and he went close to it, and said,

> *"O man of the sea!*
> *Come listen to me,*
> *For Alice my wife,*
> *The plague of my life,*
> *Hath sent me to beg a boon of thee!"*

"Well, what does she want now?" said the fish. "Ah!" said the man very sorrowfully, "my wife wants to live in a stone castle." "Go home, then," said the fish, "she is standing at the door of it already." So away went the fisherman, and found his wife standing before a great castle. "See," said she; "is not this grand?" With that they went into the castle together, and found a great many servants there, and the rooms all richly furnished and full of golden chairs and tables; and behind the castle was a garden, and a wood half a mile long, full of sheep, and goats, and hares, and deer; and in the courtyard were stables and cow houses. "Well," said the man, "now will we live contented and happy in this beautiful castle for the rest of our lives." "Perhaps we may," said the wife; "but let us consider and sleep upon it before we make up our minds." So they went to bed.

The next morning, when Dame Alice awoke, it was broad daylight, and she jogged the fisherman with her elbow, and said, "Get up, husband, and bestir yourself, for we must be king of all the land." "Wife, wife," said the man, "why should we wish to be king? I will not be king." "Then I will," said Alice. "But, wife," answered the fisherman, "how can you be king? The fish cannot make you a king." "Husband," said she, "say no more about it, but go and try; I will be king!" So the man went away, quite sorrowful to think that his wife should want to be king. The sea looked a dark gray color, and was covered with foam as he cried out,

"O man of the sea!
Come listen to me,
For Alice my wife,
The plague of my life,
Hath sent me to beg a boon of thee!"

"Well, what would she have now?" said the fish. "Alas!" said the man, "my wife wants to be king." "Go home," said the fish, "she is king already."

Then the fisherman went home; and as he came close to the palace, he saw a troop of soldiers, and heard the sound of drums and trumpets; and when he entered in, he saw his wife sitting on a high throne of gold and diamonds, with a golden crown upon her head; and on each side of her stood six beautiful maidens, each a head taller than the other. "Well, wife," said the fisherman, "are you king?" "Yes," said she, "I am king." And when he had looked at her for a long time, he said, "Ah, wife! what a fine thing it is to be king! Now we shall never have anything more to wish for." "I don't know how that may be," said she; "never is a long time. I am king, 'tis true, but I begin to be tired of it, and I think I should like to be emperor." "Alas, wife! why should you wish to be emperor?" said the fisherman. "Husband," said she, "go to the fish; I say I will be emperor." "Ah, wife!" replied the fisherman, "the fish cannot make an emperor, and I should not like to ask for such a thing." "I am king," said Alice, "and you are my slave, so go directly!" So the fisherman was obliged to go; and he muttered as he went along, "This will come to no good, it is too much to ask, the fish will be tired at last, and then we shall repent of what we have done." He soon arrived at the sea, and the water was quite black and muddy, and a mighty whirlwind blew over it; but he went to the shore, and said,

"O man of the sea!
Come listen to me,
For Alice my wife,
The plague of my life,
Hath sent me to beg a boon of thee!"

"What would she have now!" said the fish. "Ah!" said the fisherman, "she wants to be emperor." "Go home," said the fish, "she is emperor already."

So he went home again; and as he came near he saw his wife sitting on a very lofty throne made of solid gold, with a great crown on her head full two yards high, and on each side of her stood her guards and attendants in a row, each one smaller than the other, from the tallest giant down to a little dwarf no bigger than my finger. And before her stood princes, and dukes, and earls; and the fisherman went up to her and said, "Wife, are you emperor?" "Yes," said she, "I am emperor." "Ah!" said the man as he gazed upon her, "what a fine thing it is to be emperor!" "Husband," said she, "why should we stay at being emperor; I will be pope next." "O wife, wife!" said he, "how can you be pope? There is but one pope at a time in Christendom." "Husband," said she, "I will be pope this very day." "But," replied the husband, "the fish cannot make you pope." "What nonsense!" said she. "If he can make an emperor, he can make a pope, go and try him." So the fisherman went. But when he came to the shore the wind was raging, and the sea was tossed up and down like boiling water, and the ships were in the greatest distress and danced upon the waves most fearfully; in the middle of the sky there was a little blue, but toward the south it was all red as if a dreadful storm was rising. At this the fisherman was terribly frightened, and trembled, so that his knees knocked together; but he went to the shore and said,

"O man of the sea!
Come listen to me,
For Alice my wife,
The plague of my life,
Hath sent me to beg a boon of thee!"

"What does she want now?" said the fish. "Ah!" said the fisherman, "my wife wants to be pope." "Go home," said the fish, "she is pope already."

Then the fisherman went home, and found his wife sitting on a throne that was two miles high; and she had three great crowns on her head, and around stood all the pomp and power of the Church; and on each side were two rows of burning lights, of all sizes, the greatest as large as the highest and biggest tower in the world, and the least no larger than a small rushlight. "Wife," said the fisherman as he looked at all this grandeur, "are you pope?" "Yes," said she, "I am pope." "Well, wife," replied he, "it is a grand thing to be pope; and now you must be content, for you can be nothing greater." "I will consider of that," said the wife. Then they went to bed; but Dame Alice could not sleep all night for thinking what she should be next. At last morning came, and the sun rose. "Ha!" thought she as she looked at it through the window, "cannot I prevent the sun rising?" At this she was very angry, and she wakened her husband, and said, "Husband, go to the fish and tell him I want to be lord of the sun and moon." The fisherman was half asleep, but the thought frightened him so much that he started and fell out of bed. "Alas, wife!" said he, "cannot you be content to be pope?" "No," said she, "I am very uneasy, and cannot bear to see the sun and moon rise without my leave. Go to the fish directly."

Then the man went trembling for fear; and as he was going down to the shore a dreadful storm arose, so that the trees and the rocks shook; and the heavens became black, and the lightning played, and the thunder rolled; and you might have seen in the sea great black waves like mountains with a white crown of foam upon them; and the fisherman said,

> *"O man of the sea!*
> *Come listen to me,*
> *For Alice my wife,*
> *The plague of my life,*
> *Hath sent me to beg a boon of thee!"*

"What does she want now?" said the fish. "Ah!" said he, "she wants to be lord of the sun and moon." "Go home," said the fish, "to your ditch again!" and there they live to this very day.

FOR FURTHER READING

ANGELL, NORMAN. *The Story of Money.* New York: Frederick A. Stokes Company, 1929. A wise and humane historical survey, written for the layman; the best book of its kind.

BIALIK, HAYYIM NAHMAN. *And It Came to Pass: Legends and Stories About King David and King Solomon.* New York: Hebrew Publishing Co., 1938. Gathers many of the Solomon stories and tells them well and simply.

BRAUDELL, FERNAND. *Capitalism and Material Life 1400–1800.* New York: Harper and Row, 1973. A great scholar looks at the extraordinary history of everyday things, including the device called money, "which never ceases to surprise humanity."

BROWN, NORMAN O. *Hermes the Thief: The Evolution of a Myth.* University of Wisconsin Press, 1947. Provocative and penetrating insights dealing with the legendary god of commerce, exchange, secrecy, trickery, and engagement in all the forces of life. An intriguing fragment of the idea of the way in life.

DESMONDE, WILLIAM H. *Magic, Myth and Money: The Origin of Money in Religious Ritual.* New York: The Free Press of Glencoe, 1962. A bold and persuasive psychohistorical argument for the spiritual origins of the money device.

GALBRAITH, JOHN KENNETH. *The Affluent Society.* 4th ed. New York: New American Library, 1984. Justifiably a modern classic, full of insight, common sense, and wit.

——. *Money: Whence It Came, Where It Went.* Boston: Houghton Mifflin Co., 1975. A fine historical analysis of the nature of money in American society.

GINZBERG, LOUIS. *The Legends of the Jews.* Philadelphia: The Jewish Publication Society of America, 1909. A magnificent multivolume collection of legends involving all the people and events of the Bible.

GREEN, ROBERT W., ed. *Protestantism and Capitalism: The Weber Thesis and Its Critics.* Boston: D. C. Heath and Co., 1959. An excellent collection of essays for and against Max Weber's view of Protestantism and capitalism. The article by Kemper Fullerton on Calvinism and capitalism is especially helpful.

GREIDER, WILLIAM. *Secrets of the Temple: How the Federal Reserve Runs the Country.* New York: Simon and Schuster, 1987. A fascinating and comprehensive account of the meaning of money in American life.

GURDJIEFF, G. I. *Meetings with Remarkable Men.* New York: E. P. Dutton, 1969. Written on many levels, Gurdjieff's account of his own search includes a long chapter, "The Material Question," that shows how a master of the way in life confronts the money question.

HYDE, LEWIS. *The Gift: Imagination and the Erotic Life of Property.* New York: Vintage Books, 1979. A brilliant essay about the place of artistic creativity in the world of buying and selling.

HYMA, ALBERT. *The Christian Renaissance: A History of the "Devotio Moderna."* New York: The Century Co., 1924. A solid, scholarly history of the Brethren of the Common Life.

JONES, RUFUS M. *Studies in Mystical Religion.* London: Macmillan and Co., 1909. Intelligently places the Brethren of the Common Life within the broad sweep of Western religious history.

LE GOFF, JACQUES. *Your Money or Your Life: Economy and Religion in the Middle Ages.* New York: Zone Books, 1988. A penetrating analysis of the idea of usury.

MAIMONIDES, MOSES. *The Guide for the Perplexed.* Trans. M. Friedländer. New York: Dover Publications, 1956. A towering and complex work by the greatest of Jewish philosophers, opening the inner meanings of the Bible with an extraordinary balance of logic, practical moral wisdom, and mystical sensibility.

FOR FURTHER READING

OUSPENSKY, P. D. *In Search of the Miraculous: Fragments of an Unknown Teaching.* New York: Harcourt, Brace and World, 1949. The best account, by a pupil, of the teaching of G. I. Gurdjieff and of the idea of the way in life.

PHILLIPS, MICHAEL. *The Seven Laws of Money.* New York: Random House, 1974. The first book of its kind, and still the best, that tries to reestablish money as a servant rather than a master. Full of hard common sense and humanistic ideals.

ROSS, NANCY WILSON. *Buddhism: A Way of Life and Thought.* New York: Alfred A. Knopf, 1980. There are now many excellent books that explain the basics of Buddhism to the Western mind. This is one of the best.

SCHERMAN, HARRY. *The Promises Men Live By: A New Approach to Economics.* New York: Random House, 1938. One of the most interesting attempts to define the nature of money in terms that are humanly meaningful.

SCHUMACHER, E. F. *Small Is Beautiful: Economics as if People Mattered.* New York: Harper and Row, 1973. A visionary humanization of the science of economics. Keen insights into the relationship between the spiritual and the material dimensions of human life.

SIMMEL, GEORG. *The Philosophy of Money.* London and New York: Routledge, 1990. An astonishingly wide-ranging treatment of the social, psychological, and philosophical aspects of money.

TAWNEY, R. H. *Religion and the Rise of Capitalism.* New York: Harcourt, Brace and World, 1926. One of the most important studies of the issues pioneered by Max Weber, providing insights that help balance one-sided interpretations of the Weber thesis and offering a fascinating portrait of the social and religious context of the birth of modern capitalism.

WEBER, MAX. *The Protestant Ethic and the Spirit of Capitalism.* New York: Charles Scribner's Sons, 1958. Weber's revolutionary analysis of the relationship between Calvinism and modern capitalism. Required reading.